SETTING LIMITS WITH YOUR
STRONG-WILLED CHILD

SETTING
LIMITS WITH YOUR
STRONG-WILLED
CHILD

Eliminating Conflict by
Establishing Clear, Firm, and
Respectful Boundaries

ROBERT J. MACKENZIE, Ed.D.

THREE RIVERS PRESS
NEW YORK

Published in the United States by Three Rivers Press,
an imprint of the Crown Publishing Group,
a division of Random House, Inc., New York.

www.crownpublishing.com

THREE RIVERS PRESS and the Tugboat design are
registered trademarks of Random House, Inc.

Originally published in paperback in the United States by Prima Publishing,
Roseville, California, and subsequently by Three Rivers Press, an imprint of the
Crown Publishing Group, a division of Random House, Inc., New York, in 2001.

In order to protect their privacy, the names of some individuals cited in this
book have been changed. Any similarities to real names of persons is purely
coincidental.

Library of Congress Cataloging-in-Publication data is available upon request.

ISBN 978-0-7704-3659-9
eISBN 978-0-7704-3660-5

PRINTED IN THE UNITED STATES OF AMERICA

Illustrations by Tom McLelland
Cover design by Lauren Monchik
Cover photographs: Rubberball/Mike Kemp, Nathan Blaney, George Doyle, Neustockimages

10 9 8 7 6 5 4 3 2 1

Second Edition

This book is dedicated to my two wonderful sons,
Scott and Ian, who have helped me understand
and appreciate the uniqueness of our individual
temperaments and the importance of
clear, firm, respectful limit setting.

CONTENTS

ACKNOWLEDGMENTS

Special thanks goes to those who supported my workshops in major ways and to those who contributed to the writing of this book.

To Bob Trigg and Dave Gordon, past superintendents of the Elk Grove Unified School District, for funding and supporting my teacher and parent workshops for more than fifteen years.

To Ben Dominitz, publisher; Jamie Miller, acquisitions editor; Marjorie Lery, project editor; and all the other good folks at Prima Publishing for believing in my projects.

To Duane Newcomb, literary consultant, for teaching me nearly everything I know about writing books of this sort.

To Sandra Isla, graphics consultant, for assistance with the many charts and diagrams.

To Lisa Stanzione, my best friend and sounding board for testing out my ideas.

To all the parents and children I've seen over the years in my workshops and counseling work. Your experiences helped many of the ideas and methods in this book take shape.

INTRODUCTION

If you want to discover what doesn't work for you in this life, do one or all of the following three things: get married, start your own business, or raise a strong-willed child. I've done all three, but raising a strong-willed child has taught me more about myself, about others, and about the importance of setting clear, firm limits than any other experience.

I'm a proud parent of two wonderful sons. My oldest son has a temperament much like my own. He's cooperative, sensitive, and eager to please. He does what he's asked most of the time, and I've learned to depend on his cooperation. *Parenting is easy!* I said to myself for the first three years. Then, my second son was born, and everything changed. Nothing in my lifetime had prepared me for this experience.

He dawdled at mealtimes and getting dressed, resisted picking up his toys and messes, and always seemed to be the last one out the door. His schedule never seemed to match up with other family members. He had many strong traits, but the one that stuck out most prominently was his stubborn determination.

He understood what I wanted when I asked him to cooperate.

He just didn't want to do it much of the time. The simple, polite requests that worked so well with his brother didn't work with him. He was very determined to have things work out on his terms. I did my best to get him to cooperate. I repeated, reminded, warned, cajoled, gave second chances, pleaded, bribed, and bargained for his cooperation. It was exhausting, and it didn't work!

After a while, I'd lose my patience and become angry. I'd raise my voice and threaten to take away all his favorite toys and privileges for long periods of time. Sometimes, this worked. Other times, it didn't. But even when it worked, I felt awful, because I had promised myself I would never treat my children this way. Then I'd soften and revert back to the old repeating, reminding, and persuading routine that didn't work the first time. It was crazy!

I thought I was supposed to know what to do. I had a master's degree in psychology, a solid background in child development, and I was working on a doctoral degree in counseling psychology at the time. Somehow, none of this made any difference when it came to getting my youngest son to cooperate. I was doing the best I could with the guidance tools I had, but my tools weren't working, and I didn't know what else to do. I was beginning to wonder if there was something wrong with me or with him.

Fortunately, I was able to acquire the tools I needed from the real pros. In 1979, I participated in a research study on teacher effectiveness at the University of California, Davis. My job was to observe effective teachers in their classrooms and record the specific things they said and did that contributed to cooperation and achievement.

I didn't realize it at the time, but the teachers I observed were masters at setting limits. They didn't give in to students who were uncooperative or disrespectful, and they didn't try to overpower them with threats, shaming, or long, drawn-out consequences. Instead, these teachers held their ground, maintained a respectful tone, gave clear messages with their words, and supported their words with effective action. They got a high level of cooperation and respect, and they made it look easy.

Best of all, their guidance methods worked with all students, not with just the compliant ones, but also strong-willed students and those in between. These teachers were prepared to teach their rules the easy way or the hard way. It didn't matter, because they had the tools to get the job done.

The importance of this discovery didn't hit home until I started using these tools with my own sons. Even my youngest son cooperated! He tested and resisted less and started making better choices to cooperate just like his brother. The daily power struggles began to disappear. For the first time in years, I began to feel like an effective parent again. All I had lacked were the right tools to get the job done.

I believed if I could get these results, others could too. In 1985, I piloted a workshop for teachers. The response was overwhelmingly positive. The methods were clear, easy to learn, and best of all, they worked with all students, not just the compliant ones. The workshop became a book, *Setting Limits in the Classroom*, which has been tested and used successfully by thousands of teachers throughout the United States, Canada, and Europe.

In 1987, I began giving the same workshop for parents and got the same response. Once again, the workshop became a book, *Setting Limits*, which has gained increasing popularity throughout the United States, Canada, and Europe.

Looking back, I realize that I'm no different than most of the parents and teachers who attend my workshops. They don't come in search of solutions to the problems they're having with their compliant children. They come because they're wearing down from the challenges they face with their strong-willed children. Like me, these teachers and parents already have guidance tools. They just don't have the right ones. Their tools are poorly matched to the temperament and learning style of their strong-willed child.

This book will help you improve the match. *Setting Limits with Your Strong-Willed Child* provides you with the information and tools you need to understand your strong-willed child, stop misbehavior and power struggles, and teach your rules in the clearest and most understandable way. You can say good-bye to all the ineffective methods that wear you down and get you nowhere. No more repeating, reminding, reasoning, explaining, arguing, debating, lecturing, threatening, punishing, or coercing. Your child will understand what you mean when you learn how to give clear, firm messages with your words and support your words with logical consequences. This book will show you how to do that. The methods should be a refreshing alternative to the ineffective extremes of punishment and permissiveness.

This book is divided into two parts to help you answer two basic questions: (1) What's going on? and (2) What do you do about it? Chapters 1 through 5 are devoted to helping you recognize the dynamics that are operating between you and your child and the things you're doing that aren't working for you. Without this awareness, it will be difficult, if not impossible, to avoid repeating your old mistakes because most of them are made unconsciously.

Chapter 1 will help you discover your child's temperament, as well as your own, and learn how temperament affects behavior. In Chapter 2, you'll discover how your strong-willed child learns your rules and why the teaching-and-learning process often breaks down. In Chapters 3 and 4, you'll identify your approach to limit setting and determine whether your limits are firm or soft.

Chapter 5 will help you recognize your family dance. Nearly every family that operates with unclear or ineffective limits has its own special dance that it performs over and over again in conflict situations. Helping you break free from your family dance is a major goal of this book.

With an understanding of what has not worked for you, you'll be ready to learn new skills. Chapters 6 through 12 form the core of the skill-training program. In these chapters, you'll learn how to give clear messages with your words, how to stop power struggles before they begin, how to support your rules with effective action, how to manage the resistance you'll likely encounter, and how to develop support systems to keep you on track.

Stopping misbehavior is an important skill, but clear messages and consequences alone do not always motivate children or teach them the skills they need to behave acceptably. Chapters 10 and 11 will show you how to do that. In Chapter 10, you'll learn how to motivate your strong-willed child to cooperate without threats, bribes, or coercion. In Chapter 11, you'll learn a variety of simple, but effective, strategies for teaching problem-solving skills when children lack the skills to behave acceptably.

Changing behavior can be a stressful and confusing process for many parents, even when the changes are for the better. Chapters 12 and 13 provide much needed support for parents. In Chapter 12, you'll learn how to use patience as you go through the ups and downs of the change process. Chapter 13 will help you make sense of the changes as they unfold and help you see things from a broader perspective.

Learning the methods in this book will be relatively easy. Most are clear and fairly straightforward. The hardest part, for most of you, will be overcoming your compelling desire to revert back to your old bad habits and do things the way you always have. You may recognize intellectually that the methods will lead to the type of change you desire, but the new methods and the changes they bring may not feel comfortable to you or your child in the beginning. You'll likely encounter pressure and resistance, not only from your child, but also from within yourself. Chapter 9 will help you understand and cope with the resistance you'll likely encounter and prepare you for the changes that lie ahead.

You'll probably be tempted to try out your new skills as you go, but I encourage you to read the entire book before practicing your new skills with your children. Why? Because the guidance tools all fit together and complement one another. Your total skills will not be complete until you learn how to use your words and actions together.

When you complete the book, refer to the suggestions for getting started immediately following Chapter 13. These tips will help you start off at a comfortable pace and provide a schedule for adding new tools to your toolbox.

Expect to make mistakes when you begin practicing your new skills. That's okay. Mistakes are part of learning. Your goal should be improvement, not perfection, and you will improve the more you practice. Strive for consistency, but don't be too hard on yourself when you slip up. If you encounter unexpected problems, refer to the pertinent chapters for assistance. Note the specific language used to carry out the skill.

The more consistency you achieve between your guidance methods and those used by other important people in your child's life, the faster your child's behavior will improve. Share your methods with your child's teacher at school, day-care provider, relatives, friends, or others who help out with child care. Their support will pay off.

Finally, most of the examples in this book reflect actual cases from my family-counseling work. The names have been changed in all these examples to protect the privacy of those involved. The methods in this book have helped thousands of parents and teachers enjoy more satisfying and cooperative relationships with strong-willed children. If you're willing to invest the time and energy needed to learn the skills, you too can share the rewards. Enjoy *Setting Limits with Your Strong-Willed Child.*

SETTING LIMITS WITH YOUR STRONG-WILLED CHILD

1

Understanding Your Strong-Willed Child

Four-year-old Corey is a challenge. He begins his typical day by refusing to wear the clothes his mother picks out, then dawdles for the next twenty minutes while she prods and pleads with him to put them on. When he arrives at the breakfast table, he turns up his nose and complains that he doesn't like what's offered. *This is not a battle I want to fight,* his mother says to herself as she prepares Corey his own special meal. She tells her husband that she worries about Corey's nutrition, but what she really worries about is the tantrum Corey will throw if he doesn't get what he wants. Her husband thinks she's too soft on Corey and so do her two daughters. "It's not fair!" they complain. "He always gets his own way." By the time Corey makes it out the door in the morning, his mother is ready for a nap. But this is only the beginning. Round two begins in the afternoon when Corey returns from preschool. Sometimes Corey's mother wonders how long she can take it.

Six-year-old Kristal is sweet and cooperative one moment, angry and defiant the next. Little things set her off—unexpected changes, departures from routine, or simply things not working out her way. Tantrums are not uncommon. "Living with Kristal is like riding on a roller coaster," says her mother. "It's exhausting!" Kristal's parents alternate between punishing and giving in, depending upon how worn down they feel; but nothing seems to make any difference. They wonder if Kristal's behavior is normal and question whether they did something to cause her to behave this way.

Nine-year-old Alex has a short fuse and often acts before he thinks. When things don't go his way at school or in the neighborhood, Alex gets loud, calls names, threatens, and sometimes hits other kids. Alex has been suspended from school three times this year for being disrespectful to teachers and fighting on the playground. It's only December. "It's too bad they don't spank kids at school anymore," Alex's father laments. "When Alex acts like a brat at home, we give him an earful, then we paddle him. He has to learn. We've threatened to take away his TV privileges for the rest of the year if he gets suspended again."

Lynn, age twelve, is destined to be a great trial lawyer. She's bright, intense, and very persistent. Lynn will argue with anyone if she thinks there's a chance of getting things to work out her way, and she's willing to use drama, rudeness, and disrespect when she believes it will help her win her case. "I never would have imagined talking to adults the way she talks to us," Lynn's father complains. "We reason with her every way we know, but everything turns into an argument."

Do any of these children sound familiar? If your child resembles one of these, you're not alone. I see more than a hundred children each year whom parents and teachers describe as challenging, difficult, spirited, stubborn, hell-raising, a pistol, or just plain impossible. Although no single term adequately describes all, or even most, of the children I see, the one that comes closest is "strong-willed." These are normal children with extreme behavior who are hard to raise and difficult to discipline.

Strong-willed children are not part of some conspiracy to make life difficult for others. They just do what strong-willed children do. They test harder and more often, resist longer, protest louder, use more drama, and carry things further than most of us would ever imagine. They're movers and shakers, powerful kids who bring out strong reactions in others.

Teachers and principals know them as the 10 to 15 percent who cause 90 percent of school discipline problems. Parents know them as their big challenge. I know them affectionately as "my kids" because I spend a lot of my time with them, both at work and at home. Yes, I'm the proud parent of a strong-willed son. My youngest son is a delight, but he's also a workout, and he's not the least bit impressed by the fact that I write books on this subject or that I'm supposed to know what to do. At home, I get no breaks or professional immunity. He pushes hard against my rules and authority. At times, I've wondered whether his behavior is normal.

> Strong-willed children are not part of some conspiracy to make life difficult for others. They just do what strong-willed children do. They test.

Do you sometimes question whether your child's behavior is normal? Perhaps you worry that you've done something to cause your child to behave this way. If so, you'll be relieved to know that the problem, in most cases, is not parents. Most are doing the best they can with the discipline tools they have. The problem is not the child, either. Most strong-willed children are just being themselves. The real problem is a bad match between the child's temperament and the parents' discipline methods. The parents' tools are not well suited for the job. The predictable result—conflict and power struggles.

When parents arrive at my office looking for help in dealing with their strong-willed child, one of my first tasks is to assist them in understanding their child's temperament. Then we examine how their discipline tools match up with their child's temperament and discuss the predictable conflicts and friction points that develop around a bad match. That's what we're going to do in this chapter. A new perspective awaits you. You're not the problem, but you are a big part of the solution. Improving the match is well within your control.

WHO IS THIS STRONG-WILLED CHILD?

My youngest son, Ian, is a great force in our family and a great source of pride and joy. He's bright, creative, sensitive, and very determined. Sometimes, I think he's more determined to train his parents than we are to train him. He keeps us on our toes. If we are unclear, inconsistent, or indecisive when we ask him to do something, Ian lets us know. He holds out for a clearer signal.

Like most strong-willed children, Ian understands the "bottom line," and he knows how to get there. He just pushes hard until he finds it, and when he does, he pushes a little more to see whether it holds up. If it does, he stops pushing, at least for a while, and accepts the boundary. But Ian pushes a lot before he gets there. It's wearing! My older son, Scott, usually cooperates for the asking without all the pushing.

How would you react if you asked two children to cooperate in the same respectful manner and got two consistently different responses? Would you become upset? Would you question whether something is wrong?

The persistent testing that is so characteristic of strong-willed children is also what drives most parents crazy. *Why would anyone do this?* I'd ask myself. *Is this normal? I would never push anyone as hard as Ian pushes me.*

Does your child push hard against your rules and authority? Has he or she done so from an early age? Do you react in extreme ways and question whether your child is normal? Join the club. Now it's time to get better acquainted with your child. Following are some basic facts about strong-willed children that will help you better understand your child and your reactions to his or her behavior.

> The persistent testing that is so characteristic of strong-willed children is also what drives most parents crazy.

- **Strong-willed children are normal.** You've probably worried about whether your child is normal when his teacher or a well-intended relative pointed out that his behavior seems extreme. They're right, but extreme does not mean abnormal. Most strong-willed children are normal with well-defined temperament traits. They're not brain damaged, emotionally disturbed, or defective. Most have no diagnosable problems at all, though some do. In addition, no rule says you can only have one thing going on in your life at a time. Some strong-willed children also have learning disabilities, hyperactivity, and other special needs, but a strong will does not mean they are abnormal.

- **Strong-willed children are not all alike.** Each strong-willed child is a special individual with his or her own unique temperament. No two behave in exactly the same way. Sure, they all test parents and behave in extreme ways, but they don't all test in the same way or to the same degree. Some are easier. Others are more difficult. Some are almost impossible.

- **Strong-willed children are hard to understand.** Our individual temperament shapes the way we think, learn, and behave. When others think and behave as we do, we can readily identify with them and understand their experience. When others think, learn, and behave very differently from us, however, it is not easy to understand them or to identify with their behavior. *Why would anyone do that?* we ask ourselves. The behavior makes no sense from our perspective. Strong-willed children are hard to understand for exactly this reason. As you learn about your child's temperament and how that temperament shapes the way your child behaves, behavior that once seemed confusing should begin to make sense.

> When others think, learn, and behave very differ-
> ently from us, it is not easy to understand them or
> to identify with their behavior.

- **Strong-willed children require a lot of guidance and discipline.** Of course, this statement sounds obvious: Children who test frequently require frequent discipline. Yet when you accept this statement as a fact of life rather than a source of annoyance, your attitude and perspective changes. Mine did. I stopped feeling so angry and resentful when my son tested me and developed patience I didn't believe was possible. I realized that his job was to test, and my job was to guide him in the right direction. Those are the hands each of us were dealt. My new perspective didn't change his behavior, but it sure made my life a lot easier. I stopped taking it personally.

- **Strong-willed children do not respond to discipline methods that seem to work with other children.** Why do children respond so differently to the same request? One cooperates, the other resists. Is the problem the resistant child? Or the request? Most parents feel confused when their best guidance efforts work with one child but not with another. The issue is less confusing when we consider the individual temperaments involved. Compliant children will cooperate with most discipline approaches, even ineffective ones, because their underlying desire is to cooperate. They have a different learning style than their strong-willed counterparts. Compliant children permit parents a wide margin for ineffectiveness. Strong-willed children, on the other hand, do not respond to ineffective discipline. They require clear, firm, and consistent guidance. Ineffective discipline is a fast lane to power struggles with a strong-willed child.

> Ineffective discipline is a fast lane to power struggles with a strong-willed child.

- **Strong-willed children learn differently than their peers.** Strong-willed children do much of their learning "the hard way." That is, they often need to experience the consequences of their own choices and behavior before they can learn the lesson we're trying to teach. It's not enough just to announce that kicking the soccer ball in the house is not okay. Strong-willed children need to experience having the ball taken away for a while each time they decide to test the rule and kick the ball anyway. They may need to repeat this drill many times before they accept the rule as mandatory. Their behavior is not malicious, but can be very frustrating and confusing because it is so unlike that of compliant children who cooperate the first time they're asked. Parents must learn to accept that "hard-way learning" is good learning for strong-willed children.
- **Strong-willed children bring out extreme reactions in others.** How do you feel when your child challenges your rules and authority? Angry? Frustrated? Confused? Threatened? Intimidated? Embarrassed? Guilty? Inadequate? Discouraged? Exhausted? All of the above? These are all normal reactions to extreme behavior. Strong-willed children often

place strain on a marriage, cause sibling conflicts, and create other problems within the family.

> The traits of strong-willed children that drive many of us crazy can actually become strengths when we give our kids the understanding and guidance they need to choose the right path.

- **With proper guidance, strong-willed children can develop into dynamic, cooperative, and responsible individuals.** Once you discover that your child has a strong will, the next question is: How are you going to deal with it? Your options are clear. You can fight with it and try to control it. You can give in to it and let it control you. You can try some of both. Or you can accept your child's strong will as a fact of life, make peace with it, and learn better ways to guide him or her down a healthy path. The choice is yours. The traits of strong-willed children that drive many of us crazy can actually become strengths when we give our kids the understanding and guidance they need to head down the right path.

DISCOVERING YOUR CHILD'S TEMPERAMENT

When my son was born, there was no tag attached to his heel that said: Caution! Strong-willed child. Handle with Care. There were no warnings at all. I discovered his temperament the way most parents do. I watched it emerge as he grew up.

I had clues about his temperament from the beginning. He was colicky and screamed a lot during his first few months. He was picky and finicky when we introduced solid foods. Mornings were the hardest. He was slow to get going and cranky. For some reason, his schedule never seemed to match up with the rest of ours.

But Ian didn't put his cards out on the table until he was eight and a half months old. One Saturday morning, while I was sitting on the couch reading the newspaper, I saw Ian pull himself up to a standing position. *Watch out!* I thought to myself. *We're entering the furniture-walking phase.* His older brother went through this phase about the same age, and I thought I knew what was ahead. But to my amazement, Ian let go of the furniture and walked all the way across the living room! When he got to the end, he plunked down, then pulled himself up and did it again. Wow!

I called my wife in the other room to come see Ian walk. When she arrived, I tried my best to get him to do it again. I pleaded, begged, coaxed, and cajoled, but Ian wouldn't budge. He just sat there with this look on his face that said, *Watch out. I'm Ian.* Nearly two weeks went by before he walked again; but when he did, he did it the way he prefers to do most things—on his terms. Looking back, I realize this was one of those defining moments.

Ian revealed a characteristic part of his temperament well before I had an opportunity to influence him with my limit-setting or guidance methods. He has been this way ever since. This is part of his unique style of behaving. I didn't cause it. It was already there. I just discovered it.

All children have their own unique temperaments or inborn styles of behaving. This preferred style of behavior is innate. The parents' actions, lifestyle, values, or beliefs did not cause their child to behave this way. Temperament is not caused by environmental factors, but it does interact and interplay with these factors.

Does this mean your child's behavior is set and unchangeable? No. Temperament is not rigid in the sense that it's fixed in cement. It can be shaped and molded with the proper guidance, but the underlying tendency to behave in certain ways remains the same. For example, consider the preschooler who digs in his heels and refuses to cooperate when asked to pick up his messes. By the time he becomes an adult, he will have learned not to do this, but he's more likely to take a strong stand on issues that affect him, both at work and at home. He will always be temperamentally persistent, but he will learn to express his persistence in more appropriate ways.

Much of what we know about temperament is credited to the pioneering research by Drs. Alexander Thomas, Stella Chess, and Herbert Birch of New York University. Their study, which began in 1956 and continues to the present, followed 133 individuals from infancy to adulthood and examined individual differences in the way they responded to the world around them. These differences, or characteristic ways of responding, revealed the unique temperament of each child. Thomas, Chess, and Birch identified nine characteristic temperament traits that are present, in varying degrees, in all children. These nine traits that are present at birth and continue to influence a child's development throughout his or her life proved to be relatively stable predictors of how a given child responds at different times and in different situations. Let's look at each of these traits and see if you can identify your child's temperament. These traits include:

1. **Persistence.** Children show individual differences in how long they persist with tasks or resist the limits they confront. The positive side of persistence is reflected in that strong determination to stay with a task even when the task is difficult or challenging. The negative side of persistence is reflected in stubborn resistance to rules or authority. How long does your child stay with a task? A long time? A short time? How stubborn is your child when he or she wants something? How resistant is your child when he or she confronts limits? Nearly all strong-willed children are high in the trait of negative persistence.

2. **Intensity.** Some children react in mild and quiet ways when they are happy or upset, while others react very intensely. How does your child respond when happy or frustrated? Does he smile and cry softly? Laugh and cry with animation? Or shout with glee and wail with frustration? Strong-willed children can be quite dramatic. Many are high in intensity.

> Nearly all strong-willed children are high in the trait of negative persistence.

3. **Regularity.** Some children settle into routines quickly and maintain regular patterns whereas others show more variability and irregularity. How regular is your child in his or her eating, sleeping, toileting, and other daily habits? Does your child adjust well to schedules and routines?

4. **Distractibility.** Some children can sustain the focus of their attention for long periods of time. Others have very brief at-

tention spans and are easily distracted. How long can your child stay focused on a task? Is his or her attention easily diverted? Does your child shift from one uncompleted task to another?

5. **Energy and Activity Level.** General energy and activity level varies from child to child. Some are energetic and highly active. Others are passive and subdued. Most fall somewhere between the two extremes. How active is your child? How energetic? Does the motor always seem to be in high gear? Can your child downshift into lower gears when the task requires it?

6. **Sensitivity.** Children show differences in the way they respond to sensory stimulation. Some are highly sensitive and reactive. Others are less affected by the sensory stimuli around them. How does your child respond to sensory stimulation? Is he or she highly sensitive to odors, tastes of certain foods, changes in temperature, texture of clothing, sounds, bright lights, or sudden movements?

7. **Adaptability.** Some children adapt easily to changes and new situations while others find change stressful and upsetting. Transitions in the day, such as leaving home for school or entering the classroom after recess, are difficult for some children, whereas others seem unaffected. How does your child handle change? Are transitions in the day easy or stressful?

8. **Reactivity.** Some children move into new situations without hesitation or reluctance, while others stand on the sidelines, take time to get their bearings, and join in gradually. How

does your child respond to new situations or people? Does he or she join in willingly or with reluctance? Does your child tend to withdraw and avoid new situations?

9. **Mood.** Mood or general disposition also varies from child to child. Some tend to be positive and cheerful. Some tend to be serious and analytical. Others tend to be cranky and negative. How would you describe your child's basic disposition?

How is this information useful? These nine traits are the puzzle pieces that form your child's temperament. When you put them together you begin to get a picture of your child's temperament. Remember, all children show these traits in varying degrees. Some show only a few traits to an extreme degree and are easier to manage. Others show many traits to an extreme degree and are quite difficult to manage.

The research of Thomas, Chess, and Birch revealed that approximately 65 percent of all children fit one of three basic temperament types or profiles: easy or flexible, difficult or feisty, and cautious or slow-to-warm-up. Approximately 40 percent fall into the category of easy or flexible, 15 percent as cautious or slow-to-warm-up, and 10 percent as difficult or feisty. The remaining 35 percent show a combination of the three basic temperament types.

As an educational consultant, I repeatedly observe these distinct temperament types among students when I assist teachers and principals in developing effective classroom management programs and schoolwide discipline plans. Most teachers report that 10 percent of their students cause 90 percent of classroom discipline problems. These students clearly fit the profile of "difficult or feisty." In the Setting Limits Program, we refer to them as "strong-willed." They don't respond to discipline methods that work with the majority of their classmates.

The remaining 90 percent of students in most classrooms fall into two distinct groups that generally correspond to the temperament research. The 40 percent of easy students and the 15 percent of cautious students make up the 55 percent we refer to as "compliant students." They don't do a lot of testing. Their underlying desire is to please and cooperate.

The 35 percent that show a combination of temperament traits we refer to as "fence-sitters." As the name implies, fence-sitters can go either way depending upon what the market will bear. If they observe their strong-willed classmates getting away with misbehavior, fence-sitters often will join in the fun. Winning over the fence-sitters can make or break a teacher's classroom management experience.

Temperament Profiles

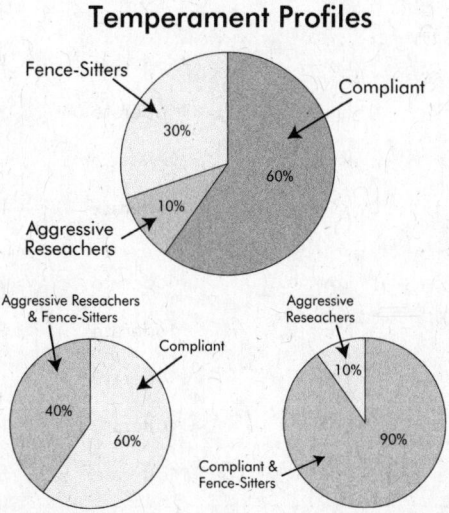

With an understanding of the basic temperament types, let's see where your child falls on the continuum of temperament traits and begin to identify your child's unique temperament. Rate your child's behavior on the scale in Table 1, which is a modified version of the rating scale designed by Stanley Turecki in his excellent book, *The Difficult Child*. Circle the ratings that best describe your child's characteristic ways of behaving.

What does your child's temperament profile look like? How many difficult-to-manage traits does your child show? Does he or she show a high rating in the area of negative persistence? If so, your child shows the defining characteristic of a strong-willed child, but let's see what else is going on. How many other ratings does your child have under the "Difficult to Manage" column?

TABLE 1. Your Child's Temperament Profile

Temperament Characteristic	Easy to Manage ⟶		Difficult to Manage
Negative Persistence	Low	Moderate	High
Intensity	Low	Moderate	High
Regularity	Regular	Variable	Irregular
Distractibility	Low	Moderate	High
Energy/ Activity Level	Low	Moderate	High
Sensitivity	Mild	Moderate	Extreme
Adaptability	Low	Moderate	High
Reactivity	Low	Moderate	High
Mood	Mild	Moderate	Extreme

One? Several? Many? The more your child has, the harder your job. Are you beginning to understand why you feel so worn out?

If you're curious, rate the behavior of other children in your family and note the comparisons. Do you think you have a compliant child? Or a fence-sitter? Or perhaps you have more than one strong-willed child in your family? Every family is unique.

Now, the good news. Your life just got a little easier. Once you understand your child's temperament, you can predict your child's behavior. You are a step closer to matching your child's temperament to more effective guidance tools.

HOW DID MY CHILD BECOME THIS WAY?

The nature-nurture debate over causes for differences in personality and temperament has raged for years. The answer is still unclear. We do know that genetic and environmental factors play important roles in the development of temperament, but the relative contributing influences of these factors is not known. The debate continues, but we can chart the thinking and research that takes us to the present.

In the 1950s, the nurture view dominated the thinking. Researchers believed that environmental influences such as parenting accounted for most of the differences in temperament among children. When children showed extreme or difficult behaviors, parents were suspected to be the cause. Parents shouldered a heavy load of responsibility for their child's behavior.

But the nurture view proved confusing to parents and researchers alike. Parents correctly pointed out that children respond differently to the same parenting methods. Some cooperate. Others don't. Why? If the problem is parenting, shouldn't all children respond the same? Researchers recognized that environmental influences alone could not adequately explain the differences they observed among children. The search continued for a better explanation.

We do know that genetic and environmental factors play important roles in the development of temperament, but the relative contributing influences of these factors is not known.

The nature view became the next focus of investigation. According to this view, differences in temperament were due largely to hereditary or inborn influences. The nature view explained why children respond differently to the same parenting and environmental influences, but it did not explain why some children with extreme traits adapt and adjust better than others.

Neither point of view, nurture or nature, could adequately account for observed differences in temperament. One overemphasized the role of parenting and left parents feeling guilty and responsible. The other underemphasized the role of parenting and left parents feeling helpless and resigned. Was there a better explanation? Yes.

Another group of researchers proposed an interactive model that incorporated the influences of both nature and nurture. According to this model, nature and nurture were two parts of the same picture. Both contributed, in varying degrees, to the development of temperament. Temperament was seen as the result of the continuous interaction between biological factors (inborn traits) and environmental factors (parenting). In other words, the child brings his or her nature into the arena, and parents provide the nurture. The interaction between these factors shapes the outcome. Parenting plays an important role, but parents have to work with the plan nature provides.

How Temperament Affects Behavior

Temperament is like a blueprint for behavior. Nature provides the blueprint when your child is born, but the plan is not fixed. It's waiting for the architect to guide it and shape it and help it take form. Parents are the architects. It's our job to work with the plan nature gives us.

Once you identify your child's temperament, you can begin to understand the blueprint. Behavior that once seemed confusing begins to make sense. The question no longer is: Why does he do that? The new question becomes: What will I do to guide him when he does what he does? Based on what you know about your child's temperament, you can predict your child's behavior and develop more effective strategies for guiding it.

For example, if I ask my son Ian to clean up his mess at the counter, I can predict, from experience, that he will test and resist my request. He'll probably say "I will" but make no effort toward getting started. What Ian really means is, *I will if I have to*, but he's not convinced he has to, so he holds out for a clearer signal. He'll dawdle and try to wait me out.

If I take the bait and ask him when he plans to pick up his mess, once again I can predict his response. He'll likely say "soon," but continue to dawdle. To Ian, soon can mean hours or possibly never if he thinks there's a chance he can avoid the job. So I have to stay in the area long enough for him to be convinced he can't avoid the job. When he's convinced, he cleans up his mess.

Does this seem like a lot to go through just to get a kid to pick up a mess on the counter? It does to me, and if I was willing to go through all these steps each time, I would be even more exhausted than I already am. But I'm not willing. I know what he's likely to do, and so does he. So I get to the bottom line quickly. The first time I notice the mess on the counter, I say, in a clear, firm, and respectful voice, "Ian, please pick up your mess at the counter now before you do anything else." Then, I stay in the area so he can't sneak off. He usually cleans up his mess.

> When we accept our child's temperament as a fact of life, behavior is much easier to understand and manage.

Most parents can predict, with good accuracy, how their child will respond in specific situations, but many parents feel confused and frustrated by the predictable response. They choose to fight with it or give in to it, rather than shape and guide it. When we accept our child's temperament as a fact of life, behavior is much easier to understand and manage.

HOW YOUR CHILD'S BEHAVIOR AFFECTS YOU

Ten-year-old Aaron is typical of many of the strong-willed children I see in my counseling work. He's bright and capable but also intense, persistent, and distractible. He can be loud, and he's not afraid to argue with adults if he thinks he can get what he wants. Yes, Aaron shows a number of those difficult-to-manage temperament traits. He arrived at my office with his parents following his third suspension for arguing and defying his teacher.

"Every year, it's the same story," Aaron's father complained. "It begins with the phone calls from the teacher, then the notes home, and finally the conferences at school. By the middle of the year, Aaron wears out his teachers. They send him to the office, and the office sends him home. His teacher and principal don't realize that we're just as worn out as they are." By the look on his face, I could see Aaron's father meant what he said.

At home, family life revolves around Aaron's difficult behavior. Everyone is affected. He argues and fights constantly with his younger sister who resents all the attention he receives. He's loud and bossy with playmates in the neighborhood, and he resists and argues with his parents whenever they ask him to do something he doesn't want to do. Chores and homework are daily battles. Aaron's mother is so exhausted at the end of the day that she has little energy left for her husband. He feels resentful and left out. She feels guilty and lonely. They're both doing the best they can.

Like most strong-willed children, Aaron brings out strong reactions from nearly everyone. His teacher feels angry, burned out, and resentful. "I've had all I can take," she complains. "When Aaron is absent, the whole atmosphere changes in my classroom." She hopes the principal will move him to another room.

His mother alternates between feelings of inadequacy and depression and feelings of guilt and overprotectiveness. "It's crazy!" she says. "When Aaron misbehaves at home or in public, I feel responsible. I take his side and defend him against his father, the school, and the neighbors." She tells herself that Aaron's behavior is just a stage that will pass but fears others will think she's a bad parent until it does. She also worries about the strain Aaron's behavior places on her marriage.

Aaron's father feels confused, frustrated, and resentful. He can't imagine how things became so out of control. Before Aaron was born, he envisioned a happy family life and a warm, wonderful relationship with his son. Nothing turned out the way he expected.

Like many parents of strong-willed children, Aaron's father has battled with his son for so long that the battles have become a way of life. He feels stuck, and he has completely personalized his son's difficult behavior. *Why is he doing this to me?* he wonders. He blames Aaron for their turbulent family life and the strains in his marriage.

To complicate matters, Aaron's parents don't agree on discipline. His mother takes a very gentle approach. She repeats, reminds, warns, cajoles, reasons, and explains, methods that work with her daughter, but not with Aaron. He digs in his heels and resists until his mother gives in.

I must be doing something wrong, his mother thinks. *This approach always works with my daughter. She's such a joy and so easy to like. I wish I had two like her.*

Aaron's father tries to balance out his wife's leniency by being very strict. He yells, blames, criticizes, and argues until he can't take it any longer, then he threatens to take away all of Aaron's toys and privileges for long periods of time. The louder he yells and the more he threatens, the more intense and resistant Aaron becomes. The ineffective discipline actually increases Aaron's unruly behavior and intensifies their power struggles. Aaron can hold out for hours.

When things become too heated, Aaron's mother steps in and rescues her son. She doesn't mean to undermine her husband's authority, but she can't stand listening to their battles. Aaron's father understands how she feels but doesn't know what else to do. He worries that Aaron is ruining the marriage.

Strong-willed children have a wearing effect upon others. When I first met him, Aaron had exhausted his parents, burned out several teachers, exasperated the school principal, and alienated half the neighborhood. His sister resented him, and his parents were on the verge of marital counseling. The impact of his extreme behavior extended beyond his immediate family into the school, neighborhood, and the community.

How has your life been affected by your strong-willed child? Do you sometimes feel exhausted? Overwhelmed? Lonely? Confused? Depressed? Discouraged? Inadequate? Embarrassed? Guilty? Protective? Responsible? Frustrated? Angry? Resentful? Stuck in power struggles? Do you worry about the strain your child's behavior places on your marriage and other family relationships? If so, you're not alone. These are common experiences reported by parents of strong-willed children.

WHAT ROLE DOES YOUR TEMPERAMENT PLAY?

We've talked about the important interaction between the child's temperament and the parent's discipline approach, but parents also bring their own unique temperaments into the interaction. How does the parent's temperament affect the interaction?

When parent and child temperaments are similar, parents have a much easier time identifying with and understanding their child's behavior. The behavior makes sense from the parent's perspective. When parent and child temperaments are very different, however, parents have a more difficult time identifying with their child and understanding the behavior. From the parent's perspective, the child's behavior makes no sense. Let's look at how these dynamics play out in Aaron's family.

Aaron's parents and his younger sister are compliant people with few, if any, difficult-to-manage traits. In most situations, they cooperate and get along with one another. Because they share similar styles of behavior, Aaron's parents can readily identify with their daughter and understand her behavior.

The dynamics between Aaron and his parents, however, are much different. Aaron is a strong-willed child with several difficult-to-manage traits. His tendency, in most situations, is to test and resist his parents' requests. Because Aaron has such a different style of behavior, his parents cannot easily identify with or understand him. His behavior makes no sense from their perspective. Their combined temperaments are like mixing AC and DC currents with no adapter. They don't mix well. The adapter, in this case, is a better understanding of their respective temperaments.

Are you ready to add an adapter to your perspective? Now that you've discovered your child's temperament, it's time to get better acquainted with your own. Return to page 16 and rate yourself on each of the nine characteristics. How does your temperament match up with your child's temperament?

INEFFECTIVE DISCIPLINE: FAST LANE
TO POWER STRUGGLES

Strong-willed children test more than other children, and because they do, parents have to use a lot more guidance and discipline. This is just a fact of life. Whatever methods you use, you will need to use them frequently. Strong-willed children need to experience your boundaries repeatedly before they accept them as mandatory, not optional.

> Strong-willed children need to experience your boundaries repeatedly before they accept them as mandatory, not optional.

If your methods are unclear or ineffective, you can expect problems because strong-willed children give parents little margin for ineffectiveness.

Let me illustrate what I mean with a personal example. If I say to my compliant son, "Scott, I hope you clean your room sometime today," I can predict what he'll do. He'll clean it up early in the day, and I won't have to say anything more. My signal was not particularly clear or firm, but Scott's underlying desire is to please and cooperate. I can get away with an ineffective message with Scott, but not with Ian.

If I tried the same vague signal with Ian, I can predict his response. He'll likely say, "I will," then put the job off as long as possible in the hope I'll forget. If he does clean it up, it will be the last act at the end of the day and only because I insist on it.

With Ian, I have to be very clear and firm with my requests. I have to say, "Please clean your room before you do anything else today." He knows from experience that I will not allow him to do anything else until the job is done. A tentative or unclear request sets both of us up for further testing and power struggles.

> The more the child tests, the more parents respond with ineffective methods, and the more deeply both become stuck in power struggles.

Ineffective guidance is an invitation to power struggles with strong-willed children. But most parents who use ineffective methods are unaware they're doing so. They don't realize their signals lack clarity and firmness and actually encourage the testing they're trying to stop. The more the child tests, the more parents respond with ineffective methods, and the more deeply both become stuck in power struggles. A vicious cycle develops. I call them family dances, but they are simply repetitive patterns of ineffective communication that play out over and over again in discipline situations.

If you've been using ineffective discipline with your strong-willed child, you've probably done your share of dancing. Family dances are stressful and exhausting. Helping you break free from your dance is a major goal of this book.

GOOD MATCHES AND BAD MATCHES

Most parents carry a picture in their mind, a set of hopes and expectations about how they want their children to behave. When the child's actual behavior matches the parents' picture, the relationship develops smoothly and naturally. Things just seem to fit.

What happens when the child's actual behavior does not match up with the parents' picture? It's time to introduce the concept of fit and discuss the adjustment parents go through when the child's behavior and the parents' picture don't match up. "Fit" is a term mental health professionals use to describe the match between a child and the important people in the child's environment, primarily the parents. The fit or match is usually evaluated on two levels:

- the emotional level, or how the parents feel about the child
- the behavioral level, or how acceptable the child's behavior is to the parents

In the earlier example, you recall that Aaron's mother felt a warm, positive connection with her compliant daughter whom she described as "a joy and easy to like." Mother and daughter enjoyed a good emotional and behavioral fit. In most healthy families, a good match develops naturally between compliant children and their parents. Easy-to-manage children are easy to like. Their behavior invites our love and affection.

But Aaron's parents had a difficult time feeling positive toward Aaron. They loved him, but they didn't like his behavior, which turned out to be very different than they expected. Aaron's parents were quite distressed by the poor emotional and behavioral fit.

"Sure, I'm disappointed," Aaron's father confessed. "I wish we could have done fun things together, but Aaron never wants to do the things I enjoy. I wish we could be close, and sometimes I feel guilty that we're not."

> Letting go of your ideal picture may be one of the most difficult tasks you'll face as a parent, but it's a necessary task.

Aaron's father didn't realize it but he was grieving the loss of the ideal son he never had. Letting go of the dream can be very painful. As Aaron's father worked through the grieving process, gradually he began to let go of the ideal picture and accept Aaron as he really was.

Letting go of your ideal picture may be one of the most difficult tasks you'll face as a parent, but it's a necessary task. Your child needs you to do it. If this means shedding tears, saying good-bye to unfulfilled fantasies, or creating new dreams for you and your child, then that's what you need to do, because holding on to what isn't real keeps you stuck.

IMPROVING THE MATCH: THE GOAL OF THIS BOOK

Thus far, we've looked at three important factors in raising a strong-willed child: your child's temperament, your temperament, and your guidance methods. Parenting is a continual interaction among these factors.

The problem many parents experience is that they invest too much time and energy trying to change the one thing they can't change—their child's temperament. We can't change temperament, but we can understand it, guide it, and shape it in positive directions.

Now, the really good news! The other two factors are solidly within your control. You can improve your guidance methods and learn better ways to manage your own temperament. That's what this book will show you how to do, but first, we need to look at the important role limits play in the teaching and learning process.

2

How Strong-Willed Children Learn Your Rules

Curt, age eight, and his six-year-old brother, Michael, know they're not supposed to fill up their squirt guns in the house, but the kitchen faucet works so much better than the hose. As they head into the kitchen with their squirt guns, their mother suspects what they're up to.

"If you fill those squirt guns in the house, I'm going to have to take them away," she says, matter-of-factly. "Is that clear, Curt?" She directs her question his way because she expects him to test.

"Oh, all right," says Curt, reluctantly. Both boys head outside to use the hose. The game continues.

A few minutes later Curt notices his mother talking with a neighbor across the street. *Now's my chance*, he thinks to himself. He sneaks into the kitchen to fill up. Michael remembers what his mother said. He decides to play it safe and fill up at the hose.

Curt's gun is almost full when his mother returns to the kitchen and catches him in the act. "Hand me the squirt gun, Curt," she says calmly. "You can have it back tomorrow if you fill up at the hose." Curt pleads for another chance, but his mother holds firm. He's not happy about it, but he knows he'll have another chance tomorrow.

Like most strong-willed children, Curt chose to learn his mother's rule the hard way. He decided to test it out for himself to see if she really meant what she said. She did. Curt and his mother will probably have to repeat this lesson several times before he's convinced that her rule is firm, but her guidance methods will certainly lead to the desired outcome.

> The hard way is the clearest way for strong-willed children to learn your rules.

Curt's mother understands that her sons have different temperaments and different learning styles, and she's prepared to teach her rules however the situation requires—the easy way or the hard way. Curt is strong-willed. She expects him to test, and she's ready to follow through with instructive consequences when he does. Like most hard-way learners, Curt requires a lot of discipline. He's a challenge to raise.

Michael, on the other hand, is a compliant child. He doesn't do much testing because his underlying desire is to please and cooperate. His mother expects him to cooperate, but she's ready to follow through with instructive consequences when he doesn't. Like most easy-way learners, Michael doesn't require much discipline. He's easy to raise.

Curt and Michael's mother doesn't waste her time with ineffective discipline. No yelling or threats. No arguing or debating. No lectures or sermons. No angry dramatic displays. She simply gives them a clear message with her words and supports her words with effective action. Her message is clear, and so is the rule behind it. She makes learning the hard way look easy.

In this chapter, you'll understand why the hard way is the clearest way for strong-willed children to learn your rules, and you'll discover why the teaching-and-learning process often breaks down. By the time you're done, you'll be a step closer to teaching your rules in the clearest and most understandable way.

CHILDREN LEARN CONCRETELY

Children do not learn like miniature adults. Jean Piaget's research on children's intellectual development has shown us that the thinking and learning of children is qualitatively different from that of adults. Children learn concretely. Their immediate sensory experience plays a powerful role in shaping their beliefs about reality.

What does this mean in everyday terms? It means that what children experience with their senses (what they see, hear, touch, and feel) determines how they think things really are. Their beliefs and perceptions about the world are based primarily on their concrete experiences.

Piaget's research has important implications for how we teach rules to children. We do this in two basic ways: with our words and with our actions. Both teach a lesson, but only our actions are concrete. Actions, not words, define the rules we really practice.

Consider Chuck's experience, for example. Eight-year-old Chuck is busy building a castle with LEGOs when the doorbell rings. His mother answers the door. "Can Chuck play at my house?" asks Kevin.

"Sure," Chuck's mother replies, "but first he needs to pick up his LEGOs." Chuck's LEGOs are spread out all over the floor. She repeats the request for Chuck and leaves the room.

She returns a few minutes later to find the LEGOs still lying on the floor. *Darn him! He did it again*, she says to herself as she reaches down to put them away for him.

When Chuck returns home a few hours later, he notices the LEGOs placed neatly in their container and smiles to himself. His observation confirms what he already knew about his mother's rule.

> What children experience with their senses (what they see, hear, touch, and feel) determines how they think things really are.

Her words said, "Pick up the LEGOs before leaving the house," but what did her actions say? Of course, they said, "You don't really have to." What did Chuck experience? It wasn't picking up LEGOs. He knows from experience that picking up before leaving the house is not really required if he can sneak out the door fast enough. Do you think Chuck will take his mother seriously next time she asks him to pick up before playing?

Let's replay the scene above with a different ending. This time, when Chuck's mother enters the room and sees the LEGOs spread out all over the floor, she walks down to Kevin's house, finds Chuck, and brings him home. Then, she sets the kitchen timer for ten minutes.

"You can return to Kevin's house when all the LEGOs are picked up and the timer goes off," she says, matter-of-factly. "When you sneak off to avoid a job, it will cost you playtime." Then, she stays in the room to monitor his compliance.

What did Chuck hear and experience this time? Are they the same message? You bet. If his mother enforces her rule in this manner consistently, Chuck will learn to take her seriously when she asks him to pick up before leaving the house.

LIMITS AND THE LEARNING PROCESS

Can you imagine how much easier life would be if children were programmed at birth with the limits and boundaries for healthy relationships? This is a wonderful fantasy, but not reality. Nobody is born with limits. We learn limits by growing up in our families. They are taught to us first by our parents and the lessons are reinforced by other important people such as teachers and care providers in the course of our growing up.

When the limits children learn at home correspond to the limits that are accepted and practiced in our schools and communities, children have a much easier time adjusting. When the limits children learn in their families are different from those accepted and practiced out in the world, the adjustment process is more complicated.

Limits don't complicate life or our interactions with others. In fact, the opposite is true. Limits simplify life. When children know how far they are allowed to go and how far others are allowed to go with them, they feel secure and comfortable in their relationships. Limits provide vital information children need to cooperate and get along.

WHY TEACHING AND LEARNING BREAK DOWN

When our words consistently match our actions, children learn to take our words seriously and accept the rules behind them. When our words do not match our actions, children learn to ignore our words and base their beliefs on what they experience. In effect, we are teaching two different rules: a rule in theory and a rule in practice.

This essential miscommunication is the source of most breakdowns in the teaching-and-learning process between children and their parents. Most parents are not even aware it's happening. They just continue teaching their rules with their words while their children learn from what they experience. Here's a typical example.

> When our words do not match our actions, children
> learn to ignore our words and base their beliefs on
> what they experience.

Five-year-old Sarah sits on the sofa and draws pictures with colored marker pens. Her mother enters the room and recognizes the perilous situation for the sofa.

"Sarah, that doesn't look like a very good idea," her mother says. "I'm afraid you might mark the sofa."

"I'll be careful, Mommy," says Sarah, convincingly.

"I know you will, honey," says her mother, "but I really wish you would work at the table where you can't stain anything."

"I will," says Sarah, "but I want to finish this one part first."

"After you finish, you'll move to the table, okay?" asks her mother. She leaves the room.

"Okay," says Sarah, but ten minutes go by and she's still sitting on the sofa drawing her pictures.

"Sarah, I thought I asked you to do your artwork at the table," says her mother with concern in her voice. "Your father and I would be very upset if any marks got on the sofa. I really wish you would do what you were asked."

"I will, Mommy," says Sarah, "but I just want to finish this one picture and then I'll move. I'm almost done."

"You better finish it quickly," says her mother. "I'm starting to get mad." She waits, tapping her foot impatiently, but Sarah keeps on drawing. Her mother is losing her patience.

"Sarah!" her mother shouts. "I've had enough of this, young lady! Do I have to take the pens away?"

"Okay, I'm finished," says Sarah as she puts her work away and leaves the sofa.

Sarah's mother sincerely believes she's communicating a message that says stop when she points out the hazards of using marker pens on the sofa. She becomes frustrated and annoyed when Sarah does not respond as expected. Actually, Sarah's mother is communicating two messages, but she is aware of only one.

With her words, she says something that resembles stop, but what does Sarah experience? It isn't stopping. Instead, she hears more words. Her mother's action message is really saying, "Go ahead and do what you want. I don't like it, but I'm not going to do anything about it, at least not for a while."

Sarah responds to the mixed message the way most strong-willed children do when they suspect their parents don't mean what they say. She ignores the words and learns from what she experiences. What is Sarah's interpretation of her mother's rule about using marker pens on the sofa? Yes, it's okay to use them as long as she can tolerate her mother's annoying reminders.

LIMIT TESTING: HOW CHILDREN DO RESEARCH

Children are natural researchers. They are astute observers of behavior. They know how to collect research data, and they know how to form conclusions based upon the data they collect. How do children like Sarah know that our spoken rules are really the rules we practice? Often, they don't know, but they do know how to find out. They test. They simply do whatever it is we asked them not to do and they wait to see what happens. This is limit testing or how children do research. The data they collect from these experiences helps them form conclusions about our rules and answer some very important research questions: What's really okay? Who's really in charge? How far can I go? What happens when I go too far?

The conclusions children reach are often different from those parents expect. Why? Because children conduct their research the same way they learn—concretely. They base their beliefs on what they experience, not just on what they are told.

Aggressive Research

Eight-year-old Brian is a typical example of the many hard-way learners I see in my family counseling work. He's bright and capable, but he resists doing what he's asked, both at home and in the classroom. He arrived at my office with his parents.

> How do children know that our spoken rules are really the rules we practice? They test.

"Brian takes everything to the limit," his father complained. "He challenges and defies most of our requests and doesn't seem satisfied until everybody is upset." I had a hunch I was about to meet a very aggressive researcher.

As his father talked, I could see Brian sizing me up. Then, he went right to work on me. In my office I have six comfortable, upholstered swivel chairs. What do you think aggressive researchers like Brian do when they arrive in an office with swivel chairs? That's right. They spin them, and sometimes they put their feet in them. I see more than a hundred chair spinners a year!

The kids know it's not okay, I know it's not okay, and their parents know it too; but the kids spin in my swivel chairs anyway. They look at their parents, then at me, then spin away and wait to see what happens. This is limit testing. When it happens, I know I'm going to learn a great deal about how the family communicates about limits. I watch the child, the parents, and the chairs for ten to fifteen minutes, and I get all the data I need about what's going on.

Brian's parents reacted to his chair spinning the way many parents do. They gave him a look of disapproval but didn't say a word. Brian acknowledged the look, stopped briefly, then resumed his spinning as soon as his parents looked away. Brian and his parents were reenacting their family dance, the same dance they go through dozens of times each week. Brian knew every step in the dance by heart.

With his behavior, Brian was asking the same questions he asks at home and in the classroom: Who's in control? How far can I go? What happens when I go too far? He was conducting his own research regarding my authority and the rules that operated in my office. Between disapproving looks, Brian continued to spin the chair. I watched to see what his parents would do next.

After a few minutes, Brian's father did what some parents do when they start to wear down and get frustrated. He reached over and stopped the chair with his hand. Brian's mother gave a series of disapproving looks. Both messages elicited the same response from Brian. He acknowledged their gestures, stopped briefly, then resumed his spinning as soon as they looked away.

Brian's parents were doing their best to say "Stop!" but Brian knew that stopping was not really expected or required. The data he had collected over the years had convinced him that compliance with their rules was optional, not required. All their words and gestures were just meaningless steps in a drama. The spinning continued.

Ten minutes went by, and Brian still had not received a clear or firm message from his parents. Finally, his exasperated mother turned to me and said, "See what he does! This is the same thing he does at home and in the classroom!"

At this point, I intervened and attempted to provide some clear answers to Brian's research questions. In a matter-of-fact voice, I said, "Brian, you can sit in my chairs if you follow two rules: don't spin them and don't put your feet in them. I'm confident you can if you choose to, but if you decide not to, you'll be sitting in my orange chair for the rest of the session." I keep an old, plastic chair in my office for chair spinners.

What do you think Brian did? Sure, he did the same thing most strong-willed children do. He tested, but not right away. A few minutes later, he gave the chair a full spin and looked at me for a reaction.

With his behavior, he was saying, *I heard your words. Now, let's see what you do.* This is aggressive research. He was collecting hard data in the form of experience to determine whether I really meant what I said.

I always do the same thing in these situations. I pulled out the old plastic chair, sat it down next to Brian, and remained standing.

"This will be your chair for the rest of the session," I said. No yelling or threatening. No warnings or second chances. I just looked at him expectantly and waited for him to move into the orange chair.

Brian did what most strong-willed children do when they confront a firm boundary. He made the acceptable choice, but he didn't do it in a respectful manner. He rolled his eyes, gave me a look of disgust, and murmured something under his breath I'm sure wasn't a compliment. Then he complied with my request. He gave me the right behavior but the wrong attitude in an attempt to hook me into a power struggle. The bait was tempting and skillfully presented, but I didn't bite.

What did Brian learn from this experience? I provided him with the hard data he needed to answer his research questions. He knew how far he could push me and what would happen if he pushed too far. He received all the information he needed to make an acceptable choice. By the time the session was over, he understood that I meant what I said. My rule and expectations were clear. With this encounter behind us, it was time for his parents and me to talk about temperament and learning styles.

TEMPERAMENT AND LEARNING STYLES

All children test limits to determine our rules and expectations. This is normal. But not all children test limits or learn rules in the same way. Temperament has a lot to do with how children conduct their research.

> All children test limits to determine our rules and expectations. This is normal. But not all children test limits or learn rules in the same way.

Compliant children don't do a lot of testing because they don't require a lot of hard data to be convinced to accept and follow our rules. Their underlying desire is to please and cooperate. Most are willing to accept our words as all the data they need and cooperate when they're asked. Compliant children are easy to teach because they do most of their learning the easy way. They permit us a wide margin for ineffectiveness in our guidance and discipline methods.

Fence-sitters can be swayed to cooperate or to test depending upon what they observe going on around them. Fence-sitters are not big risk takers, but they are skillful researchers. They get most of their research accomplished by watching their siblings or classmates. When fence-sitters observe their strong-willed siblings or peers consistently getting away with violating rules or challenging authority, that's when fence-sitters shift into gear and start testing more aggressively. If fence-sitters observe strong-willed children not getting away with violating rules or challenging authority, then fence-sitters usually choose to cooperate. They are persuaded by the firm limits they observe.

Strong-willed children, on the other hand, are the real "movers and shakers" in the world. We call them "aggressive researchers" because they frequently test limits and authority. They require a lot of data in the form of experience before they are convinced to accept and follow our rules. To them, the word *stop* is just theory. They want to know what will happen if they don't stop, and they know how to find out. They continue to test and push us to the point of action to see what happens.

Strong-willed children are difficult to teach because they do much of their learning "the hard way"; that is, they have to repeatedly experience the consequences of their choices or behavior before they are willing to accept our rules and authority. This is just a fact of life. It's how they learn. Each time they test they collect another important piece of research data they put into the conclusion column that helps them form their beliefs about our rules and authority. They simply require a lot of data to be convinced.

Is persistent aggressive research really normal? The answer is yes. This is normal behavior for strong-willed children. This is what they do. It's our job to provide them with the data they need to arrive at the desired conclusion.

Strong-willed children are the best measure of the effectiveness of any guidance and discipline program because they leave us no margin for ineffectiveness. We have to be at the top of our game and use discipline methods that are well matched to their temperament and learning style. If not, we will pay a dear price with exhaustive testing and power struggles.

SAME MESSAGE, DIFFERENT RESPONSE

Because they learn rules differently, compliant children, fence-sitters, and strong-willed children often respond differently to the same messages from their parents. This can be very confusing. Let me illustrate this with a personal example.

My oldest son, Scott, is compliant. Most of the time, he cooperates for the asking. My youngest son, Ian, is strong-willed. He requires a lot of hard data before he's convinced that I mean business. My boys conduct their research differently, and I've learned to adjust my signals accordingly.

Both my boys like to listen to the TV with the volume cranked up. When Scott does this, I simply say, "Scott, the TV is too loud. Turn it down, please." He always does, at least he has so far, and I've learned to count on his cooperation. He accepts my words as all the data he needs.

If I use the same message with Ian, I know from experience what he's likely to do. Sometimes he ignores me and waits for a clearer signal, or he might say the words I want to hear, "I will," but continues to do what he wants. What Ian really means is, "I will if I have to, but I didn't hear that I have to." So he continues to test.

Like most strong-willed kids, Ian is searching for the bottom line to determine what the market will bear. So I've learned to provide him with the data he needs to make an acceptable choice. When the TV is too loud, I say, "Ian, turn the TV down, please, or I'm going to have to turn it off."

When Ian hears the word off, he gets up and does the same thing his brother does. He turns the volume down. Why? Because he doesn't want to experience the consequence of his poor choice not to comply. He knows from experience that I will turn the TV off.

I did not achieve my credibility with Ian overnight. I had to earn it with years of consistency. When he was younger, he ignored many of my requests, and I had to follow through and turn the TV off. Each time I did, I was usually confronted with complaints about how mean or unfair I was; but after he collected enough of these experiences, he learned that I meant what I said and started turning the TV down as requested. Eventually, we worked it out. The process wasn't fun or easy for either of us, but he learned that my boundary was firm, and he began making the right choice to cooperate.

Ian still tests more than his brother does, but he also cooperates most of the time when he encounters a firm boundary and gets the data he needs to make an acceptable choice. I've come to accept his aggressive research as a fact of life. I don't take his testing personally. I'm prepared to teach my rules the hard way or the easy way, whichever gets the job done.

> When your words are consistent with your actions,
> your child will begin to tune in to your words and
> take them seriously.

If you have a strong-willed child, you will have to work hard to keep your boundaries firm and provide your child with the data he or she needs to make an acceptable choice. Strong-willed children believe what they experience more than what they are told. When your words are consistent with your actions, your child will begin to tune in to your words and take them seriously. When this happens, you've taken a big step in the right direction, but you still need to make sure that your words and actions are teaching the lessons you intend.

WHAT WE DO IS WHAT WE TEACH

Whatever methods you use to teach your rules, you will have to use those methods frequently with your strong-willed child. Why? Because strong-willed children are action learners. They require large amounts of hard data in the form of experience before they're convinced you mean what you say. If your methods are ineffective, you may be teaching a lesson you don't intend. This is what happened to Steven's parents. When I first met them, their fourth grader had already been suspended from school four times for hitting, and it was still October. The year had barely begun.

"Living with Steven is like living with a time bomb waiting to explode," said his frustrated mother. "He knows it's not okay to hit, but he does it anyway. He hits his younger brother, he hits other kids in the neighborhood, and he hits kids at school. We've talked to him over and over again, but it doesn't seem to sink in."

"What exactly do you say to Steven when he hits his brother?" I asked, curious about their verbal messages.

"Well, I get a little loud," his father confessed. "It makes me angry to see Steven mistreating his younger brother. I let him know very clearly that I'm not going to tolerate it."

"What do you do to get that message across?" I asked.

"We paddle him when he needs it," replied his father. "We don't believe in all this permissive stuff going on today. Kids need to know that you mean business."

"How many times a week does Steven need that kind of reminder?" I asked.

"Two or three times, and sometimes more," his mother replied. "He needs to know when he's gone too far."

"With that many reminders, why do you think Steven is having such a difficult time learning your rules?" I asked.

"We suspect he has some kind of learning problem," his mother replied. "We're thinking about having him tested."

As I got to know Steven, I could see he didn't need testing. The problem wasn't learning. It was teaching. In fact, Steven was a very capable learner. He was mastering all the lessons his parents were teaching him. He was good at yelling, threatening, and intimidation. He knew how to hit to get others to cooperate, and he was becoming very skillful at blaming others when he got caught.

> Strong-willed children are action learners. They require large amounts of hard data in the form of experience before they're convinced you mean what you say.

Clearly, Steven understood his parents' words when they told him not to hit, but their spoken rules were not the rules they practiced. What did they practice? Hitting—lots of it. That was the way they solved problems, and that was the real lesson Steven was learning. By their example, they were teaching a different lesson than they intended.

Parents who rely too heavily on words also experience breakdowns in the teaching-and-learning process. They tend to confuse their words for actions and don't understand why their message doesn't get across. Natalie's mom is a good example. She arrived at my office very frustrated by all the testing and resistance she was encountering from her strong-willed daughter.

"Natalie is a self-centered and disrespectful twelve-year-old," her mother complained. "She knows my rules but doesn't care to follow them. When I try to explain why I have those rules, she tunes me out and does what she pleases." Natalie's mom shared an incident that happens almost every morning before school.

"Natalie knows she's not supposed to play her radio loudly in the morning, but every morning, it's the same thing. She blasts her music so loud you can hear it across the street. It drives me crazy."

"What do you do when that happens?" I asked.

"First, I tell her to turn it down," said her mother, "but that doesn't do any good. I tell her over and over again, but she never listens."

"What do you do next?" I inquired.

"I get really angry. I walk into her room and tell her to turn it down or turn it off. Sometimes I threaten to take her radio away," said her mother.

"Does she cooperate then?" I asked.

"She may turn it down a little," said her mother, "but you can still hear it throughout the house. After a while, she just turns it up again."

"Do you take it away then?" I asked, wondering if eventually she does get around to her action step.

"I haven't yet," she replied, "but that day isn't far off. I just shut her door. She can ruin her own ears."

Natalie's mom doesn't realize that she's actually communicating two rules about playing the radio loudly—one with her words and another with her actions. Her words say, "Turn it down," but her actions say, "You really don't have to if you don't want to." Natalie's choice is clear. This lesson isn't likely to change until her mom provides Natalie with different data.

The examples of Steven and Natalie illustrate how easily the teaching-and-learning process can break down when our words are inconsistent with our actions or when our words and actions are ineffective. In each case, the children collected data, formed conclusions, and learned lessons their parents didn't intend. Their parents believed they were teaching their rules with their words, but the real lesson was being taught with their actions.

Do you find yourself teaching the same lessons over and over again without success? Do you suspect you might be teaching a different lesson than you intend? If so, Chapter 3 will help you confirm your suspicions and get you pointed in the right direction. Teaching rules is much easier when you use the right tools: clear words combined with effective action.

3

How Parents Teach Their Rules

When it comes to teaching rules, most parents operate somewhere on a continuum of approaches. On the one extreme is the autocratic or punitive approach. The limits are firm, but the methods are not very respectful. On the other extreme is the permissive approach. The methods are respectful, but the limits are not very firm. Some use a mixed approach and use some of each extreme. Still others have managed to strike a balance between the two extremes and use an approach that is both firm and respectful.

Each approach is premised on a different set of beliefs about how children learn, the parents' role in the training process, and the proper distribution of power and responsibility between parents and children. Each approach uses different methods and teaches different lessons about cooperation, responsibility, communication, and problem solving.

What is your approach? Do you operate from one of the extremes? Or do you switch back and forth and do some of both? Perhaps you've found a balance that allows you to be firm and respectful at the same time? Is your approach well matched to the temperaments and learning styles of your children? This chapter will help you find out. By examining the methods others use, you'll discover your approach and learn how well your approach is matched to the temperament and learning style of your strong-willed child.

If I could, I'd like to help you discover your approach the way I help parents in my counseling work. I ask them to pick a typical misbehavior that occurs in their home. Then, I ask each parent to describe, step-by-step, exactly what they say and do when their children behave this way. As each parent describes what happens, I diagram on a blackboard each step in the interactional sequence. A visual picture of each parent's methods begins to emerge.

Unfortunately, we cannot draw your diagram together in a book, but we can do the next-best thing. We can examine the experiences and diagrams of other parents who use similar methods to help you discover your approach. Let's begin by looking at how a parent handles a common problem—a sibling quarrel—using the punitive approach.

THE AUTOCRATIC OR PUNITIVE APPROACH (FIRM, BUT NOT RESPECTFUL)

Imagine the following scene. It's a Saturday morning. The parents are upstairs trying to catch a few more hours of sleep. Two children, ages five and eight, are downstairs watching their favorite cartoon show. The five-year-old decides to get more comfortable. He stretches out on the couch, and his feet touch his sister. She gives him a kick, and he screams. Then she stretches out and touches him. He gives her a kick, and she screams. As the parent arrives on the scene, the two kids are pushing and shoving and fighting for control of the couch.

Mom: (in a loud voice, almost yelling) "What's going on here? Can't you guys watch your show without acting like a couple of brats?"

Brother: "I was sitting on my side, and she kicked me."

Sister: "No. He was trying to spread out on my side. When I tried to make him move, he kicked me."

Brother: "That's not true!"

Mom: (angered) "If you both were on your own sides of the couch, there wouldn't be a problem. So one of you must be lying. Tell me the truth. Who was really on the other side of the couch?"

Sister: "He was."

Brother: "No. She was."

Mom: "I knew I couldn't trust you guys. I've heard all the lying and squabbling I'm going to listen to. If I hear any more arguing or fighting from you two, I'm going to take away bikes for the whole day, and there will be no dessert after dinner. Do you understand?" (yelling now) "Knock it off!"

Sister: "What a crab!"

Brother: "Yeah." (laughs at the comment)

Mom: "That's not funny! You both earned yourselves a day without bikes and dessert. Keep it up if you want more."

Sister: "I bet you enjoy making life miserable for others."
Brother: "Yeah!"
Mom: (yelling) "That's enough!" (She gives each a swat and
threatens to ground them if they say anything more.)

Sound familiar? If it does, you have plenty of company. The punitive approach is still one of the most widely used training models.

> Parents who use the punitive approach often find
> themselves in the roles of police detective, judge,
> jailer, referee, and probation officer.

Parents who use the punitive approach often find themselves in the roles of police detective, judge, jailer, referee, and probation officer. They investigate the misbehavior, determine guilt, assign blame, and impose penalties that tend to be harsh and drawn out. Parents direct and control the problem-solving process, which tends to be loud, angry, and adversarial. Cooperation is achieved through fear, threats, and intimidation. It's a win-lose dynamic. Parents usually win.

The underlying belief is that discipline needs to hurt before children can learn from it. Methods include investigation, interrogation, accusations, threats, criticism, shaming, blaming, spanking, grounding, and taking away favorite toys and privileges for days or weeks at a time.

How do children respond to punitive discipline? Compliant children usually cooperate out of fear and intimidation. Strong-willed children often rebel and retaliate. Fence-sitters do a little

EXAMPLES OF PUNITIVE DISCIPLINE PRACTICES

- Spanking, slapping, whipping, and other forms of corporal punishment
- Making children stand in a corner
- Washing children's mouths out with soap
- Taking away favorite toys and privileges for long periods of time
- Shaming and blaming children in front of their siblings
- Threatening, intimidating, and humiliating children
- Grounding children for long periods of time
- Sending children to time-out for several hours
- Using sarcastic or demeaning language
- Calling children names or hitting them to show them how it feels

of both. Most children feel angry and resentful and perceive the methods as hurtful and humiliating. The punitive approach is poorly matched to the temperaments and learning styles of all three groups.

Let's examine a diagram of the interaction between the parent and the two siblings in the earlier example (see Figure 3.1). The parent's behavior is on the left side of the diagram, and the children's behavior is on the right.

At point A, the parent arrives on the scene upset and intervenes with detective work. Her tone is adversarial. The focus is on right and wrong, guilt and blame, good guys and bad guys. The kids pick up on this dynamic quickly and appeal to the parent while accusing each other of lying. The detective work leads nowhere, which makes the parent even angrier. She accuses both of lying.

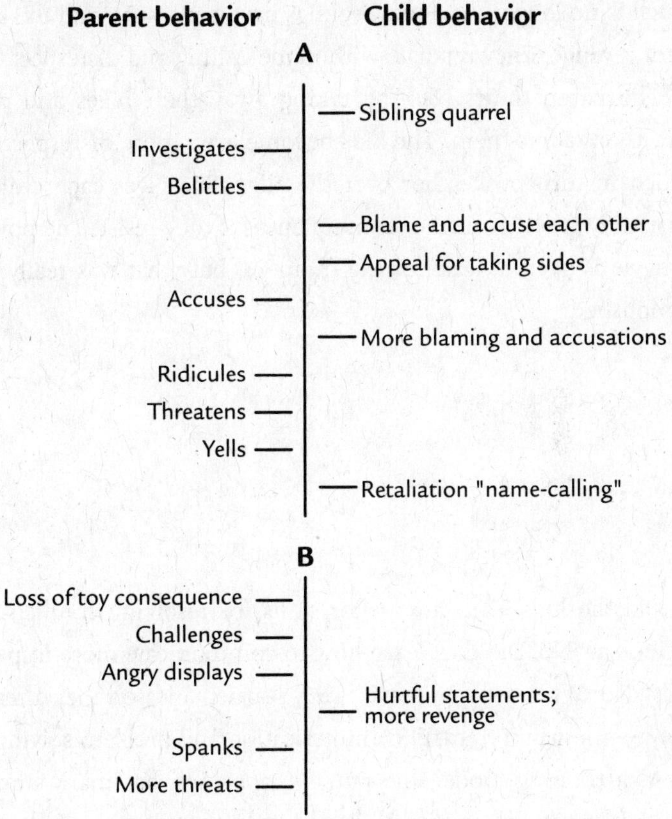

Diagram

Parent behavior   **Child behavior**

A

— Siblings quarrel

Investigates —
Belittles —

— Blame and accuse each other
— Appeal for taking sides

Accuses —

— More blaming and accusations

Ridicules —
Threatens —
Yells —

— Retaliation "name-calling"

B

Loss of toy consequence —
Challenges —
Angry displays —

— Hurtful statements;
more revenge

Spanks —
More threats —

Figure 3.1   Diagram of a Punitive Interaction

By midpoint in the interaction, her anger and frustration take over. She has completely personalized the conflict. The original sibling quarrel is now secondary to the parent-child conflict that dominates the interaction. What started off as problem solving has deteriorated into a hurtful and escalating power struggle.

At point B, the parent tries to end the conflict by threatening to take away their bikes and dessert, but it's too late. Sharing the couch is no longer the issue. Feelings have been hurt, and the kids want revenge. They retaliate with name-calling and disrespect.

The parent hurts back by taking away their bikes and dessert, then taunts them. The kids become even more disrespectful, which in turn pushes her over the edge. She gives each child a swat and threatens further consequences if they resist. The power struggle is over, at least for the moment, but what was really accomplished?

> As a training model, the punitive approach has many limitations; it doesn't teach positive lessons about responsibility, problem solving, or respectful communication.

Did the kids learn any better skills for resolving conflicts on their own? No. Did they learn how to communicate more respectfully? No. What did they learn? They learned a lesson they already knew—a lesson in hurtful communication and problem solving.

As a training model, the punitive approach has many limitations. It usually does stop misbehavior eventually, but it doesn't teach positive lessons about responsibility, problem solving, or respectful communication. Why not? Because parents make all the decisions, and parents do all the problem solving. The methods parents use in the punitive model encourage hurtful communication, demonstrate poor problem solving, and teach children to be dependent upon adults.

What do you think will happen next time the two siblings in our example have a conflict? Sure, one of them will scream for Mom or Dad to come solve the problem. If Mom or Dad doesn't show up in time, the kids will use the methods they know best: yelling, threatening, blaming, name-calling, and hitting.

Can you imagine what it would be like if our traffic laws were enforced with this approach? Visualize yourself driving through a stop sign or a red light. A cop sees you and pulls you over. As he approaches your car, he shouts insults and angrily writes out a ticket. But before he returns to his car, he smacks you twice with his nightstick.

How would you respond to this kind of treatment? Would you turn to the officer with a look of gratitude and say, "Thanks, I needed that. I understand your point, and I'll try harder to stop in the future." Probably not. Would you feel like cooperating with someone who treated you so disrespectfully? Again, probably not.

When it comes to humiliation, children respond much like

adults. They understand the rule, but they dislike the way the message is delivered.

The punitive approach works best with the kids who don't need it: compliant kids who have an underlying desire to please and cooperate. But the approach is poorly matched to the temperaments and learning styles of strong-willed children and many fence-sitters. It makes them angry and resentful and incites them to retaliate. The cooperation parents achieve comes at a high price—injured feelings, damaged relationships, and angry power struggles.

> If the punitive approach has so many limitations,
> why do so many parents continue to use it?

If the punitive approach has so many limitations, why do so many parents continue to use it? Most parents who use punishment were raised that way themselves. It feels natural and familiar, and they don't question its effectiveness. When things break down, they assume the problem is with the child, not with their methods.

Kyle's dad is a good example. He arrived at my office with his ten-year-old son and announced, "Kyle is going through some kind of rebellious stage. He won't do anything I tell him."

Kyle and his father had been locked in a power struggle for nearly a month. Both sides were so angry with each other that they weren't even speaking.

The problem began when Kyle arrived home nearly two hours late from school one day. He told his parents he was playing basketball and simply lost track of the time. Kyle's father was determined to see that the problem didn't happen again. He suspended Kyle's after-school play privileges for two weeks.

> Most parents who use punishment were raised that way themselves. It feels natural and familiar, and they don't question its effectiveness.

When Kyle tried to protest the decision, his father sent him to his room. Kyle got mad. "You're a tyrant!" he shouted, and he kicked a hole in his door. Kyle's father shouted back and informed Kyle he was grounded until further notice and that his allowance would be withheld for two months to pay for the door. Kyle refused to do his chores.

Three weeks passed, and they were still stuck. No chores had been done, and Kyle spent most of his time sulking around the house. His parents were miserable too. Both sides blamed the other, and neither side was willing to budge. It was hard to tell who was being punished most, Kyle or his parents.

"How would your father have handled this problem?" I asked Kyle's father, hoping to take a little pressure off Kyle.

"I would have been spanked as soon as I got home, and then I would have been grounded for a couple of weeks," he replied.

"Did that kind of discipline ever seem excessive to you?" I asked.

"Sometimes," he replied, "but that was my father's way of teaching me a lesson. Lots of parents did that when I was young; and kids learned from it too."

Like many parents raised with punishment, Kyle's father was taught that consequences had to be painful for children to learn. He was applying this same belief with his son.

"Did your father's lessons ever make you angry?" I asked.

"Frequently," he replied. "I can remember thinking he was a real tyrant at times. We had our share of quarrels, too." Kyle began to get interested.

"So your father's methods made you angry and rebellious, too," I observed. "Were your quarrels with your father similar to the one you're having now with Kyle?" He looked at Kyle and smiled. He was beginning to see that Kyle's resentment was not the problem—his methods were (see Table 2). He was ready to learn some better ways to get his message across.

TABLE 2. The Autocratic or Punitive Approach

Matchups	Poorly matched to temperaments and learning styles of strong-willed and fence-sitters.
Parents' beliefs	If it doesn't hurt, children won't learn. Children won't respect my rules unless they fear my methods. It's my job to control my children. It's my job to solve my children's problems.
Power and control	All for parents.
Problem solving	Problem solving by force. Adversarial. Win-lose (parents win). Parents do all the problem solving and make all the decisions. Parents direct and control the process.
What children learn	Parents are responsible for solving children's problems. Dependency on adults, disrespect. Hurtful methods of communication and problem solving.
How children respond	Anger, stubbornness, revenge, rebellion, withdrawal, fearful submission.

THE PERMISSIVE APPROACH (RESPECTFUL, BUT NOT FIRM)

Permissiveness emerged in the 1960s and 1970s as a reaction against the hurtful and autocratic nature of the punitive approach. Many parents were looking for a more respectful method of raising children based on democratic principles of freedom, equality, and mutual respect.

Putting these principles into practice, however, was not as easy as it sounded. This was uncharted territory for those of us who grew up with the punitive model. How do you do it? Is it a simple matter of relaxing your rules and expectations and giving children more freedom and control? That's what many parents tried, but the experiment backfired because a vital ingredient was left out—firm limits.

Freedom without limits is not democracy. It's anarchy, and children raised with anarchy don't learn respect for rules or authority or how to handle their freedom responsibly. They tend to think of themselves first and have an exaggerated sense of their own power and authority.

Let's return to the sibling conflict and see how this problem is handled from the permissive approach. As the parent arrives on the scene, the kids are fighting for control of the couch.

Mom: "Hey guys, I don't like all this yelling and screaming. It sounds like a battle zone around here." (She walks out of the room, but the quarrel continues.)

Mom: (entering the room once again, annoyed) "Did you guys hear what I said? Would you keep the noise down and stop all the hassling? Okay?" (She leaves but the quarrel continues.)

Mom: (entering the room a third time) "How many times do I have to tell you? Do you think I enjoy repeating myself? Can't you guys just be nice to each other for a change? I can't stand living in a house where people argue and shout all the time! Someday, you'll regret the way you're treating each other. Now please, try to get along!" (The quarrel continues.)

Brother: "I was sitting here, and she kicked me."

Sister: "His feet were on my side. When he tried to kick me, I kicked him back."

Mom: "Why don't you guys take turns sharing the couch?"

Brother: "Okay. It's my turn first." (He places his feet on the edge of the couch, taunting his sister.)

Sister: "No, it's my turn first!" (She places her feet on the far edge of her side, nearly touching her brother.)

Mom: (exasperated and yelling) "That's it! I've had it with you two." (She threatens to turn the TV off and tells the kids to get off the couch until they decide to cooperate.)

Brother: "That's not fair! We didn't do anything wrong."

Sister: "Yeah, we were just sitting here."

Mom: "No, you were about to start a fight."

Brother: "We were just playing."

Sister: "Yeah."

Mom: "If you both promise to keep your feet to yourselves and stay on your own side, you can stay on the couch with the TV on."

Brother: "I promise."

Sister: "I promise, too."

Mom: "Good. No more fighting, okay? I really mean it." (Within minutes, the quarrel resumes.)
Brother: "She kicked me harder this time."
Sister: "He kicked me first."
Mom: "Okay, if fighting is the only thing you know how to do, then go ahead and battle it out, but do it quietly." (She leaves, exasperated.)

Permissive parents constantly shift gears and use different verbal tactics to convince and persuade children to cooperate. The underlying belief is that kids will cooperate when they understand that cooperation is the right thing to do. The assumption generally holds for compliant children who do most of their learning the easy way. But the assumption does not apply to strong-willed children and many fence-sitters who do much of their learning the hard way. These children require more than words to be convinced.

Permissive methods involve a lot of repeating, reminding, warning, second chances, reasoning, explaining, pleading, cajoling, lecturing, arguing, bargaining, debating, negotiating, compromising, and other forms of persuasion. Consequences or actions, if they are used at all, are typically late and ineffective. Basically, it's lots of words and very little action. The methods are respectful, but not very firm.

How do children respond to permissive discipline methods? Compliant children usually cooperate, not because the signals are clear, but because their underlying desire is to please and cooperate anyway. Compliant children give parents a wide margin for ineffectiveness.

EXAMPLES OF PERMISSIVE DISCIPLINE METHODS

- Ignoring or overlooking unacceptable behavior
- Allowing children to misbehave when you are in a good mood
- Giving warnings, second chances for misbehavior
- Arguing, debating, and negotiating with misbehaving children
- Repeating, reminding, and giving long explanations
- Offering bribes and special rewards for cooperation
- Pleading and begging for cooperation
- Allowing children to treat you disrespectfully
- Allowing children to treat each other disrespectfully
- Giving in to tantrums or angry drama
- Cleaning up messes for children
- Making excuses for children's misbehavior
- Avoiding confrontations
- Allowing children to misbehave in public
- Cajoling children into cooperating
- Giving long lectures to correct misbehavior
- Inconsistent follow-through for misbehavior

The opposite is true for strong-willed children and many fence-sitters. When they encounter messages that lack firmness or clarity, they usually test to see what the market will bear. They tune out, ignore, challenge, defy, argue, debate, dawdle, procrastinate, or just dig in their heels and push for the walls. They know from experience that if they resist long enough, there's a good chance their parents will compromise away their limits or give in altogether.

From a training perspective, permissive methods have limited instructive value because children don't make the cause-and-effect connection between what we say and what we do. They hear the words *no* or *stop*," but they don't experience the action that supports them and gives them meaning. To kids, the message sounds something like this: "It would be nice if you cooperated, but you really don't have to."

Would you cooperate with this message? I might. I'm compliant, but most strong-willed children and many fence-sitters don't because compliance is optional, not required. Instead, they tune out and ignore the words and push things to the point of action.

> Permissive parents constantly shift gears and use different verbal tactics to convince and persuade children to cooperate. The underlying belief is that kids will cooperate when they understand that cooperation is the right thing to do.

As a training model, permissiveness is poorly matched to the temperaments and learning styles of strong-willed children and fence-sitters. It doesn't accomplish any of our basic training goals. It doesn't stop misbehavior. It doesn't teach respect for rules or authority, and it doesn't teach the lessons we intend about responsibility, respectful communication, or cooperative problem solving. The methods inspire testing and power struggles. Permissiveness is humiliating to parents.

Let's examine a diagram of the interaction of the two siblings quarreling over the couch (see Figure 3.2). The first thing you probably notice is the length of this diagram. Permissive parents invest a great deal of time and energy in methods that don't work. This parent is no exception. She begins at point A with a lot of repeating and reminding. The kids respond by ignoring her. So she

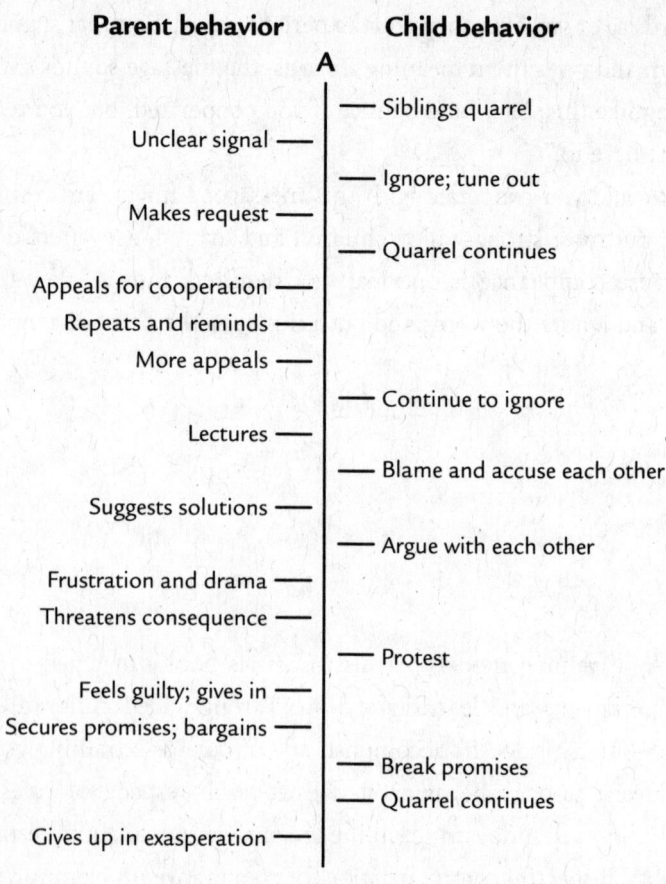

Figure 3.2   Diagram of a Permissive Interaction

tries lecturing and pleading, but that doesn't work either. The kids continue to ignore her.

So the parent suggests a reasonable solution—taking turns—but neither child is willing to cooperate if the solution means letting the other go first. The parent becomes frustrated and shifts gears again. She threatens to turn off the TV and make the kids get off the couch. When they protest, she gives in.

Next, the parent tries bargaining for their cooperation. Promises are made, then broken, and she finally gives up and leaves the room discouraged. She never did succeed in stopping their misbehavior or teaching them better ways to resolve their disputes.

Why didn't the siblings cooperate? The reason is simple. They didn't have to. Cooperation was optional, not required. Their parent was unwilling to support her words with effective action. Instead, she relied on words alone to get her message across.

Can you imagine what things would be like if our traffic laws were enforced with permissiveness? Visualize yourself driving home once again. You approach a red light, but there isn't another car in sight. So you run it. Each time you approach an intersection with no other cars around, you do the same thing. Eventually, a cop sees you and pulls you over.

> As a training model, permissiveness is poorly matched to the temperaments and learning styles of strong-willed children.

He approaches your car, smiles, tips his hat, and informs you that you ran four stoplights. Then, he proceeds to lecture you on the importance of obeying traffic laws.

"Those signals are intended for your safety," he says, "and the safety and protection of other motorists. If everyone ran stoplights, we would have accidents all over our streets, injuries, and higher insurance rates." Then he pleads with you to try harder to follow those signals in the future. When the lecture is over, he gets in his car and drives off. If our traffic laws were enforced in this manner, do you think people would take them very seriously? Not likely.

Permissive parents are a lot like the cop in my example. They give lots of warnings, reminders, and persuasive reasons why kids should cooperate. Parents may threaten to write tickets, and sometimes they actually do, but most of the time kids talk their way out of it, and parents let things pass with a warning.

Is a warning a strong enough signal to stop you from doing something you really want to do? Let's test it out. When you approach an intersection and the light is yellow, but you can safely make it through, do you always stop at the yellow light, every time? Most drivers don't, and neither do kids when parents hold up these signals to try to stop misbehavior.

Kids don't stop for the same reason adults don't. Stopping is optional, not required. Most of us wait for the signal that really matters, the red light. Why? Because we associate this signal with an action that means something—a ticket, a collision, higher insurance rates, or something worse.

Kids are no different. They respect the signals that matter, the ones that have a direct and meaningful effect upon them. Without tickets (consequences) to hold them accountable, kids have little cause to take their parents' rules seriously.

Permissiveness is a guidance system based on yellow lights. Stopping is optional, not required. Kids know it, but permissive parents are unaware that their signals don't really require stopping. They sincerely believe that all their repeating, reminding, warnings, and words of persuasion are equivalent to a red light.

Why are permissive parents so reluctant to use consequences in their training? Most have the best of intentions. They're not trying to be vague. They simply want to teach their rules "the easy way," with words alone, and avoid the frustration that comes with

meaningful action. Permissive parents believe that the temporary frustration that accompanies consequences may damage their children psychologically.

Let's do a little reality testing. Are you accustomed to always getting your way out in the world? When you don't, do you feel good about it? Aren't we supposed to feel frustrated when we don't get what we want? Isn't that how we learn to delay immediate gratification and adjust to reality? When parents prevent children from experiencing the consequences of their poor choices and behavior, parents also prevent important learning.

> When parents prevent children from experiencing the consequences of their poor choices and behavior, parents also prevent important learning.

James, age five, is a good example. He was getting off to a rough start in kindergarten when I first met him. The note his teacher sent was revealing: "James is very disruptive and uncooperative in class. He pushes everything to the limit. When I ask him to join an activity, he usually ignores me and does what he wants. When I insist, he cries or throws a tantrum. He seems to think classroom rules don't apply to him."

James's mother also was frustrated. "He's the same way at home," she complained. "He refuses to get dressed in the morning. He won't come in when I call him for dinner, and getting him to bed is a nightmare by itself. I have to ask him over and over again, and most of the time, he just ignores me and does what he wants."

Like many strong-willed children raised with permissiveness, James was accustomed to getting his way and had learned a full repertoire of skills to make that happen. He was an expert at tuning out, ignoring, resisting, avoiding, dawdling, arguing, debating, bargaining, challenging, and defying. When those tactics didn't work, James played his power card. He threw a tantrum. His mother usually felt guilty and gave in.

James's intentions were not malicious. He did it because it worked. His experiences had taught him this: "Rules are for others, not me. I make my own rules, and I do what I want." James operated on these beliefs, both at home and in the classroom.

It wasn't hard to understand why James had such an exaggerated sense of his own power and authority. At home, he ran the show. His mother's "stop signs" didn't require stopping. When he

TABLE 3. The Permissive Approach

Matchups	Poorly matched to strong-willed children and fence-sitters.
Parents' beliefs	Children will cooperate when they understand that cooperation is the right thing to do.
Power and control	All for children.
Problem solving	Problem solving by persuasion. Win-lose (children win). Parents do most of the problem solving.
What children learn	Rules are for others, not me. I do as I wish. Parents serve children. Parents are responsible for solving children's problems. Dependency, disrespect, self-centeredness.
How children respond	Limit testing. Challenge and defy rules and authority. Ignore and tune out words. Wear parents down with words.

misbehaved, he knew he'd hear a lot of repeating, reminding, lecturing, and threats . . . but none of those "warning" signals really required stopping. His training had not prepared him for the real stop signs he encountered out in the world (see Table 3).

THE MIXED APPROACH (NEITHER FIRM NOR RESPECTFUL)

As the name implies, the mixed approach is a combination of the punitive and permissive training models. The mixed approach is characterized by inconsistency. It combines the worst elements of the two extremes and brings out the most extreme reactions in parents and children.

Parents who use this approach do a lot of flip-flopping back and forth between punishment and permissiveness in search of a better way to get their message across. They know how to be respectful but not without being permissive. They know how to be firm but not without being punitive. They don't know how to be firm and respectful at the same time, so they flip-flop back and forth.

Try to imagine what our traffic laws would be like if they were enforced with the mixed approach. When you run a red light, sometimes the cop gives you a lecture and lets it pass with a warning. Other times, he screams insults at you, writes out a ticket, and threatens to hit you with his club. How do you know what will happen from one time to the next? You don't. How would you respond?

If you're compliant, you probably won't risk running red lights very often. If you're a fence-sitter, you'll decide what to do based on what you see others getting away with. If you're strong-willed,

> ### EXAMPLES OF MIXED DISCIPLINE PRACTICES
>
> - Ignoring misbehavior until you can't stand it anymore, then using harsh consequences
> - Allowing children to misbehave sometimes
> - Threatening consequences but failing to follow through
> - Using different consequences for the same misbehavior
> - Asking children to be quiet, then yelling at them
> - Using punitive and permissive practices under the same roof
> - Giving warnings and second chances, then punishing

you'll probably run red lights frequently and find ways to retaliate when you get caught.

There are many variations to the mixed approach. The most common variation is the one in which parents begin permissively, then they wear down, lose their patience, and resort to punitive tactics—threats, shaming, blaming, long and drawn-out consequences. Other parents begin punitively, but give in and resort to permissive tactics when they encounter complaints or resistance. Still others remain loyal to one approach for longer periods of time. They try permissiveness for weeks or months until they can't stand being tuned out and ignored any longer, then they crack down and use punishment until they can't stand how tyrannical they sound. Then, they switch back to permissiveness. It's a roller-coaster ride. The cycle of flip-flops just takes longer to repeat itself.

The mixed approach is characterized by inconsistency. It combines the worst elements of the two extremes and brings out the most extreme reactions in parents and children.

Another common variation occurs when parents differ in their respective approaches. One parent might be punitive, the other permissive, but their combined methods constitute a mixed approach (see Table 4).

To kids, this is like living under the same roof with two governments operating simultaneously. One government takes the hard line. The other takes the soft line. Kids figure out that the rules are different between their parents and learn to play one government against the other.

Trent, age nine, is a good example. He knows he's supposed to finish his chores before he goes out to play, but his friends are in the street playing baseball, and he really wants to join them.

TABLE 4. The Mixed Approach

Matchups	Poorly matched to all temperaments and learning styles.
Parents' beliefs	Alternates between permissive and punitive thinking. Characterized by inconsistency.
Power and control	Varies from one incident to the next.
Problem solving	Inconsistent. Alternates between punitive and permissive practices.
What children learn	Parents are inconsistent. Parents don't mean what they say. Parents don't follow through. Testing is the only way to find out what's okay. Children learn ineffective problem solving and communication skills.
How children respond	Varies from one incident to the next. Rules and expectations are unclear. Ignore, tune out, explode with defiance.

Trent's mom is permissive. If he asks her for permission, he knows the answer will be a dependable yes. Trent's dad is punitive. If Trent asks him for permission, Trent knows the answer will be a predictable no. If you were Trent, who would you ask? Of course, you'd go to Mom every time.

If Dad discovers that Mom allowed Trent to play before completing his chores, how will Dad respond? Sure, he'll likely think she's too lenient. He'll probably try to balance her out by being more strict. How will Mom respond if he does? She'll likely think he's being too strict and try to balance him out by being more lenient. In an attempt to balance each other out, parents often end up driving each other even further in their respective extreme directions. The inconsistency between parents sets the whole family up for testing and conflict.

Let's return to our sibling conflict and see how the problem is handled with the mixed approach. Once again, the parents are upstairs trying to sleep. The kids are downstairs, arguing and fighting for control of the couch.

Mom: (hears the quarrel but tries to ignore the noise; five minutes pass; the quarrel continues; parent decides to intervene.) "Hey guys, it's pretty loud in here. Would you try to hold the noise down a little, please?" (She leaves. The quarrel continues.)

Mom: (entering the room again, annoyed) "Did you guys hear what I just said? I'm getting tired of coming in here and talking to you guys. Do you understand? Would you keep it down, please? Okay?" (She leaves again, but the quarrel continues.)

Mom: (entering the room a third time, very annoyed) "How many times do I have to ask you? Why can't you two be nice to each other?"

Brother: "I was just trying to stretch out and she kicked me."

Sister: "No, I was trying to stretch out and he kicked me."

Mom: "I suspect one of you is not telling me the truth. Now who's lying? You know how I feel about lying."

Brother: "She is."

Sister: "No, he is."

Mom: "I've had enough of this! You both are acting like brats. If I hear another peep out of either of you, I'm going to take away your bikes and dessert for the rest of the day." (She gives them each an angry look.) "If that's what you want, try me." (She leaves the room, but a few moments later the youngest sibling lets out a scream.)

Mom: (enters the room, and explodes) "I've had it! You both just lost your bikes and dessert for the rest of the day. Do you want to lose your TV privileges too?"

Brother: "You're mean!"

Sister: "No, wicked is a better word."

Mom: (yelling) "Okay, you both just lost your TV privileges too."

Brother: "That's not fair!"

Sister: "She enjoys making others miserable."

Mom: "You got what you deserve. If I hear any more out of either of you, you both will be grounded to the house for the rest of the day, and no friends will be allowed in the house." (She shoots an intimidating glance at each child. The quarrel ends.)

Did the kids' behavior cause the parent to explode or did she set herself up by allowing things to go too far? Let's answer these questions by examining a diagram of the interaction (see Figure 3.3).

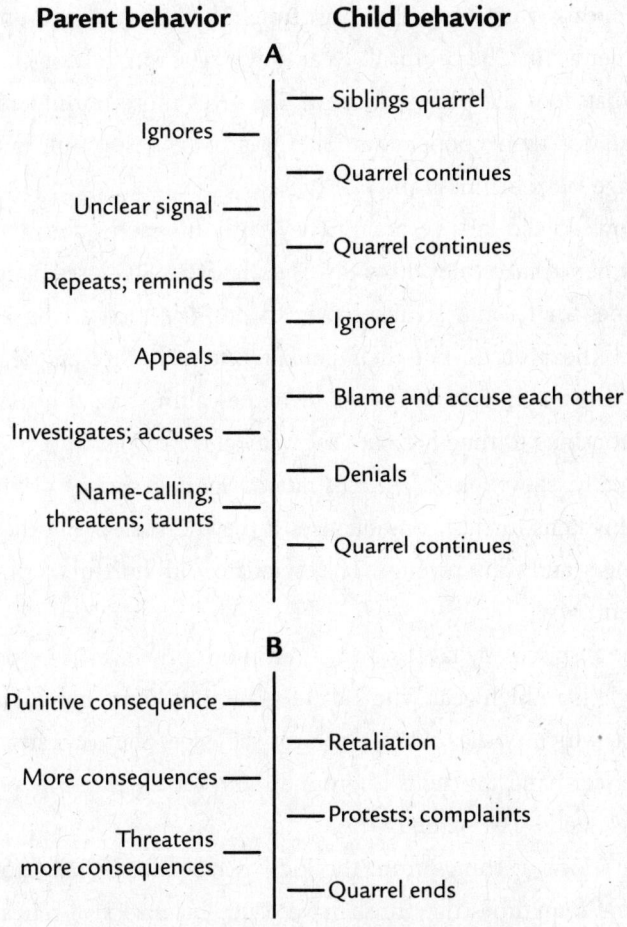

Figure 3.3   Diagram of a Mixed Interaction

What happens the first time the quarrel gets too loud? Do the kids receive a clear message to stop? No. The parent ignores the noise and hopes it will stop. The quarrel continues.

What happens the second time? The parent appeals for their cooperation and leaves the room. The quarrel continues.

What happens the third time? The parent reenters the room and repeats what she said the last time. The kids tune out and ignore her again. She begins to wear down. The quarrel continues.

What does the parent do next? She gives more reminders and appeals for their cooperation. She tries to be respectful, but her message lacks firmness and clarity.

How do the kids respond? They tattle on each other and try to get her to take sides. It works. She's hooked. She loses patience, becomes angry, and switches over to punitive tactics. She investigates and accuses, but their denials just make her angrier and more frustrated. So she resorts to name-calling and threats. The kids continue to tune her out. The quarrel continues.

Finally, she explodes in frustration. She takes away privileges and threatens further consequences if they don't stop. But the kids are angry and want revenge. They retaliate with hurtful comments of their own.

She responds by taking away even more privileges. The power struggle is in high gear. The kids retaliate with more hurtful comments, which pushes the parent over the edge. She plays her final power card and threatens to ground them for the day. The power struggle ends. The parent wins.

Let's look at things from the kids' perspective. What happens the first four times they misbehave? They hear a lot of repeating, reminding, and appeals for their cooperation, but nothing happens to make them stop. Why should they take her seriously? They don't.

What happens the fifth time? Finally, the parent is ready to act, but she's allowed things to go too far. Her anger and frustration take over. She explodes and ends up using the punitive tactics she tried so hard to avoid. She wants to be firm and respectful, but she lacks the skills to be both at the same time.

THE DEMOCRATIC APPROACH (FIRM AND RESPECTFUL)

Effective limit setting requires a balance between firmness and respect. The punitive approach is firm but not respectful. The permissive approach is respectful but not firm. The mixed approach is neither firm nor respectful.

These approaches are based on win-lose methods of problem solving and on faulty beliefs about learning, and they fail to accomplish our basic training goals. They don't stop misbehavior. They don't teach children the skills they need to solve problems on their own. And they don't teach the lessons we intend about responsibility, communication, or respectful problem solving. These approaches invite testing and rebellion and are poorly matched to many temperaments and learning styles.

> The democratic approach is a win-win method of problem solving that combines firmness with respect and accomplishes all of our basic training goals.

Is there a better alternative? Fortunately, there is. The democratic approach is a win-win method of problem solving that combines firmness with respect and accomplishes all of our basic training goals. It stops misbehavior. It teaches responsibility, and it conveys, in the clearest way, the lessons we want to teach about responsibility, problem solving, and respectful communication.

Best of all, the democratic approach works with all children, easy-way learners, hard-way learners, and those in between. The approach gets the job done in less time, with less energy, and without injuring feelings, damaging relationships, or provoking power struggles in the process.

Don't be confused by the term "democratic." I'm not suggesting decision making by consensus or problem solving by compromise, nor that you abdicate your parental authority. The term "democratic" is used to illustrate how boundaries are established.

The punitive approach provides limits without much freedom or choice. The permissive approach provides freedom and choice without clearly defined limits. The democratic approach is simply the balance between the two extremes. It's not too broad, and it's not too restrictive. It provides children with freedom and choice within clearly defined boundaries.

The democratic approach is a healthy, balanced blueprint for guidance and development. It provides opportunities for healthy testing and exploration but within clearly defined boundaries to guide children's choices and learning.

The democratic approach succeeds where others fail because it's clear. Children hear our words and experience the action that supports them without all the anger, drama, strong emotion, and power struggles that interfere with good communication and learning. The message is clear, and so is the rule behind it.

> The teaching-and-learning process is cooperative, not adversarial.

The underlying belief is that children learn best when encouraged and allowed to experience the consequences of their own choices and behavior. Children are encouraged to make choices, experience the outcomes of their choices, and learn from their experiences.

The teaching-and-learning process is cooperative, not adversarial. Parents don't act like broken records trying to wear kids down with words, and they don't act like police detectives, judges, referees, or probation officers trying to force or coerce kids into cooperation. Instead, parents take a teaching role and guide a natural learning process. They give clear messages with their words, encourage cooperation, teach skills, and follow through with instructive consequences that are logically related to the behavior.

The democratic approach is particularly well matched to the temperaments and learning styles of strong-willed children and fence-sitters. When used consistently, it teaches them to tune in to your words, make better choices, and cooperate more often. It won't change their temperament or how they do their research, but it will provide them with the data they need in the clearest and most understandable way. Whether they choose to learn the easy way or the hard way, it doesn't matter. The democratic approach teaches the lesson in whatever way your child chooses to learn it (see Table 5).

EXAMPLES OF DEMOCRATIC DISCIPLINE PRACTICES

- Separating children who are quarreling, fighting, or antagonizing each other
- Removing toys temporarily when children use toys in an unacceptable manner
- Turning off the TV when children refuse to turn it down
- Encouraging children to make better choices
- Sending children to time-out for aggressive or hurtful behavior toward others
- Acknowledging cooperation and good choices
- Removing a privilege temporarily when children misuse or abuse that privilege
- Separating children from activities temporarily when they are disruptive
- Expressing confidence in children's capabilities
- Sending children to time-out for defiant behavior
- Removing a soccer ball from a child kicking it in the house
- Holding children accountable for cleaning up their own messes
- Catching children cooperating and celebrating their compliance
- Expressing your confidence that your children can make good choices
- Accepting children, not their unacceptable behavior
- Showing forgiveness when a discipline incident is over

Let's return to our now-familiar sibling conflict and see how this problem is handled with the democratic approach.

Mom: (in a matter-of-fact voice) "Guys, stop the yelling and arguing. I'm sure we can find a way to share the couch without

TABLE 5. The Democratic Approach

Matchups	The democratic approach is well matched to all temperament and learning styles.
Parents' beliefs	Children are capable of solving problems on their own. Children should be given choices and allowed to learn from their choices. Encouragement is an effective way to motivate cooperation.
Power and control	Children are given only as much power and control as they can handle responsibly.
Problem solving	Cooperative. Win-win. Based on mutual respect. Children are active participants in the problem-solving process.
What children learn	Responsibility. Cooperation. Independence. Respect for rules and authority. Self-control.
How children respond	More cooperation. Less limit testing. Resolve problems on their own. Regard parents' words seriously.

fighting, but do you guys need a little time to cool off first before we talk?"

Brother: "I can talk."

Sister: "I'm ready, too."

Mom: "What's another way to handle this problem without yelling and fighting about it?"

Brother: "I don't know, but I was sitting on my side and she kicked me."

Sister: "No, he put his feet on my side. When I tried to make him move, he kicked me."

Mom: "We can set the timer and each of you can have the couch to yourself for fifteen minutes, or you guys can share the couch and keep your feet on your own side. What would you like to do?"

Brother: "I'll share."

Sister: "So will I."

Mom: "Good choice. I knew you guys could work it out, but if there's any more fighting over the couch, you'll both have to sit on the floor."

Unlike the other examples, this parent succeeds at stopping her children's misbehavior and teaching the lessons she intends. She accomplishes all this without conflicts and power struggles. Let's examine a diagram of the interaction (see Figure 3.4).

Notice how short the diagram is. Effective guidance takes less time and energy and yields better results. This parent is working with a plan. She knows what she's going to do, and she's prepared for whatever she may encounter. No time is wasted on ineffective lobbying or detective work.

Her first step is to give a clear message about the behavior she wants to stop. In a matter-of-fact voice, she asks them to stop yelling and fighting. Then she gets right to work creating a climate for cooperation by expressing confidence in their ability to work things out. Her words are encouraging. Her message is clear and direct. In two brief sentences, she creates a climate of cooperation and respect.

This parent understands that successful problem solving rarely occurs in an atmosphere of anger, so she provides her children with the skills they need to manage their hurt feelings. She asks if they need a cool-down period before talking.

The cool-down period, in this instance, is presented as a choice, and the exercise of that choice teaches children to be responsible for managing their angry feelings. If the frustration level had been greater, the cool-down time would have been presented as mandatory rather than optional.

When the parent is sure emotional control has been restored, she checks in with her children to determine whether they have the skills to resolve the problem on their own. Their responses indicate they don't, so she presents several solutions in the form of a choice. By choosing the solution themselves, the children learn responsibility for their own problem solving.

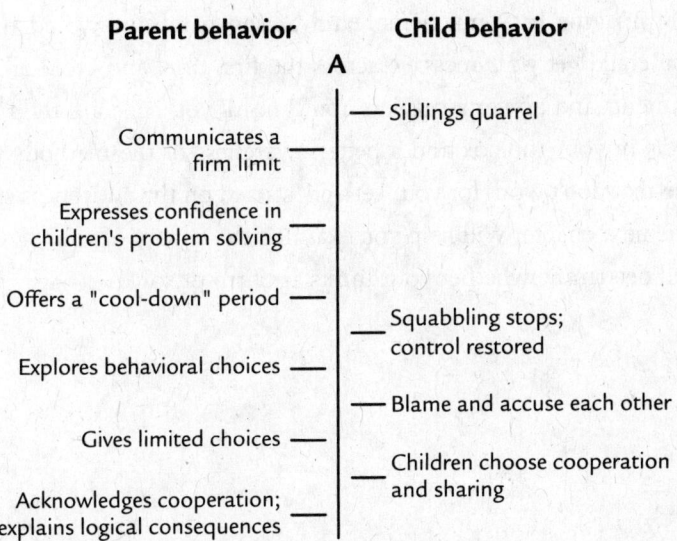

Figure 3.4   Diagram of a Democratic Interaction

The guidance lesson ends the way it began—in an atmosphere of cooperation and mutual respect. All goals were accomplished. The parent stopped the misbehavior, modeled respectful communication and problem solving, and taught the skills her children needed to solve problems on their own. No arguments or power struggles. No one was blamed or singled out. She was so effective that consequences were not even needed, but she was equally prepared to make the kids sit apart on the floor had they decided to continue quarreling over the couch. Either way, they would have learned the rule she intended to teach.

> Successful problem solving rarely occurs in an atmosphere of anger.

Can you see yourself handling problems like this parent? Can you imagine how much more rewarding parenting would be if you could get your message across the first time and avoid all arguments and power struggles? You can. All you need are the right tools in your toolbox and a better awareness of the methods you use that don't work for you. Let's get started on the awareness step. The next chapter will help you examine the quality of your signals and determine whether your limits are firm or soft.

4

Are Your Limits Firm or Soft?

When you say no to your kids, does it really mean no? If you ask the kids, often they'll tell you that no really means yes, sometimes, or maybe. The problem, in most cases, is unclear communication limits. Many parents believe they're holding up a red light when they say no, but the kids see it as green or flashing yellow because they know compliance is optional, not required.

Limits come in two basic varieties, firm and soft, each of which sends a different message to children about our rules and expectations. Firm limits are clear signals. Words are supported with effective action, and compliance is both expected and required. Children raised with firm limits learn to tune in to our words, to take them seriously, and to cooperate more often when asked.

Soft limits, on the other hand, are mixed messages or unclear signals about our rules and expectations. Words are not supported with action. Compliance is optional, not required. Children raised with soft limits learn to tune out and ignore our words and to push us to the point of action more often. Soft limits are a setup for testing and power struggles with strong-willed children and many fence-sitters.

> Children raised with firm limits learn to tune in to our words, to take them seriously, and to cooperate more often when asked.

What kind of signals are you using to get your children to cooperate? Are your red lights really red lights? Or are they green or yellow? This chapter will help you find out. You'll learn the specific things you say and do that don't work for you, and you'll understand why children respond to your signals the way they do.

SOFT LIMITS: WHEN NO MEANS YES, SOMETIMES, OR MAYBE

Five-year-old Andrew knows he's not supposed to have sweets before dinner, but while his mother is busy on the phone, he sneaks into the cookie jar and helps himself to a handful. When his mother discovers what he's doing, she intervenes. "Andrew! You know you're not supposed to have cookies or sweets before dinner. You'll ruin your appetite." Andrew looks apologetic but continues to eat the cookies. His mother continues reasoning with him.

"If I allowed you to eat sweets anytime you want," his mother adds, "you'd never be hungry at meals and you wouldn't get the nutrition you need. If you feel like eating something sweet before dinner, would you let me know first? Okay? I'll try to come up with something that doesn't ruin your dinner." Andrew nods as he gulps down the last few cookies in his hand. "All right, honey," says his mother, "you'll ask next time, won't you?" Andrew nods again.

Andrew's mother is using soft limits to communicate her rules about eating sweets before meals. By the time she finishes talking, she believes her message has gotten across, but has it? What did Andrew really learn about eating sweets before dinner?

> Children raised with soft limits learn to tune out
> and ignore our words and to push us to the point of
> action more often.

Andrew understood his mother's words and gave many of the appropriate responses, but he also finished off a handful of cookies while his mother lectured. What Andrew learned is that eating sweets before dinner is actually okay, as long as he can endure his mother's annoying lectures. The limits Andrew's mother allowed conveyed a different message than she intended.

Soft limits are rules in theory, not in practice. They invite testing because they carry a mixed message. The words seem to say stop, but the action message says that stopping is neither expected nor required. Andrew understood this clearly and responded the way most strong-willed children do when they encounter "warnings." He acknowledged the signal but continued to do what he wanted.

From a training perspective, soft limits are ineffective because they don't give children the information they need to connect the dots and make the cause-and-effect connection between what we say and what we do. The signals simply fail to get the message across. Worse yet, soft limits often achieve the opposite of their intended effect. They invite testing, escalating misbehavior, and power struggles.

Soft limits come in a variety of forms. They can be ineffective verbal messages or ineffective action messages. Sometimes they are both at the same time. All share the common feature of being ineffective at communicating our intended message. Compliance is neither expected nor required. Let's look at some typical examples.

> Soft limits are rules in theory, not in practice. They invite testing because they carry a mixed message.

Wishes, Hopes, and Shoulds

Maddie, age four, knows she's not supposed to play with her father's new CD player, but she thinks she knows what to do. She turns on the power and pushes different buttons to get some music. Her mother enters the room.

Wishes, hopes, and shoulds are another way of saying that stopping would be nice, but you don't really have to. When strong-willed children hear these messages, often they test for clarification.

"Maddie, I really wish you wouldn't play with Daddy's new CD player. I'm afraid you might break it." Maddie ignores her and continues to push buttons. Her mother tries again.

"Maddie, Daddy doesn't like you playing with his electronic equipment. He asked you not to touch it. Remember, honey?" Maddie continues to play with the controls.

"Maddie! I'm getting angry," says her mother. "I really hope you stop before I become even angrier." Maddie still tries to get it to work.

Did you hear a clear message that Maddie is expected and required to stop playing with the CD player? Maddie didn't. Wishes, hopes, and shoulds are another way of saying that stopping would be nice, but you don't really have to. When strong-willed children hear these messages, often they test for clarification. This is exactly what Maddie did when she ignored her mother and continued to play with the controls.

Repeating and Reminding

Matt, age twelve, sits in the living room watching his favorite television show with the volume turned up high.

His annoyed father yells from the other room: "Matt! Turn the TV down."

Matt ignores the request. Several minutes pass.

His father yells again. "Matt, how many times do I have to tell you? Turn the TV down. Are you deaf?"

Matt continues to ignore him, so his father yells again. "Turn it down! The neighbors can hear the TV from across the street." Again, no response.

Finally, Matt's father enters the room, stands between Matt and the TV, and, with one hand on the on/off button, says, "Turn it down or I'll turn it off." Matt gets up and turns the volume down.

What happened the first time Matt ignored his father's request? Nothing. Matt got what he wanted. The second and third requests followed the same pattern. If Matt's father didn't mean what he said the first three times, why should Matt take his father's words more seriously the fourth time? He doesn't.

His father's words say, "Turn it down," but the action message says, "I'm not going to do anything about it, at least not for a while." If you are a strong-willed twelve-year-old who wants to watch your show with the volume high, which message would you follow? Like most of his strong-willed peers, Matt doesn't turn the TV down until he has to. Parents who repeat and remind are actually teaching their children to tune out and ignore.

Warnings and Second Chances

Darryl, age seven, calls his younger brother a butthead. His mom intervenes.

"Darryl, it's not okay to call your brother names, especially that name. It's not nice."

"He is a butthead," Darryl insists, with a mischievous smile. He enjoys the strong reaction.

"You may not talk to your brother or anyone else like that!" says his mom in a serious tone. "Do you understand me? That's a warning."

Darryl decides to push it. "Butthead! Butthead! Max is a butthead!" he says in a singsong voice.

Now his mom is really angry. "Stop it now!" she shouts. "I really mean it. This is your last warning. If I hear that word again, you'll spend the rest of the day in your room."

"Yeah," Max chimes in, trying to provoke his brother.

"Okay, he's a butt face," says Darryl, pleased with his cleverness.

"That's it!" shouts his mom. "You're in your room for the rest of the day."

"That's not fair!" protests Darryl. "I called him something else. You're changing the rules."

"You knew what I meant," his mom insists, "but I'll give you one last chance. If I hear any more name-calling, you'll spend the day in your room."

How many times did Darryl call his brother a name? What happened each time he did? He got more warnings and second chances. If calling names is really not okay, why did she permit it to happen six times without a meaningful consequence?

Reasoning and Explaining

Ten-year-old Janet has been told not to use her Rollerblades without wearing knee and elbow pads, but she decides to do it anyway and gets caught.

"Rollerblades are really dangerous, Janet," says her concerned father. "You might injure yourself. Knees and wrists take a long time to heal."

"Safety pads are really dorky," complains Janet. "None of my friends have to wear them, and they haven't been hurt."

"They've been lucky," her father replies. "Your mother and I are not willing to take those risks with you. We want you safe. I hope you consider the risks next time you decide to skate without your pads."

Janet's father believes his reasons and explanations will convince his daughter to use her safety gear, but what happens if she isn't convinced? The worst thing that will happen is that Janet will have to listen to more of his reasons and explanations. She can live with that.

If Janet's father really expects her to wear safety gear, he needs to support his words with effective action and take away the Rollerblades for a while each time she decides to skate without them.

Speeches, Lectures, and Sermons

Sandra, age eleven, knows she's supposed to go directly home after school but decides instead to hang out with her friends. She arrives home nearly two hours late.

"Where have you been, young lady?" says her concerned mother. "This is the third time this week. I was worried. I called the school, and I was about to call the police."

"I went with Susie and Alice to get a yogurt," Sandra replies. "I kinda lost track of the time."

"That's so inconsiderate," replies her mother. "What would our house be like if all of us showed up whenever we pleased?"

Did you hear a clear message that showing up late would not be tolerated? Sandra didn't. Will the lecture help her arrive on time in the future? Not likely, especially if she really wants to hang out with her friends. Sandra understands that showing up late is worth it if she can tolerate the annoying lecture. Sandra is not likely to take her mother seriously until her mother removes Sandra's after-school play privileges for a few days or more each time she shows up late.

Statements of Fact

Six-year-old T.J. is supposed to take off his dirty shoes before he enters the house, but he's in a hurry and walks in anyway. He leaves a trail of muddy footprints all the way to the kitchen.

"You make me so mad!" says his mother when she notices the mess. "This carpet is hard to clean. I'm tired of cleaning up your messes." T.J. hurries out the door.

Do you think these statements will dissuade T.J. from entering the house next time he's in a hurry? Probably not. He knows he can count on his mother to clean up the mess. If she really wants him to stop wearing dirty shoes in the house, she needs to make him clean up his messes each time it happens.

Ignoring the Misbehavior

Three-year-old Allison has discovered the pleasures of blowing bubbles in her cup at mealtimes. Her parents try to ignore this annoying behavior in the hope that it will go away, but Allison hasn't stopped. Mealtimes aren't much fun for Allison's parents.

> What makes us think that the absence of a green light is equivalent to a red light? At best, it's a yellow light, and we know how strong-willed children respond to yellow lights.

What makes us think that the absence of a green light is equivalent to a red light? At best, it's a yellow light, and we know how strong-willed children respond to yellow lights. When we ignore misbehavior, we're really saying: It's okay to do that. Go ahead. You don't have to stop.

If Allison's parents really want her to stop blowing bubbles, they need to provide the right signal. They need to say stop with their words, and follow through by taking the cup away for a while each time she decides to test.

Unclear Directions

Eli, age nine, shows up late for dinner on a regular basis. His parents are annoyed. As he heads out the door to play, his mother reminds him, "We're eating at 6:00 P.M. Don't stay out too late."

What does "too late" mean to a nine-year-old who wants to stretch out his playtime? 6:15? 6:30? 6:45? Or later? And who decides? Eli only knows what the market will bear, and so far, he has managed to arrive home late on a regular basis.

> Unclear or open-ended directions invite testing and
> set both parents and children up for conflict.

Unclear or open-ended directions invite testing and set both parents and children up for conflict. If Eli's parents want to teach him to return to the house at 6:00 P.M., then they need to be clear with their words and their actions. They need to say, "Eli, you need to be home by 6:00 P.M. If you're not home by that time, we'll revise your return time to 5:00 P.M. and work on that until you get it right." Now, Eli has the data he needs to make a better choice.

Ineffective Role Modeling

Curt, age ten, and his brother, Chris, age eight, get into a heated argument over a video game. Their quarrel disturbs their father, who enters the room to check it out. When he arrives, he sees both boys hitting and shoving and calling each other names.

"Knock it off!" their father shouts. "Can't you guys share the game without acting like a couple of brats?" He gives each a swat on the seat and leaves the room. "Keep it quiet for a while!" he shouts.

What did the boys learn from this? They were trying to resolve a conflict by yelling, hitting, and name-calling. Their hassling disturbed their father. What did he do? He tried to resolve their conflict with more yelling, hitting, and name-calling. In effect, he was teaching them to do the same thing he was punishing them for.

Pleading, Begging, and Cajoling

Four-year-old Cheri is capable of dressing herself, but each morning before preschool, she goes into a stall.

"Come on, Cheri," urges her mother. "Please hurry. You're going to be late again." But Cheri just sits on the floor in her underwear, unconcerned. Her mother tries again.

"If you get dressed quickly, you'll make me really happy," encourages her mother. "I like to be proud of my big girl." Cheri picks up one sock and puts it on very slowly.

"That's what I like to see," says her mother, but it takes Cheri nearly five minutes to get one sock on. Time is running out.

"You did such a good job with that sock," remarks her mother. "Let's see if you can put on the other sock even faster." Cheri picks up the other sock and begins the task again. Five more minutes go by. Finally, both socks are on.

"That's my big girl!" exclaims her mother. "You're almost there! All you have left is your skirt, blouse, and shoes."

"It's too hard to put my skirt on," Cheri complains, hoping her mother will do it for her.

"You put it on just fine yesterday," says her mother. "Come on, show me how a big girl does it." Cheri senses the desperation in her mother's voice. There isn't much time left. Cheri goes even slower.

"Okay," says her mother. "Let's start with the blouse. I know you can do that." Cheri sits with her arms crossed, pouting. "Please, honey," her mother begs. "I'll tell Daddy what a good job you did."

Five more minutes go by. Finally, Cheri has her blouse on. Three minutes remain. Now her mother truly is desperate.

"I really need you to hurry," pleads her mother. "We're running out of time." No luck. Cheri continues to stall. Her exasperated mother gives in and dresses Cheri quickly so they can get out the door on time.

> Parents who plead, beg, and cajole children to
> cooperate are really saying: Do the job when you
> feel like it.

Parents who plead, beg, and cajole children to cooperate are really saying: Do the job when you feel like it. Who decides when or if the job gets done at all? The children. Cheri knows compliance is optional, not required, so she delays the job and gets the maximum attention possible.

If Cheri's mother really expects her daughter to get dressed in a timely manner, she needs to keep her words brief and move on quickly to her action step. She needs to inform Cheri in the morning that she has twenty minutes to get dressed. Then she needs to set the kitchen timer and stay out of it. No pleading. No begging. No cajoling. If Cheri is not fully dressed when the timer goes off, her mother should collect the remaining items of clothing, put them into a grocery bag, gather Cheri, and head out the door. Cheri will scramble to get dressed.

> The morning dawdle routine is not for public
> consumption. It's for Mom and Dad.

The morning dawdle routine is not for public consumption. It's for Mom and Dad. Parents can usually resolve the problem quickly by removing themselves from the equation and putting the responsibility for getting dressed on the child's shoulders where it belongs.

Bargaining and Negotiating

Nathan, age thirteen, is supposed to mow lawns on Saturdays before he does anything else, but he decides to take off with his friends and tell his parents he forgot. As he walks out the door, his mom reminds, "Don't forget to mow the lawns before you leave."

"But, Mom, do I have to?" Nathan asks. "The grass is not that long."

"You were supposed to mow them last weekend, but you didn't do them then," his mom reminds. "Remember? You promised you'd mow them today."

"Why can't I mow them this afternoon?" asks Nathan. "I'll get 'em done this weekend. I promise."

"If you mow them before lunch, you'll have the rest of the day to spend with your friends without anything hanging over you," says his mom.

"But I don't want to do them before lunch," Nathan complains. "Can't we compromise? I'll mow the front lawn this afternoon and the back lawn tomorrow. I promise." He senses her wearing down.

> To children, particularly strong-willed children, negotiable feels a lot like optional.

"Okay," she concedes in frustration, "but I'm not going to let you do this every time. Do you understand?"

"I understand," says Nathan.

What Nathan really understands is that his mother's rule about mowing lawns on Saturdays is negotiable. To children, particularly strong-willed children, negotiable feels a lot like optional. What do you think will happen next time Nathan doesn't feel like mowing lawns? Parents who bargain over their limits on a regular basis invite children to test and redefine their rules.

Arguing and Debating

Four-year-old Robert hates to clean up his messes. You can imagine his reaction when his mother announces, "It's time to pick up your toys and get ready for bed."

"I don't want to," he complains. "I'm tired."

"I'm sure you are," says his mother, "but you know the rules. It's your job to pick your toys up when you're done playing with them."

"Sometimes you don't pick up your things," Robert counters. "I don't see why I have to pick up my things if you don't pick up yours."

"You know that's not true," says his mother. "I always pick up after myself."

"Not your sewing stuff," says Robert.

"I'm not done with that project," replies his mother. "Now please, do what you're asked."

"That's not fair!" protests Robert.

"I've had enough of your arguing, young man!" says his mother. "You know the rules. Now do it."

"They're stupid rules," Robert snaps back.

What is the message Robert's mother sends by arguing and debating over her rules? What is not happening while the arguing and debating is going on? Of course, Robert isn't picking up. That won't happen until the argument is over, and some arguments can go on for quite a while.

By participating in a verbal sparring match with her son, Robert's mother is really saying that her rules are subject to argument and debate. She's inviting a power struggle by encouraging Robert to test her limits.

Bribes and Special Rewards

Trips to the mall are a nightmare for Justin and Tina's mother. Every time she takes her six-year-old twins, they plead and beg for treats, and throw a tantrum when they don't get them. A well-intended neighbor suggests bribing them.

Perhaps she's right, their mother says to herself. The next day before she leaves for the market, she makes the kids an offer: "If you use an indoor voice and cooperate during our trip, I'll buy you each a toy."

The kids like the offer. To their mother's surprise, they have a problem-free trip to the market. *Wow! This really works!* their mother says to herself.

She makes two more outings that week. Each time, she offers toys as bribes, and each time, the kids cooperate.

By the end of the month, their mother has paid out nearly $70 in new toys. She begins to question the wisdom of her approach.

Nobody paid me to cooperate when I was a child, she says to herself. The more she thinks about it, the madder she gets.

> When parents offer bribes and special rewards in
> return for cooperation, what they're really saying
> is cooperation is optional and contingent upon
> receiving a reward.

The next outing to the mall, she makes an announcement in the car: "You guys have shown me you can cooperate in public. I shouldn't have to buy you toys anymore to get you to do what you're supposed to do."

"That's not fair!" protests Tina. Justin agrees.

"If you don't buy us toys, we're not going to cooperate," he threatens. That's when their mother realizes she has been sending them the wrong message.

When parents offer bribes and special rewards in return for cooperation, what they're really saying is cooperation is optional and contingent upon receiving a reward. Often, cooperation stops as soon as the reward is withheld.

Inconsistency Between Parents

If Mom says, "Pick up your toys before you go out to play," and Dad says, "Let him go, dear. His friends are waiting," and holds the door open for the child's escape, what message does the child receive about the rules he's expected to follow?

In effect, there are two sets of rules operating. Mom's rule says, "Do it, please," and Dad's rule says, "You don't have to." Whose rule prevails? Yes, Dad calls the shots in this case.

What will happen next time the child is asked to pick up his toys before he goes out to play? He'll probably test to see which rule

is in effect. If Mom asks, the child will likely respond, "Dad says I don't have to do it." If Dad asks, the child will likely say, "But last time you said I didn't have to do it." In either event, inconsistency between parents sets all three up for conflict.

FIRM LIMITS: WHEN NO REALLY MEANS NO

Five-year-old Maggie and her mother wait in line at the checkout counter. Maggie grabs a candy bar off the rack and looks at her mom.

"Put it back, Maggie," says her mother. "You know what I said about asking for treats at the checkout counter."

"Please?" Maggie pleads. "Just this once?"

"No," her mother says, matter-of-factly. "Put it back, please."

Maggie decides to play her drama card. She throws a tantrum.

"Excuse me," Maggie's mother says to the clerk. "I'll be back in a few minutes." She picks her crying daughter up off the floor and carries her out to the car. No yelling. No screaming. No threats or angry lectures. And no giving in. After five minutes of crying and whimpering, Maggie regains her composure.

"Are you ready to finish our trip?" asks her mother. Maggie nods.

They return to the store, pay for the groceries, and leave.

Eight-year-old Patrick also encounters a firm signal when he decides to test his father's request not to blow whistles at the table. One morning at breakfast, Patrick finds a whistle as a prize in his cereal box. He takes it out, puts it to his lips, and gives it a couple of blows to see if it works. It works too well. His brothers cover their ears and yell for him to stop. Patrick enjoys all the commotion and continues to blast away.

MORE EXAMPLES OF INEFFECTIVE VERBAL MESSAGES
(SOFT LIMITS)

- "It's time to take a bath, okay?"
- "Would you try to be nice once in a while?"
- "Come on, get your act together."
- "Do me a favor and cooperate for once."
- "Can't you see I'm on the phone?"
- "I don't like your attitude."
- "You better shape up!"
- "How would you like it if I interrupted you?"
- "You're acting like a jerk!"
- "It's time to fly right."
- "I don't believe it! You almost cooperated."
- "Wipe that smirk off your face."

When their father walks into the room, he sees what's going on. "Patrick, please don't blow the whistle in the house," he says, matter-of-factly. "That's an outdoor toy."

Patrick gives his father a defiant look but complies and puts the whistle down. As soon as his father leaves the room, however, Patrick picks up the whistle and lets out several more defiant blasts. His father returns and, without any further comments, takes the whistle away.

Patrick's father and Maggie's mother are using firm limits to communicate their rules and expectations. Their words say stop and their actions convey the same message. Both children receive a very clear message. They hear stop and they experience stopping. Compliance is both expected and required. Both children receive the data they need to make a more acceptable choice next time.

MORE EXAMPLES OF INEFFECTIVE ACTION MESSAGES (SOFT LIMITS)

- Allowing children to walk away from a mess
- Cleaning up children's messes for them
- Dressing children who can dress themselves
- Ignoring misbehavior in the hope that it will go away
- Overlooking misbehavior when you're in a good mood
- Slapping children to show them how it feels when they hit others
- Rescuing children from the consequences of their misbehavior
- Making excuses for children when they misbehave
- Blaming ourselves or others when our children misbehave
- Relaxing standards in the hope some work will get done
- Giving in to tantrums

Firm limits send clear signals to children about our rules and expectations. Children understand that we mean what we say because they experience what they hear. Words are consistent with actions. They learn to regard our words seriously, test less, and cooperate more often for the asking. The result—better communication, less testing, and fewer power struggles. Firm limits are your ticket to better cooperation with strong-willed children.

CHAPTER SUMMARY

Limits come in two basic varieties: firm and soft (see Table 6). Firm limits (when no means no) are highly effective signals because they convey to children the seriousness of our resolve and the clear

EXAMPLES OF EFFECTIVE VERBAL MESSAGES
(FIRM LIMITS)

- "Stop hitting now."
- "We don't eat Popsicles in the living room."
- "Take your shoes off the sofa, please."
- "Put away your LEGOs before you go outside to play."
- "Be home by 5:30."
- "You can play by the rules or find a different game to play."
- "Turn the TV down, please, or I'll have to turn it off."
- "If you kick your ball in the house, I'll have to take it away."
- "If you throw your food, your meal is over."

EXAMPLES OF EFFECTIVE ACTION MESSAGES
(FIRM LIMITS)

- Using a time-out consequence for a child who hits
- Removing the Popsicle from a child who ignores your request not to eat it in the living room
- Putting away LEGOs for three or four days at a time when children don't pick them up
- Temporarily revising return time to 4:30 for a few days when a child fails to return home at 5:30 as requested
- Not allowing a child to participate in a game for a while when he or she fails to play by the rules
- Turning the TV off when children refuse to turn it down
- Removing the soccer ball for the rest of the day when the child decides to test by dribbling the ball in the house
- Not replacing a toy that was lost or broken due to carelessness

boundaries they're searching for. Children raised with firm limits test less because they understand that compliance is both expected and required.

TABLE 6. Comparison of Firm and Soft Limits

	Firm Limits	Soft Limits
Characteristics	Stated in clear, direct, concrete behavioral terms.	Stated in unclear terms or as "mixed messages."
	Words supported by actions.	Actions do not support intended rule.
	Compliance expected and required.	Compliance optional, not required.
	Provide information needed to make acceptable choices and cooperate.	Do not provide information needed to make acceptable choices.
	Provide accountability.	Lack of accountability.
Predictable outcomes	Cooperation.	Resistance.
	Decreased limit testing.	Increased limit testing.
	Clear understanding of rules and expectations.	Escalating misbehavior, power struggles.
	Regard parents' words seriously.	Ignore and tune out parents' words.
Children learn	No means no.	No means yes, sometimes, or maybe.
	I'm expected and required to follow the rules.	I'm not expected to follow the rules.
	Rules apply to me like everyone else.	Rules are made for others, not me.
		I make my own rules and do what I want.
	I am responsible for my own behavior.	Adults are responsible for my behavior.
	Adults mean what they say.	Adults don't mean what they say.

> Firm limits are your ticket to better cooperation
> with strong-willed children.

Soft limits (when no means yes, sometimes, or maybe) are rules in theory, not in practice. They come in a variety of forms, but all invite testing and resistance as children attempt to clarify what we really expect and require. Soft limits are a predictable setup for testing and power struggles with strong-willed children and many fence-sitters.

5

The Family Dance

If you use unclear or ineffective limits with your strong-willed child, you undoubtedly have developed your own special dance that you perform over and over again in conflict situations. Family dances come in a variety of forms. There's a permissive version that tends to be wordy and drawn out, a punitive version that tends to be angry and dramatic, and a mixed version that involves a little of both. No matter what form they take, all dances are ineffective attempts to set limits and get children to cooperate.

These learned patterns of ineffective problem solving lead to escalating conflicts and power struggles. Over time, the dance becomes such a familiar and deeply ingrained habit that family members experience it as their normal way of communicating. They are not even aware they are dancing.

Families, such as the ones we'll follow in this chapter, can easily become stuck in these destructive patterns of communication.

Without awareness and new skills, they have little choice but to keep on dancing the only dance they know. Awareness is the first step toward breaking free.

> No matter what form they take, all dances are ineffective attempts to set limits and get children to cooperate. These learned patterns lead to escalating conflicts and power struggles.

If you suspect you've become stuck in a family dance, this chapter will help you begin to break free. You'll learn how your dances begin, how they end, and what keeps them going. Most important, you'll gain the awareness you need to step off the dance floor and move on to more effective methods of communication and problem solving.

WHAT DO KIDS GET FROM DANCES?

Imagine you're five years old. You can't read or tell time. You're not allowed to play more than a block from your house, but each time your parents ask you to pick up your toys, you fuss and complain, and your parents go into a dance. They plead and cajole, warn and remind, reason and explain, and if you continue to resist, they yell and threaten to take away all your toys and privileges for long periods of time.

Wow! Look at them go! you say to yourself. *They look really upset!* The drama is terrific, but you know, from past experience, that they probably won't follow through on any of their threats. Even if they do, the entertainment is worth it.

If you could generate all this drama and excitement by simply resisting a request, how do you think you'd feel? Powerful? Sure. In control? You bet. Entertained? Yes again.

Family dances are like soap operas for kids, an ongoing source of live entertainment. The kids are the producers and directors, and the parents are the lead actors. The script is well rehearsed. Everyone knows his or her part and how things will likely play out, but play out they all do, over and over again, in each conflict situation.

> Family dances are like soap operas for kids, an ongoing source of live entertainment.

To helping professionals like myself, family dances are reinforcement errors or things parents say or do, often unconsciously, that encourage and reward their children's unwanted behavior. Dances provide children with two types of rewards. The primary payoff is getting their own way or winning the power struggle. If you're five, and you don't want to pick up your toys, getting Mom or Dad to do the job for you is a pretty good deal. Even if they don't, you still get the live entertainment that leads us to the next reward. The secondary payoff for children is all the negative attention, power, and control they receive by getting their parents to dance. The dance itself is a reward.

If you regularly dance with your children, you've probably become stuck in this vicious cycle of unintentionally rewarding the misbehavior you're trying to stop.

If you regularly dance with your children, you've probably become stuck in this vicious cycle of unintentionally rewarding the misbehavior you're trying to stop. The pattern is not likely to change until you recognize what you're doing and start withholding the rewards that keep it going. It's up to you to stop the dance. Awareness is the first step. Let's look at how one couple discovered their dance.

A PERMISSIVE DANCE

Mike and Sherry are parents of two children, Justin, age six, and Brook, age nine. Their home is a busy place. Both parents work full-time jobs outside the home, and the kids are involved in many extracurricular activities. The parents arrived for counseling because they felt worn down by Justin's resistant behavior and all the yelling and arguing that took place in their home.

"Justin's first response to anything is no," Sherry complained. "When we tell him no, he argues with us. Before we know it, we're yelling at him, he's yelling back at us, and his sister is yelling at all of us to stop. Is this normal behavior? He drives us all crazy. I don't know if I can take it anymore."

Mike was feeling equally discouraged. "We try to be fair and reasonable with Justin, but he takes advantage of us and treats us disrespectfully. Our house is in a constant state of uproar. I don't know what it takes to get through to him."

Mike and Sherry didn't realize it, but they had been dancing with Justin for a long time. They were stuck in an escalating pattern of conflicts and power struggles that left them worn out and discouraged. My first task was to help them get acquainted with their various temperaments. We completed a temperament profile for each family member.

Justin's profile was typical of many strong-willed children. He showed high ratings in negative persistence, reactivity, and intensity. He pushes hard on everyone. His sister, Brook, on the other hand, profiled as a compliant individual with no difficult traits. Her underlying desire is to please and cooperate. Mike's profile was similar to Brook's, while Sherry tended to be strong-willed, intense, and reactive like Justin.

Their temperament profiles provided insights into their family dynamics. I could understand why Mike had such a difficult time understanding Justin. Their temperaments were very different. In conflict situations, Mike's underlying desire is to cooperate. He responds well to reason and tries to work toward a mutually acceptable solution. Justin's desire, on the other hand, is to have things work out on his terms, and he's willing to go to extremes to make it happen. Justin has little interest in being reasonable if that means he might not get his own way.

I could also understand why Sherry reacts so strongly to Justin. Their temperaments are very similar. Both are intense and reactive. In conflict situations, they are like two charged particles reacting off each other. Both are very determined to prevail over the other. I shared these impressions with Mike and Sherry.

My next task was to see how their guidance methods match up with Justin's temperament and learning style. I asked both parents to pick one of Justin's typical misbehaviors and describe, in a very step-by-step manner, exactly what they say and do when he behaves this way. Without hesitation, both parents agreed that Justin's resistance in the morning was the hardest part of the day. Each day starts off on a sour note.

"Okay," I said, "describe what happens in the morning when you ask Justin to get ready for school."

Sherry went first. As she described their morning routine, I diagrammed out each step in the interactional sequence. Visual diagrams are a great way to help parents become better acquainted with their dance. When Sherry finished, we took a few minutes to reflect upon her diagram (see Figure 5.1). Sherry's eyes got wide when she saw the length of her diagram.

"Wow!" she exclaimed. "I get exhausted just looking at it. I do that all day long."

"Yes. That's a long, drawn-out dance," I replied, giving it the label it deserved. "I can see why you feel so worn-out."

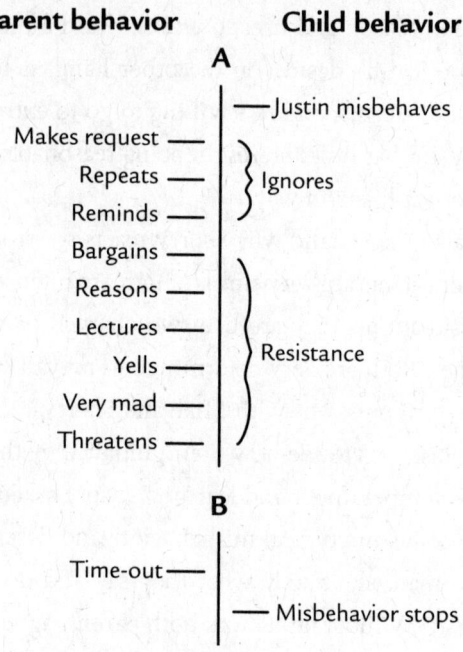

Figure 5.1   Sherry's Diagram

For many parents, family dances are like saving stress coupons. When they collect enough of them, they can redeem them for prizes: headaches, stomachaches, depression, and a variety of other upsets. Sherry had been saving coupons for quite a while.

> For many parents, family dances are like saving stress coupons. When they collect enough of them, they can redeem them for prizes: headaches, stomachaches, depression, and a variety of other upsets.

Her diagram was revealing. From the time she first intervenes to the time she finishes, she tries many different forms of persuasion, but none of them stop Justin's misbehavior. She typically begins by repeating and reminding, but her requests are usually ignored. Next, she tries bargaining, reasoning, and lecturing with the same result. Justin's resistance continues.

The more she talks, the madder she gets, until lecturing turns into yelling, and bargaining gives way to threats. When she reaches her boiling point, she sends him to his room to finish dressing and tells him that he has to leave the house at 7:45 A.M. without breakfast if he's not ready. Justin's misbehavior usually stops at this point. If he finishes on time, he gets breakfast. If not, he leaves the house with a plastic bag full of toast or dry cereal.

As both parents looked on, I returned to Sherry's diagram and drew a circle around all the steps that used words. I labeled these "Verbal Steps." They took up nearly all her diagram. Then, I drew a box around the word time-out at the end of her diagram and labeled this as an "Action Step." The box occupied a very small portion of her diagram (see Figure 5.2).

"Between point A and point B, you try many different steps to get Justin to cooperate," I observed. "Which one stops the misbehavior?" Sherry's eyes were fixed squarely on the box at the end of her diagram. The pattern was clear. She spends most of her time and energy doing things that don't work.

I summarized what her diagram was telling us: "From your initial request at point A to your eventual action step at point B, Justin pushes hard against your words to see how far he can go. The harder he pushes, the more you talk, and the angrier you become.

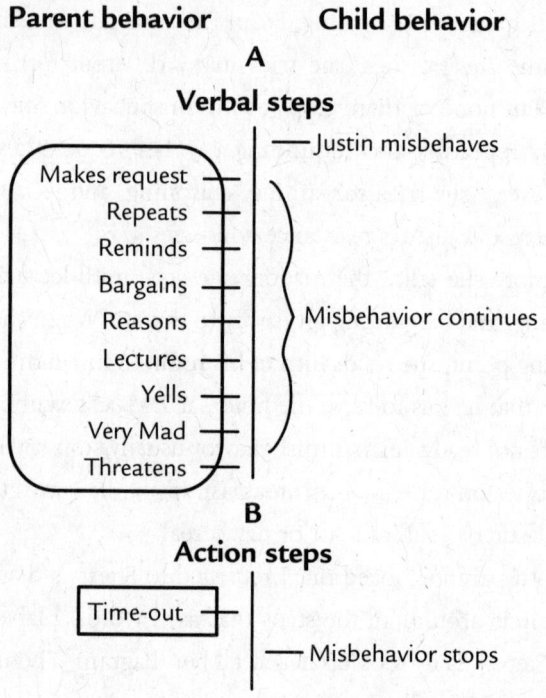

Figure 5.2   Sherry's Diagram: Verbal and Action Steps

When you finally reach your boiling point, you stop your dance with your action step."

Sherry nodded.

"At what point does your message become clear?" I asked.

She pointed to her action step.

"Exactly," I said. "That's when misbehavior stops and cooperation begins. That's the firm boundary Justin is searching for. Things improve when you get there."

Sherry understood the point I was trying to make. She could see that her guidance methods were poorly matched to the temperament and learning style of her strong-willed son. A look of relief came over her face.

Next, I wanted to help Sherry discover the origin of her dance. I asked her to describe what her parents did when she misbehaved as a child. As she described their methods, I diagrammed them out on a board and placed their diagram next to hers. When she finished, I stepped back and gave her a chance to take them in. She looked surprised.

"I believed I was handling discipline differently than my parents," Sherry exclaimed. But the diagrams told a different story. Except for the endings, their diagrams were nearly identical. Sherry ended her dances with time-outs, whereas her parents used spankings. She was doing the same dance with a different ending.

Many parents are surprised to realize how much they rely on their parents as models for child training. Some, like Sherry, try to modify their methods to correct what they perceive to be their parents' mistakes. If they believe their parents were too harsh, they might compensate by becoming more lenient. If they believe their parents were too lenient, they might compensate by becoming harsher. Most often, they end up doing the same basic dance with a different ending and passing the script on to their children.

It was time to get acquainted with Mike's dance. I asked him to describe how he handled Justin's resistance in the mornings. As he described what he did, I diagrammed the interaction (see Figure 5.3). When his diagram was complete, I paused for a moment so we all could take it in.

"Does this dance look familiar?" I asked.

"It certainly does," Mike replied. "I've probably done that dance a thousand times. I know every step by heart."

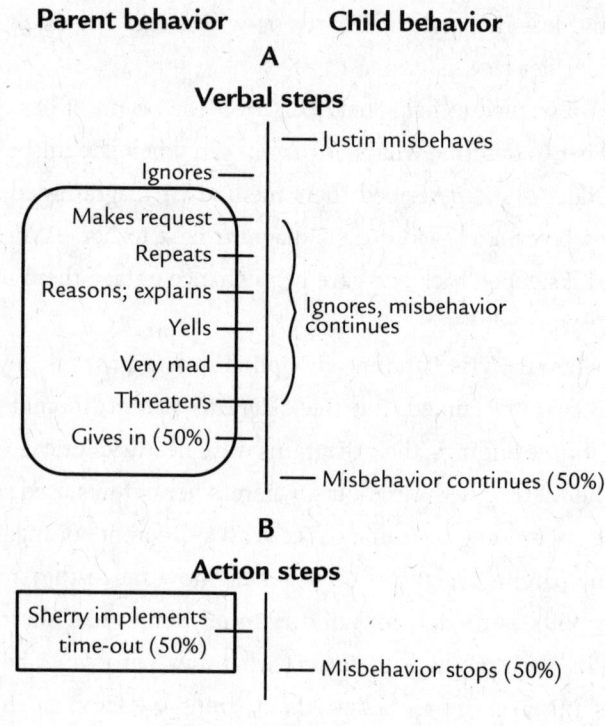

Figure 5.3   Mike's Diagram

At first glance, Mike's diagram resembled a mixed dance, but the lack of an action step was the defining feature. He was doing a permissive dance with mixed features. His dance was loud, angry, and dramatic; but it was basically all talk and no action.

Mike usually begins by trying to ignore Justin's misbehavior to avoid a confrontation. This never works. After a few minutes, Mike wears down and makes his initial request in an angry tone that Justin promptly ignores. Mike hates to be ignored but tries his best to maintain his composure. Next, he tries repeating and reminding, then reasoning and explaining. Justin continues ignoring.

This is when Mike loses his temper. He starts shaming and blaming, yelling and threatening, but Justin is not impressed with all the drama. He digs in his heels and yells back.

About half the time, when things get too loud, Sherry steps in and sends Justin to his room, which stops the misbehavior. Other times, Mike walks away in frustration. Justin gets his biggest rewards from dancing with Mike.

I returned to Mike's diagram and drew a circle around all the steps that involved words and labeled them "Verbal Steps." The circle occupied his entire diagram. The action step that eventually stops his dance belongs to Sherry and only happens 50 percent of the time.

Mike's diagram was complete, so I summarized what it was telling us. "Justin pushes hard against your words to see how far he can go. The harder he pushes, the more you talk, and the angrier you become. Finally, when you reach your explosion point, you walk away in frustration, or Sherry ends your dance for you." He nodded. Mike recognized his permissive dance, and he could see that his methods were poorly matched to Justin's temperament and learning style.

Next, I wanted to help Mike discover where his dance originated. I asked to him to describe what his parents did when he misbehaved as a child. As he spoke, I diagrammed their methods and placed their diagram next to his.

The two diagrams were similar with one conspicuous exception. Mike ended his dances by giving up and walking away. His parents ended their dances with spankings. In all other respects, Mike's dances were just as loud, angry, and dramatic as those of his parents.

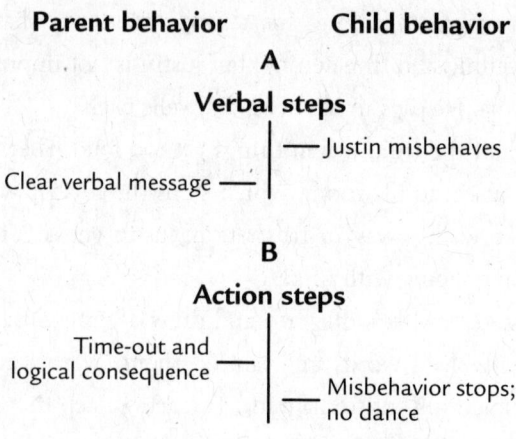

Figure 5.4   Mike and Sherry's New Diagram

The most difficult part was behind us. Mike and Sherry recognized their dances and the scripts they acquired from their families of origin. They were ready to learn new skills and get off the dance floor.

The best way to stop a dance is to begin with a clear message and put our verbal and action steps closer together. I returned to Sherry's original diagram to illustrate the process.

"Remember how Sherry spent most of her time getting bogged down with a variety of ineffective verbal messages?" I asked. "Justin resists all these signals until Sherry reaches her action step. This is when his misbehavior stops and cooperation begins. You can avoid dances altogether by beginning with a clear signal at point A and moving on directly to your action step at point B, without all the ineffective steps in between. Next time Justin resists you in the morning, simply ask him to finish the job in his room and not return until he's done. The signal is clear. No dance, and no payoffs for misbehavior." Mike and Sherry's new diagram soon looked like Figure 5.4. So can yours.

A PUNITIVE DANCE

Rick and Linda, parents of two children, Cody and Lisa, ages seven and thirteen, had a dance I won't soon forget. I caught my first glimpse of it in the reception room before they even made it back to my office.

"Come on, Lisa," Linda said to her thirteen-year-old when they were called in, but Lisa just sat there with her arms folded tightly.

"You go in," Lisa said to her parents. "You're the ones who need counseling, not me."

"If you would do what you're told once in a while, we wouldn't be here at all," her mother shot back, angrily.

"No, you'd find something else to yell about," Lisa retorted. "That's what you do best."

"I'm not going to listen to your disrespectful back talk," said Linda.

"Oh yeah! What are you going to do? Ground me? It doesn't seem to bother you when you treat me disrespectfully," Lisa shot back.

"I'm the parent," countered Linda.

"No, you're the dictator," said Lisa, still in her chair.

"That's enough, Lisa," Rick intervened. "Come on. It's time to go back to his office." Reluctantly, Lisa accompanied her parents back to my office, but before we were seated, the dance started up again.

"See what she's like?" Linda complained, trying to get me to take sides.

Before I could establish a neutral position, Lisa got in one last barb. "Yeah, you're a real pleasure to be around, too," she sneered.

"I can see you're all pretty angry and frustrated," I said, trying to take the focus off Lisa. "I'm not very good at solving problems when I'm feeling that way. Let's take a few minutes to calm down." I gave each of the kids an interest inventory to complete and handed the parents some forms to look over while we waited.

The session had barely begun, but we were already getting acquainted with a technique they would need to use fairly often to interrupt their dances: the cooldown. When calm was restored, I asked Rick whether the argument that happened earlier was similar to the arguments that happen at home.

"It has been happening all the time since Lisa was grounded six weeks ago," he replied. Rick described the events that led up to their appointment.

The problem began when Lisa arrived home with her midsemester progress report. She was getting Ds in science and math, her hardest subjects. When Linda saw the progress report, she got angry. "Ds are not acceptable grades in this house!" she declared.

"I've got six weeks until the end of the semester," said Lisa. "That's plenty of time to get them up."

"You have more time than you think," Linda countered, "because you're not going anywhere after school until those grades come up." Lisa was grounded to the house.

When she tried to protest her mother's decision, her mother threatened to take away even more privileges and informed Lisa that the matter was final. Lisa exploded. "You're mean and unfair!" she shouted.

So Linda took away Lisa's phone privileges, too, for the same period. "Keep it up if you want to lose even more privileges," Linda taunted.

Lisa ran to her room and slammed the door.

That evening, Rick tried to mediate the dispute, but things just got worse. First, Linda blamed Lisa for being lazy and disrespectful. Then, Lisa accused Linda of being mean and unfair. Linda started shouting, and Lisa shouted back. In the heat of the exchange, Lisa called Linda "a bitch." Lisa regretted it the moment she said it, but it was too late. Linda was about to slap Lisa in the face when Rick stepped in. He took away one of the privileges Lisa loved most: her Saturday skating, gone until further notice.

"I didn't know what else to do," said Rick, clearly frustrated. Lisa was already grounded to the house on weeknights, and she'd lost her phone privileges, too. "She's too big to spank, but I couldn't let her get away with it, either." Like Linda, Rick dug them all in a little deeper with his punitive consequences.

> Angry, dramatic guidance methods can quickly escalate into power struggles with strong-willed children.

I was curious to see how their various temperaments influenced the outcomes of these conflicts. I asked them all to help me complete a temperament profile for each family member. Most families enjoy this exercise.

Their temperament profiles were revealing. Rick and Cody had similar profiles. Both were compliant with few extreme or difficult traits. Linda profiled as a strong-willed person who tends to be moody, reactive, and intense. Lisa's profile was a more extreme version of Linda's. Together, they were an explosive combination.

We discussed the compatibility and friction points of their various temperaments and how angry, dramatic guidance methods can quickly escalate into power struggles with strong-willed children. The parents were relieved to hear that Lisa's extreme testing and resistance was normal. They also gained a greater appreciation for Cody's compliance.

"Let's see how your guidance methods match up with your children's temperaments," I suggested. I started with Rick.

"What do you usually do when Lisa or Cody misbehave?" I asked. As Rick described his methods, I diagrammed them on the blackboard.

"First, I tell them to stop," he said.

"In the same tone of voice you're using now?" I asked.

He nodded.

"Do they stop?" I asked.

"No, I usually have to raise my voice to get their attention," Rick replied.

"What do you do next?" I asked.

"I usually tell them again," he replied.

"Do they cooperate then?" I inquired.

"Cody does," he replied, "but not Lisa. She argues and asks why she should do what I ask."

"How do you feel at this point?" I asked.

"I get angry," said Rick. "I usually end up saying something like, 'Can't you just do what I ask without arguing for a change?'"

"Don't leave out the threats and angry lectures," added Lisa.

"Yes, I guess I do a little of that, too," Rick confessed.

"A little?" said Lisa, rolling her eyes.

"Okay, I probably do a lot of it, but it wouldn't happen if you would just cooperate the first time you were asked," Rick replied.

"Then what happens?" I asked, wondering if his consequences were getting close.

"When Cody pushes me too far, he usually gets spanked," Rick replied. "Sometimes, I take away his privileges for a week or two. When he's done something really bad, I spank and take away privileges, but I don't need to spank Cody very often. He usually cooperates. I stopped spanking Lisa when she turned twelve. Now, I usually take away her phone, TV, stereo, time with friends, skating privileges, or ground her to the house for a few weeks."

"Does that stop her misbehavior?" I asked.

"It does at the time," said Rick, "but then we have to live with an angry, resentful child until her punishment is over. Sometimes, I think it's harder on us than on Lisa." Linda nodded in agreement.

Rick's diagram was complete. I stood back and gave everyone a chance to look it over. "Look familiar?" I asked.

"You've captured something," said Rick. "I'm not sure what it is, but whatever it is, I'm doing a lot of it."

"I call them dances," I replied, "and you're not alone. There are a lot of parents doing dances to get their children to cooperate. Let's look at the steps in your dance."

I returned to Rick's diagram and drew a circle around all the steps that relied on words and labeled them "Verbal Steps." They took up most of his diagram. Next, I drew a box around the steps that involved action and labeled these "Action Steps." These took up only a small section at the end of his diagram (see Figure 5.5).

"You use two types of steps to get your kids to cooperate: verbal steps and action steps," I said. "Which one stops the misbehavior?"

"My action steps at the end," Rick replied.

"Exactly," I said. "Your action steps stop the dance for a while. Now, let's look at how you're feeling when you're doing these steps. Earlier, you said you felt angry when your kids try to argue with you. The arguments lead to lectures and threats. It sounds like things just get hotter until you end your dance with action steps."

Rick nodded. He could see that the more he talked, the more Lisa resisted, and the angrier he became. He spent most of his time saying and doing things that didn't work.

"Now, let's take a look at your action steps," I suggested. "Your action steps stop Lisa's misbehavior for the moment, but she gets angry and resentful and retaliates. Then you end up doing many shorter versions of the same dance without action steps."

"That's where I get stuck," Rick admitted. "I don't know what else to do at that point. There isn't much left to take away, but I

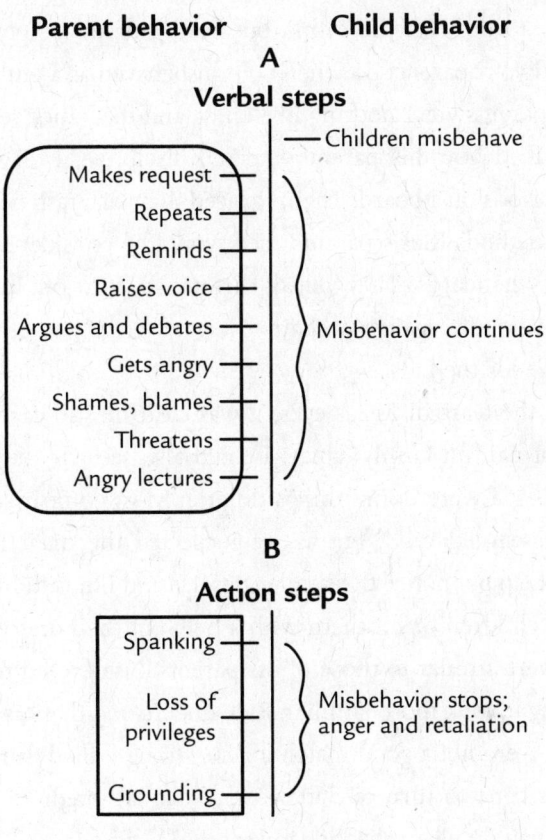

Figure 5.5   Rick's Diagram

can't just let her get away with it either. She needs to know that we expect her to cooperate."

I agreed, then asked, "If there is a way to get that message across without hooking into her anger and resentment, would you be willing to use it?"

"Of course," Rick replied. "I'm tired of all the power struggles."

"Good," I said, "because that's exactly what I'm going to show you how to do. Now, let's find out how your dance got started. What did your parents do when you misbehaved as a child?"

"My parents were nothing like Linda and me," Rick replied. As he described how his parents handled discipline, I diagrammed their methods on a board. Then, I placed their diagram next to his.

The methods Rick's parents used would be considered abusive by today's standards. They yelled, threatened, took out a belt, and cracked it loudly against a chair to create terror and fear. Then, they came for the kids.

From the tears in Rick's eyes, it was clear he still carried scars from that painful family dance. I could also see why he believed he and Linda were doing things differently. In comparison, their methods seemed mild; but as we inspected the diagrams, Rick couldn't help but notice the similarities. He and Linda didn't terrorize their children or hit them with a belt; but their angry, hurtful dances were similar to those of his parents. Lisa's resentment was beginning to look more familiar. Rick understood that his punitive methods were not a good match for his strong-willed daughter.

It was time to turn our attention to Linda's methods. "Linda, what do you do when the kids misbehave?" I asked.

"I do almost everything Rick does," replied Linda, "but I don't have the patience he does. I start off angry and yell from the beginning, and I stay that way the whole time."

I drew a diagram for Linda similar to Rick's except that I wrote "starts off angry" at the beginning of Linda's diagram. "Is that it?" I asked, when the diagram was complete.

"I think you left out a few things," Lisa chimed in. "What about the taunting and the challenging? You're always telling me, 'Go ahead, do it again. I dare you.' Dad doesn't do that."

"Yes, I get a little carried away sometimes," Linda admitted, "especially when she continues to argue after I threaten to take away her privileges."

I went back and made the correction on Linda's diagram. Then, as before, I drew a circle around all the verbal steps and a box around her action steps. Linda's diagram was complete (see Figure 5.6). "Is that the dance?" I asked.

She nodded. We all took a minute to look it over.

Linda's dance was louder and more emotional than Rick's, but in many ways it was very similar. She spent most of her time stuck in a verbal sparring match with Lisa. The more she talked, the more Lisa resisted, and the angrier Linda became. When she decided things had gone far enough, Linda ended the dance with hurtful consequences: spankings, grounding, or long-term loss of privileges.

"Strong-willed children respond best to clear, firm messages without a lot of drama or strong emotion. What would happen if you went directly from point A to your action step at point B and eliminated all these other steps in between?" I asked.

"There would be a lot less arguing," Linda acknowledged.

> Strong-willed children respond best to clear, firm
> messages without a lot of drama or strong emotion.

"And a lot less anger, too," I added. "Eliminating all those steps would stop Lisa's misbehavior with less time and energy, but Lisa would still feel angry and resentful about your action step. Now, let's suppose you used some new action steps that stop her misbehavior but don't make her angry or resentful. Would there be any need to dance?"

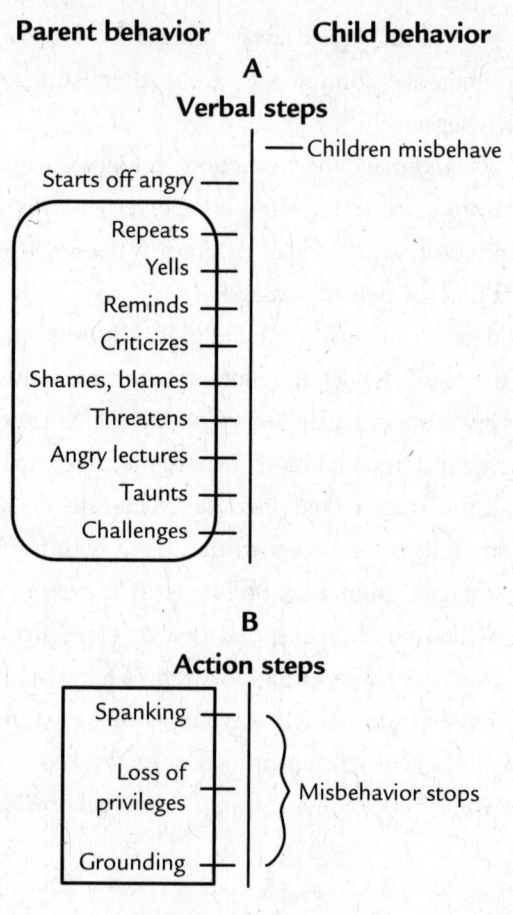

Figure 5.6   Linda's Diagram

"You make it sound so simple and easy," she said.

"I think you'll find that the methods are simple and easy to use," I replied. "The hardest part is stopping yourself from doing your old dance. You've already taken the most important step by becoming aware of it. Now, let's look at how you learned your dance." I asked Linda to describe what her parents said and did when she misbehaved as a child.

"I know where I got my flair for dramatics," said Linda. "My mom was always yelling and screaming at us about one thing or another. She did a lot of nagging and reminding. We usually cooperated, eventually; but if we didn't, she took away our privileges or grounded us to the house. I remember being grounded for weeks at a time over little things."

"How did you feel when that happened?" I asked.

"Angry and resentful," she replied.

"Like Lisa?" I asked.

Linda understood what I meant. "I was a lot like Lisa," Linda said, "and I also did a lot of rebelling when I thought my mom was unfair. I loved her, but our relationship was stormy."

"Was it anything like your relationship with Lisa?" I inquired.

Linda smiled again. She could see that the dance she did with her mother was a lot like the dance she was doing with Lisa. The relationships that developed around those dances were also very similar.

"What methods did your father use?" I asked.

"My father punished us, but he never yelled or threatened or acted angry in any way," said Linda. "He just told us to stop, and if we didn't, he spanked us, not very hard, but hard enough to make us stop misbehaving. When we got older, he also took away our privileges and grounded us, but not for weeks at a time like my mom. He tried very hard to be fair."

Linda was using a combination of her parents' methods. Her verbal steps resembled those used by her mother, while her action steps incorporated both of her parents' methods.

Rick and Linda left that session with new awareness. They recognized their punitive dances and understood that their guidance methods were poorly matched to their daughter's temperament. They were ready to learn better ways to get their message across.

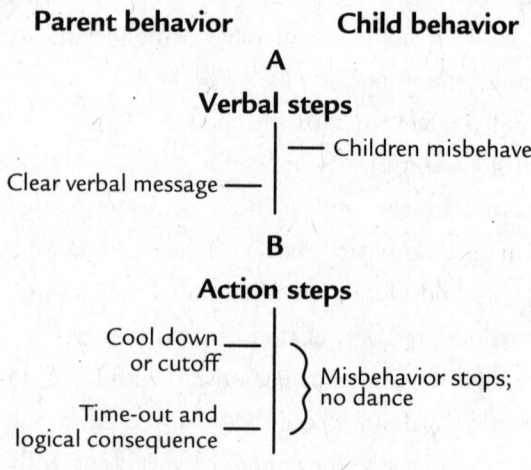

Figure 5.7   Rick and Linda's New Diagram

In the sessions that followed, they learned how to start off with a clear, brief message (see Chapter 6, "How to Be Clear with Your Words") and how to use the cool-down and cutoff techniques (see Chapter 7, "Stopping Power Struggles Before They Begin") when Lisa tried to hook them into power struggles. Then they learned how to use more effective consequences (see Chapter 8, "Supporting Your Rules with Logical Consequences"). They exchanged spankings, grounding, and long-term loss of privileges for time-outs and logical consequences. Their new diagram soon looked like Figure 5.7. So can yours.

A MIXED DANCE

Of all the dances parents do with their children, the mixed dance is the loudest, most dramatic, and most destructive. It combines the worst features of the two extreme approaches and brings out the most extreme behavior in strong-willed children. It encourages them to push hard against our rules and authority, then explode at us at the end when they encounter our harsh consequences. The wear and tear on parents is considerable.

> Of all the dances parents do with their children, the mixed dance is the longest, loudest, most dramatic, and most destructive.

There are several variations of the mixed dance. Some parents start off punitively in each guidance situation but retreat into permissiveness when they encounter sufficient resistance from their children. Others stick with one approach for longer periods of time. They try permissiveness for weeks or months until they can't stand being resisted or ignored any longer. Then they wear down, become frustrated, and resort to punitive methods until they can't stand how tyrannical they sound. Then, they switch back to permissiveness. The cycle of flip-flops may last weeks, even months.

The most common variation of the mixed approach is the one where parents start off permissively with lots of repeating, reminding, warning, cajoling, reasoning, and explaining but then wear down and resort to punitive tactics such as shaming, blaming, yelling, spanking, grounding, or taking away every favorite toy or privilege for long periods of time.

Connie, a single parent of two boys, ages four and six, is a good example of this common variation of the mixed dance. She arrived at my office exhausted.

"My four-year-old is going to drive me into a mental hospital," she began. "Everything turns into a battle—getting dressed in the morning, meals, baths, picking up toys, or getting him to stop teasing his brother. Keith ignores me, tunes out, argues, defies, calls me names, and throws tantrums when he doesn't get his own way. His older brother, Taylor, never behaves like this. Taylor always does what I ask."

Based on what she shared, I had some good suspicions about the temperaments involved, but I wanted to check them out for myself. Connie and I completed temperament profiles for each family member.

My suspicions were confirmed. Connie and Taylor profiled as compliant individuals with no difficult or extreme traits. In conflict situations, their underlying desire is to please and cooperate. Because their temperaments were very similar, Connie identified with Taylor and understood his behavior. Their temperaments were a good fit.

Keith, on the other hand, would be a workout for any parent. He tends to be moody and intense and showed high ratings in negative persistence. Like most strong-willed children, Keith does most of his learning the hard way. His profile validated something Connie suspected but never really understood. She still had one pressing question.

"Is he normal?" she asked.

> Strong-willed children need clear, firm limits to
> guide them in the right direction.

"He seems normal to me," I replied, "but he also shows some very difficult-to-manage temperament traits." Connie looked relieved to hear the word *normal*.

"Strong-willed children need clear, firm limits to guide them in the right direction," I added. "Let's see how your guidance methods match up with Keith's temperament and learning style." I asked Connie to describe exactly what she says and does when Keith teases Taylor. As she described her methods, I diagrammed them on the board. There was barely enough space on the board for her entire diagram (see Figure 5.8). When it was finished, she stared in disbelief.

"I can't believe I do all that stuff," she said. "I must go through that a dozen times a day."

"Yes, that's an exhausting dance," I agreed. I got tired just diagramming it.

Connie begins her dances with lots of repeating and reminding, but Keith usually tunes her out. Next, she tries reasoning and explaining, which works with Taylor but not Keith. He continues to ignore her.

Next, she tries to bargain for Keith's cooperation by offering him bribes in exchange for doing what she asks. Sometimes this works, but most of the time Keith digs in his heels, becomes more resistant, and argues for a better deal.

This is when Connie's anger and frustration take over. Before she knows it, she's yelling, screaming, shaming, blaming, and threatening to spank or take away all his toys or privileges. Keith

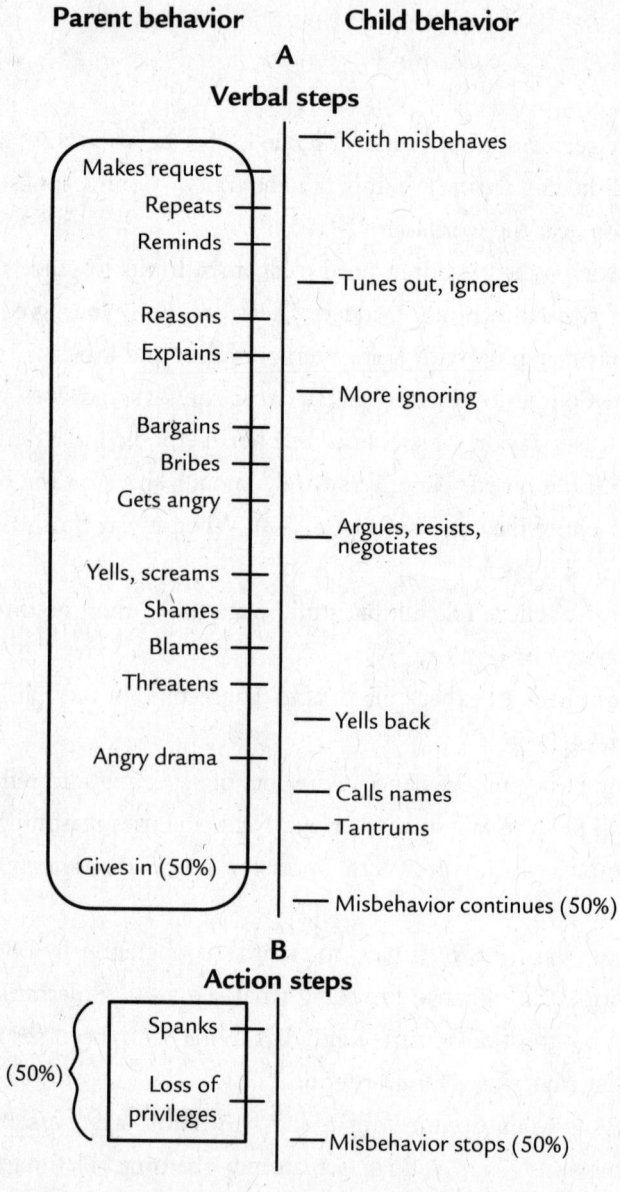

Figure 5.8   Connie's Diagram

is not impressed with the drama. He usually yells back, calls her names, or throws a tantrum if she doesn't give in. Fifty percent of the time Connie does follow through on her threats. The other 50 percent she wears down and lets things pass with an angry lecture or warning.

"Your dances get pretty hot," I observed. "When do you find yourself getting angry?"

"I started off calmly for years," she replied, "but it didn't make any difference. Now I start off angry and stay that way the whole time, but I don't show it until Keith starts to argue with me. That's when I lose my patience and begin yelling." Her waning patience was testimony to the wear and tear of her angry mixed dance.

At the beginning of Connie's diagram, I wrote "starts off angry." Her diagram was complete, so I summarized what it was telling us.

"The more you talk, the more Keith tests you, and the angrier you become. Finally, when you reach your boiling point, you explode at Keith, and he explodes back at you. Fifty percent of the time, you stop your dances with your action step; and 50 percent of the time you let things pass with a lecture or warning." Connie nodded in agreement. She could see her methods were not a good match to her son's learning style.

"Now, let's find out where your dance originated. What did your parents do when you or your siblings misbehaved?" I asked.

"My mother handled most of the discipline in our house," Connie replied. "I was the cooperative child. I didn't require much correction, but my sister did. My mother did a lot of repeating and reminding, reasoning and explaining, bargaining and negotiating, and she was a screamer. When things went too far, she threatened to turn matters over to my father, who usually spanked us."

"That's interesting," I observed. "Your mother was permissive, and your father was punitive. Together, their methods constituted the mixed approach. Notice any similarities?"

Connie understood she was repeating her parents' dance. She started off permissively like her mother, but ended punitively like her father. She incorporated both their approaches into her own mixed dance. It was time to show Connie how to get off the dance floor. I returned to her diagram.

"There are sixteen steps in your dance," I said, "but only two of them stop Keith's misbehavior. Which steps stop your dance?" Connie pointed to her action steps.

"Right," I replied. "Keith takes your action steps seriously, but your consequences hurt and add fuel to the power struggle. What would happen if you started off with your request at point A and followed through immediately with an action step at point B that didn't hurt or make him resentful?"

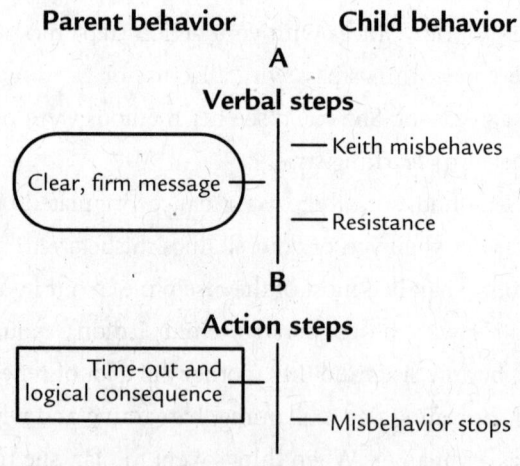

Figure 5.9   Connie's New Diagram

Connie understood where I was heading. By eliminating all the ineffective steps between points A and B, she could stop Keith's misbehavior and gain his cooperation quickly without all the anger, drama, or power struggles. Connie's new diagram soon looked like Figure 5.9. So can yours.

CHAPTER SUMMARY

Family dances are destructive patterns of communication and problem solving that are passed on from generation to generation. They all begin with unclear or ineffective messages. They're all fueled by anger, resistance, misunderstanding, and resentment; and they all lead to escalating conflicts and power struggles.

To parents, family dances are an ongoing source of frustration, stress, and discouragement. To children, dances are a rich source of live entertainment. To helping professionals, family dances are reinforcement errors, or things parents say and do that encourage and reward children's unacceptable behavior.

Over time, family dances become such a familiar and deeply ingrained habit that family members experience them as their normal way of doing things. They're not even aware they are dancing. Awareness is the first step toward breaking free.

The best way to stop a dance is not to start one. We should begin with a clear message and avoid the tempting baits children use to hook us into power struggles. That's what the next chapter will begin to show you how to do. It's time to hang up your dancing shoes and move on to more effective methods of communication.

6

How to Be Clear with Your Words

A clear message begins with your words, and most often, that's where communication breaks down because parents say and do more than is needed. Anger, drama, and strong emotion can easily sabotage the clarity of your message and reduce the likelihood of cooperation. It's not only what you say that matters; it's how you say it. Your words are an important guidance tool.

This chapter will show you how to use that tool in the clearest and most effective way. By following a few simple guidelines, you'll learn how to give your aggressive researcher the information he or she needs to make an acceptable choice and cooperate from the beginning.

Let's look at how two parents use their words to handle a typical situation. Imagine the following scene. Two six-year-olds, Matthew and Thomas, climb on a play structure while their mothers watch from a bench. All goes well until Thomas decides to show off by jumping off the edge of a raised platform, narrowly missing several children playing below. Thomas's mother intervenes.

"Thomas! What's wrong with you?" she shouts. "You could have injured those children. Can't you just climb on the bars like other normal children? Do you always have to be such a show-off?" She shakes her head in disgust. "If I see you do that again, I'm going to be very angry. Do you understand me?" She shoots him a stern glare. Thomas returns to the play structure.

> Anger, drama, and strong emotion can easily sabotage the clarity of your message and reduce the likelihood of cooperation.

Did Thomas hear a clear message that says jumping off the play structure is not okay? No. Did he hear that he has to stop jumping off the play structure? No. What did he hear? He hears that his behavior makes his mother angry. Does that require stopping? No. What is the worst thing that might happen if he does it again? His mother will become even angrier.

If you were a strong-willed six-year-old who really enjoys jumping off play structures, would this message deter you? Not likely. You might even be curious how many times you could jump before your mother actually did something to make you stop. The ineffective message sets Thomas and his mother up for testing and conflict.

Now, let's look at how Matthew's mother handles the same situation when Matthew decides to copy Thomas and jumps off the edge of the play structure. She approaches Matthew in a calm manner and gives him a clear message. "It's not okay to jump off the play structure, Matthew," she says, matter-of-factly. "If you do it again, you'll have to get down and find something different to do. Is that clear?"

Matthew nods.

No shaming. No blaming. No shouting. No drama. The focus of her message is on the behavior—not on attitude, feelings, or Matthew's worth as a person. Her words are specific and direct. Her tone is matter-of-fact. She simply tells him what she wants him to do and what will happen if he doesn't.

Matthew has all the information he needs to make an acceptable choice and cooperate. He may or he may not, but either choice will lead to good learning if his mother follows through. Her clear message sets up an instructive lesson.

GUIDELINES FOR GIVING CLEAR MESSAGES

The key to giving a clear message with your words is to say only what needs to be said in a clear, firm, and respectful manner. The following tips will help you get started.

Keep the Focus on Behavior

> Our primary goal in guidance situations is to reject unacceptable behavior, not the child performing the behavior.

Our primary goal in guidance situations is to reject unacceptable behavior, not the child performing the behavior. Therefore, we should begin our message with the focus on the right thing—behavior, not on attitude, feelings, or the worth of the child. Messages that shame, blame, criticize, or humiliate go too far. They reject the child along with the misbehavior and obscure the clarity of the message. The focus is misdirected.

For example, if you want your five-year-old to stop poking her brother at the dinner table, a clear message would be, "Keep your hands off your brother, please," or "Stop poking your brother," not "How would you feel if someone poked you during mealtime?" or "Why do you have to be such a pest?" or "Nobody likes you when you act like that!" These messages fail to provide the essential information your five-year-old needs, namely that poking her brother at mealtimes is not okay and must stop.

If you want to get your ten-year-old to stop shouting in the house, your message should be, "Use an indoor voice, please" or "We don't shout in the house." It should not be "Would you try to be a little more considerate?" or "How would you feel if I disturbed what you were doing?"

Be Specific and Direct

A clear message should inform children, specifically and directly, what it is you want them to do. If necessary, tell them when and how to do it. The fewer words, the better.

> Without a specific and direct message, your child's behavior will probably fall short of your expectations.

For example, if you want your nine-year-old to clean up his mess on the counter before he goes out to play, your message should be, "Clean up your mess at the counter, please, before you do anything else. That means putting your silverware and bowl in the sink and wiping off the counter."

If instead your message was, "I hope you do a better job cleaning up today," or "Please leave the counter a little cleaner today," who decides what "a better job" or "a little cleaner" means—you or your child? Without a specific and direct message, your child's behavior will probably fall short of your expectations.

If you want your twelve-year-old home for dinner by 6:30, your message should be, "Be home for dinner by 6:30, please," rather than "Don't be too late," or "Try to get back on time." If you use either of these latter two messages, who decides what "too late" or "on time" means—you or your twelve-year-old? Both messages leave the door open for testing.

Use Your Normal Voice

The tone of your voice is very important. A raised, irritated, or angry voice sends the wrong message—loss of control. That's when children are most likely to increase their testing because they realize you're hooked and beginning to dance.

> Your tone should convey that you are firm, in control, and resolute in your expectation that they must do what you've asked them to do.

Your tone should convey that you are firm, in control, and resolute in your expectation that they must do what you've asked them to do. The best way to communicate this expectation is simply to state your message matter-of-factly in your normal voice.

Firm limits are not stated harshly. It's not necessary to yell, scream, or raise your voice to convince your children that you mean what you say. If needed, your actions will convey that message more powerfully than your words will. Just say what you want them to do in your normal voice and be prepared to move on quickly to your action step.

> Managing anger and strong emotion is a skill you can learn; but like most new skills, the learning process requires time, patience, and lots of practice.

Sound easy? It is for some parents, but not for others—particularly those who grew up in homes where yelling, screaming, and angry dances were commonplace. Over time, the feelings of anger and frustration and the urge to yell become deeply ingrained habits and nearly automatic responses. These old habits won't disappear overnight just because you're inspired to do things differently. You have to work at it. Managing anger and strong emotion is a skill you can learn; but like most new skills, the learning process requires time, patience, and lots of practice. The more you practice, the faster your skills will improve. Chapter 12, "Patience: The Remedy for Anger and Frustration," will describe how to help manage your intense feelings.

Specify the Consequences for Noncompliance

Remember, strong-willed children are aggressive researchers. They want to know the bottom line or how far they can go when they decide to test or resist your rules. When you ask them to stop misbehaving, often they're wondering, "Or what?" "What are you going to do if I don't?" Parents can prevent a lot of testing and power struggles by providing children with all the information they need to make an acceptable choice from the beginning.

If you expect your child to test, tell your child, in your normal voice, what will happen if he or she doesn't cooperate. This is not a threat. You're just being clear by providing your child with all the information he or she needs to make an acceptable choice to cooperate.

> If you expect your child to test, tell your child, in your normal voice, what will happen if he or she doesn't cooperate.

For example, if you want your seven-year-old to stop riding his scooter in the busy street, but you expect him to test and do it anyway, your message should be, "Don't ride your scooter in the street, please. If you do, I'll have to put it away for the rest of the day."

Now, your child has all the information he needs to make an acceptable choice. He knows what you expect and what will happen if he doesn't cooperate, at least in theory. If he decides to test by riding in the street again, you simply follow through and put the scooter away.

If you want your ten-year-old to turn down the volume on his video game but expect him to test, your message should be, "Turn the volume down, please, or I'll have to put the game away for the rest of the afternoon." Now, your child has all the information he needs to make an acceptable choice and turn it down. If he decides to test, you simply follow through and put the game away.

If you want your strong-willed three-year-old to stop blowing bubbles in her cup at the dinner table but expect her to test, your message should be, "We don't blow bubbles in the cup during meals. If you do it again, I'll have to take the cup away for the next five minutes." If she decides to cooperate, wonderful, but if she decides to test, follow through and take the cup away for five minutes. Either way, your daughter will be a step closer to learning the lesson you're trying to teach.

CHAPTER SUMMARY

Effective guidance begins with a clear message with our words, and most often, that's where communication breaks down. Anger, drama, and strong emotion can easily sabotage the clarity and meaning of your message. You don't need a lot of words, and you don't need drama or strong emotion to show you mean business. You only need to be clear.

A clear verbal message focuses on behavior, not on attitude, feelings, or the worth of the child. Your message should be specific and direct and delivered in a firm, respectful tone. If you expect testing, inform your child in advance what will happen if he or she doesn't cooperate. Clear guidance messages reduce testing and dances and set up instructive learning experiences for children of all temperaments and learning styles.

7

Stopping Power Struggles Before They Begin

The best way to stop a dance is not to start one. We should begin with a clear message, resist the tempting baits children use to hook us into power struggles, and hold firm. Hannah's dad does this very effectively in the following example. You can, too, but you shouldn't expect your strong-willed child to give up his or her testing quickly.

Hannah is only nine, but she can dance circles around most adults. She can argue and debate like a courtroom attorney or develop sudden hearing loss and tune out even the clearest request. She knows just the right moment to cry or become upset when she thinks her parents are wearing down or close to giving in. Hannah can hook adults into power struggles faster than any child in her neighborhood.

But Hannah's parents are catching on to her tricks. They're beginning to see her behavior for what it is—part of a dance—and they're ready to get off the dance floor. One Saturday morning, as Hannah begins her usual chores, she gets an invitation to go skating with some friends. "Can I go, Dad?" she asks.

"Yes," he replies, "but you have to finish your chores first." Hannah is halfway down the hall before he finishes his sentence. *Did she hear what I said?* he wonders. *I'd better check in to make sure.*

> The best way to stop a dance
> is not to start one.

When he arrives at Hannah's room, she's busy getting dressed for the rink. "Did you hear what I asked you to do before you go?" he asks.

Hannah looks at him blankly. She really did tune out. So he repeats his original request. "I said you to have to finish your chores before you go."

"But, Dad! My friends will be here in twenty minutes," Hannah protests. "I can do my chores when I get back." Her dad is tempted to argue the issue, then stops himself.

"We're done talking about it, Hannah," he says, matter-of-factly, and leaves the room.

He doesn't mean it, Hannah says to herself. *He'll come back and remind me a few more times, then we'll argue, then my friends will come, and he'll have to let me go. The plan has always worked before.*

As predicted, Hannah's dad does return in a few minutes, but instead of reminding and arguing, he surprises her with an announcement. "You have fifteen minutes to finish your chores," he says. "I'll set the timer. If they're not done, you can't go." Then, he leaves the room.

Hey! What's going on? Hannah asks herself. *No reminders? No arguments? No pleading or cajoling? He's not supposed to do that.* She's in shock. Quickly, she scrambles to finish her chores so she can leave when her friends arrive.

As you begin to use your new tools, your child will likely challenge even your clearest request and do everything he or she can to get you back out on the dance floor, just like Hannah did with her parents. You'll probably be tempted to go along with it, too. This chapter will show you how to resist the urge. You'll learn how to recognize the bait, avoid the hook, and stay off the dance floor. Let's begin with the baits and how to avoid them.

> As you begin to use your new tools, your child will likely challenge even your clearest request and do everything he or she can to get you back out on the dance floor.

WHEN KIDS TUNE OUT, CHECK IN

One of the best ways to hook adults into power struggles is to tune out and ignore their requests. When this happens, adults are left wondering, *Did my message get across? Am I being ignored? Is it time to move on to my action step?*

The check-in procedure is a simple way to answer these questions without getting hooked into the old repeating and reminding routine. When in doubt, check in with your child by saying one of the following:

"Did you understand what I said?"

"Were my directions clear?"

"Tell me in your words what you heard me say."

For example, six-year-old David is watching his favorite cartoon show when his mother calls from the other room, "David, it's time to turn off the TV and wash up for dinner." No response. David continues to watch his program.

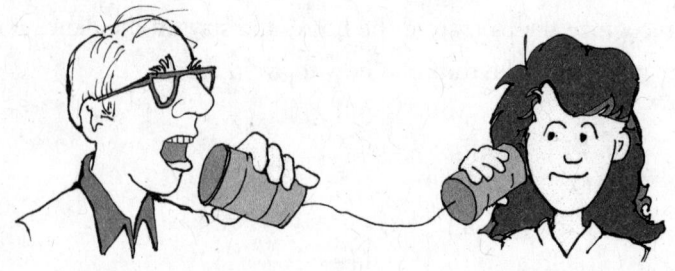

Did he hear what I said? his mother wonders. *If he did, he sure doesn't act like it.* She decides to check in. She walks into the room, stands between David and the TV, and looks him directly in the eyes.

"What did I just ask you to do?" she asks, matter-of-factly.

"Turn off the TV and wash up for dinner," he replies.

"Then do it, please," says his mother, "or the TV will be off-limits for the rest of the evening." David turns off the TV and goes to wash up.

What got into her? he wonders. *What happened to all the warnings, reminders, and threats? I should have gotten at least another ten minutes.*

In this example, David understood his mother's request but decided to ignore it. He was testing. He fully expected her to repeat and remind many times before he would actually have to turn off the TV. By checking in, David's mother eliminated any ambiguity in the message. Her expectation was clear and so was the cost for noncompliance.

Let's add a new twist to the example above. Let's say that when David's mother checks in, he looks at her with a blank stare because he really was tuned out, completely. What should she do?

She should give him the information he missed the first time and be ready to turn off the TV if he doesn't cooperate. When the message is clear, it's time to act.

The check-in procedure also is useful in situations where children give the right words but the wrong behavior. Ruben, age nine, is a good example. He knows he's not supposed to put his shoes on the couch but decides to do it anyway. His father sees him.

> The check-in procedure is useful in situations where children give the right words but the wrong behavior.

"Ruben, take your shoes off the couch, please," his father says.

"I will," says Ruben, but a few minutes go by, and his shoes are still on the couch. His father decides to check in.

"Ruben, what did I ask you to do?" his father inquires.

"I will," says Ruben as convincingly as the first time, but he makes no move to do so. His father clarifies the message.

"Your words say you will, but your actions say you won't. Let me be more clear. If you don't take your shoes off the couch now, you'll have to sit somewhere else," says his father. This message is very clear.

Rats! He didn't go for it, Ruben says to himself as he takes his shoes off the couch.

WHEN KIDS ARGUE, CUT IT OFF

The time for arguing and debating is not when your rules are being tested or violated. That's the time for action. If you take the bait and engage your child in an argument or debate over your rules, what you're really saying is that your rules are negotiable.

> If you take the bait and engage your child in an argument or debate over your rules, what you're really saying is that your rules are negotiable.

As mentioned earlier, to strong-willed children and many fence-sitters, negotiable feels a lot like optional, and optional rules invite testing. Parents who are willing to engage children in verbal sparring matches over their rules are opening themselves up for power struggles. How do you avoid the power struggle?

The cutoff procedure is a respectful method for ending an argument or discussion before it develops into a power struggle. When your child tries to hook you into arguing or debating over your rules, end the discussion by saying one of the following:

"We're done talking about it. If you bring it up again, you're going to have to spend the next five minutes by yourself in your room." (Follow through with a time-out consequence if your child continues.)

"The time for discussion is over. You can do what I asked or you can spend the next five minutes in your room getting ready to do it. What would you like to do?" (Time-out consequence)

For example, twelve-year-old Elliot knows he's not supposed to use his father's expensive camera without permission, but he really wants to take some pictures of his friends doing bicycle tricks. He heads out the door with the camera. His mother sees him.

"Elliot, is that your father's expensive camera?" she asks.

He nods.

"Aren't you supposed to ask before you use it?"

Elliot nods again. "I forgot," he says. "Can I use it, please? I want to get some pictures of my friends doing bike tricks."

His mom holds firm. She knows that if she gives in, he's going to try it again. "Not today," says his mom. "Maybe tomorrow if you ask permission first."

"Come on, Mom," Elliot pleads. "Can't you give me another chance? Please? I'll ask next time, I promise."

"Sorry, Elliot," says his mother. "Not this time."

"But that's not fair," he argues. "My friends are doing their tricks now. Can't you make an exception?"

The bait was skillfully presented. Elliot's mother was about to bite and debate the issue of fairness when she remembers what she read about family dances. *Oh no*, she says to herself. *We're not going through this again.*

There's nothing wrong with discussing your rules, but make sure that the discussion follows your child's compliance.

"Put it back, Elliot," she says, matter-of-factly. "If you bring it up again, you'll have to spend the next ten minutes by yourself in your room." Her answer is very clear. Elliot grumbles but puts the camera back where he got it.

If you've been permissive in the past, you'll probably feel compelled, like Elliott's mom, to give reasons and explanations when your child challenges your requests by asking, "Why?" There's nothing wrong with discussing your rules, but make sure that the discussion follows your child's compliance. Say something like the following:

"I'd be happy to tell you why after you do what I asked you to do." (Then arrange a time for the discussion.)

In most cases, you'll find the issue is not about why. The real issue is whether they have to do it at all. If they can wear you down in a discussion or debate, then compliance might be optional, not mandatory. By requiring compliance before the discussion, you eliminate the potential for a power struggle. Consider the following.

Julie, age eight, knows she's supposed to do her homework before she goes out to play, but decides to play first. She heads out the door.

Her mother intervenes. "Have you finished your homework?" her mother asks.

"Yeah," Julie replies.

Her mother is suspicious. "May I see it, please?" asks her mother.

Julie is caught. "I can do it later," says Julie. "I really want to play with my friends."

"I understand," says her mother, "but you know the rule— homework first, then playing."

"Why?" Julie asks. "Give me one good reason why I should have to do it now."

"I'd be happy to give you a reason after you do what you're supposed to do," says her mother.

What's going on? Julie asks herself. No arguments? No debates? Not even a discussion? She heads off to finish her homework so she can join her friends. If Julie had continued arguing, her mother would have let her know that any further discussion would result in a time-out.

WHEN KIDS CHALLENGE, GIVE LIMITED CHOICES

Alex, age eight, receives a remote control four-wheel-drive truck for Christmas. He can't wait to play with it, but first his father goes over some ground rules.

"You can run the truck anywhere in the front or backyards except the flower beds. Keep the truck out of the flower beds, please," he says.

"I will," says Alex, and he does, too—for a while. But Alex soon discovers that the bedding areas have the best terrain for his four-wheeler. There are mounds and redwood bark and all kinds of flowers and shrubs to navigate around. The temptation is more than he can resist. When his father goes into the house, Alex runs his truck through the flower beds. His father sees him and gives Alex some choices.

"You can run your truck where you were asked, or I'll have to put the truck away for the rest of the afternoon," says his father, matter-of-factly. "Those are your choices. What would you like to do?"

"I'll keep it out of the flower beds," Alex replies.

"Good choice," says his father. "Thanks for cooperating."

Alex's father is using limited choices, a highly effective method for helping children become aware of their choices when they decide to challenge or test our rules. The way Alex's father sets this situation up, Alex cannot avoid being responsible for his choices and behavior. The rule is clear and so are the consequences for noncompliance. Alex has all the information he needs to make an acceptable choice to cooperate. He may or he may not, but either way, he will experience the lesson his father is trying to teach.

> Using limited choices is a highly effective method for helping children become aware of their choices when they decide to challenge or test our rules.

The following examples illustrate some of the many ways limited choices can be used. Often, this guidance approach leads to good choices and cooperative behavior, but I've also tried to include examples where the child decides to test or defy so you can see how to follow up with a logical consequence.

Jill, age five, makes grunting noises at the table to amuse her two brothers. Her mother asks her to stop, and she does briefly, then starts up again. Her mother gives Jill some limited choices.

"You can stop making noises at the table," says her mother, "or you can spend the next five minutes in your room getting yourself ready to cooperate at the table. What would you like to do?" Jill decides to cooperate.

Philip, age eight, cheats at a table game. When his sisters ask him to play fairly, Philip ignores them. They complain, and their father intervenes.

"Philip, you can play by the rules or find something different to do. What would you like to do?"

"I'll play fair," says Philip, but five minutes later he's cheating again. His sisters complain, and their father supports his words with effective action.

"Philip, you're going to have to find something else to do," says his father. "You can't play that game anymore today."

Two brothers quarrel loudly over some baseball cards. A few shoves are exchanged, then they start to yell. Their mother intervenes.

"Guys, can you work this out quietly or do you need some time to cool off in your rooms?" she asks. They decide to work out their dispute quietly.

Maria, age twelve, plays her radio in her room with the volume cranked up. It's so loud the rest of the family can't hear their TV program downstairs. Their mother intervenes.

"Maria, turn your down radio, please," her mother says. "We can't hear our show."

Maria glares at her in defiance. So her mother gives her some limited choices.

"You can turn the radio down, or I'll have to turn it off and keep it in my room for a while," says her mother. "What would you like to do?"

Maria's options are clear. Reluctantly, she decides to turn down the radio.

"Thanks," says her mother.

WHEN KIDS DAWDLE, USE A TIMER

Ten-year-old Kimi is an aspiring artist who hates to clean up after herself. She sprinkles glitter on her latest masterpiece, proudly displays it to her parents, then heads off to watch TV in the other room. Her art supplies are scattered all over the kitchen counter. Her father intervenes.

"Kimi, you need to put away all your art supplies now before you do anything else," he says, matter-of-factly. He's been through this drill before.

"I will," says Kimi, "but I need to use the bathroom first." She disappears for about ten minutes. Her father becomes suspicious. When he investigates, he finds Kimi in another room playing a game on the computer. He checks in.

GUIDELINES FOR USING LIMITED CHOICES

1. Restrict the number of choices you present. Limit the options to two or three, and be sure the desired corrective step is one of them. For example, if you don't want your child to throw the Frisbee in the house, you might say, "You can throw the Frisbee in the front yard or the backyard, but if you throw it in the house, I'm going to have to take it away. What would you like to do?"

   If your child attempts to introduce other choices that are not acceptable, you should respond, "Those are your choices and your only choices. What would you like to do?" Strong-willed children often try to turn limited choices into one of their favorite games, *Let's Make a Deal*.

2. Remember, the choices are your limits. State them firmly with no wiggle room, or you may invite limit testing. For example, if you don't want your child to eat a drippy Popsicle anywhere in the house except at the kitchen table, you should say, "You can eat the Popsicle at the kitchen table or outdoors, but if you eat it anywhere else in the house, I'll have to take it away." Choices presented with soft limits sabotage the effectiveness of this technique.

3. Make your child responsible for the decision. After presenting limited choices, ask your child, "What would you like to do?" This question places the hot potato of responsibility on your child's lap, not yours.

4. When your child states his or her intention to comply but fails to do so, follow through with the stated consequence. For example, if you say, "You can ride your scooter on the sidewalk or the driveway but not in the street. If you ride it in the street, I'll have to put it away for the rest of the day." These choices are clear. If your child decides to challenge or test your rule by riding it in the street, follow through and take away the scooter as stated.

"Kimi, did you hear me ask you to put away all your art supplies before you do anything else?" he asks.

"I will," Kimi replies, in an annoyed voice, but she continues to sit in front of the computer. She's testing to determine what "now" really means. Fifteen minutes? Twenty minutes? Possibly never? She knows how to find out. She continues to dawdle.

Without any further words, her father walks over and turns off the computer. "I'll set the timer for ten minutes," he says. "If the job isn't done when the buzzer goes off, you'll spend the next ten minutes in your room getting ready to come back and finish it. Is that clear?"

Rats! Kimi grumbles to herself. She can't see any way out of it. Reluctantly, she heads to the kitchen to clean up her mess.

The timer also came in handy when six-year-old Colin decided to go into his usual morning stall while getting dressed. He expected his mother to do her usual warning, cajoling, pleading, begging, and bribing routine; but she surprised him with an announcement. "We're leaving for school in twenty minutes, ready or not," she says. "I'll set the timer."

What happened to all the pleading, begging, prodding, and special treats if I hurry? Colin wonders. *She can't be serious.*

When the buzzer goes off, Colin has one sock, his underwear, and a T-shirt on. "Time to go," says his mother, matter-of-factly. She gathers up the remaining clothes and school items, places them in a shopping bag, and ushers Colin out the door. He races for the car hoping none of his friends see him and dresses in the backseat. Colin will probably take his mother more seriously next time she sets the timer to help him get out the door.

IGNORE ATTITUDE, NOT MISBEHAVIOR

Grumbling, mumbling, eye rolling, door slamming, and looks of impatience or disgust are tempting baits that are hard for most adults to resist. If you bite and respond on the child's level, then you're back in the dance and what have you taught? A lesson in disrespect? They already know that. When your child tries to hook you with a disrespectful attitude, remember Anthony's mother in the next example. Ignore the attitude, not the misbehavior.

Anthony, age twelve, knows he's not supposed to play computer games before completing his homework, but his mother is in the other room, so he decides to do it anyway. She hears him and intervenes.

Ignore the attitude, not the misbehavior.

"Anthony, turn the computer off, please, and finish your homework," she says, matter-of-factly. "If you don't, the computer will be off-limits for the rest of the evening."

Anthony gives his mother a look of disgust, rolls his eyes, mumbles something under his breath, and lets out a big harrumph. "It's not fair!" he complains. "Evan's mom lets him play computer games before he does homework. I don't see why I should have to follow your stupid rule."

Anthony's mother holds firm and waits. *I'm the adult. He's the kid,* she reminds herself. *I'm not going to get hooked by his bad attitude.*

When Anthony sees she isn't going to budge or dance, he reluctantly makes the right choice to cooperate. He turns off the computer and begins his homework.

"Thank you, Anthony," says his mother.

Anthony did his best to hook his mother with his disrespectful attitude, but she didn't take the bait. Instead, she held her ground, maintained her composure, and remained focused on getting what she wanted—his cooperation.

Does ignoring a child's disrespectful attitude mean that it's okay? No, it's not okay. It doesn't feel good, and we don't like it. But if you reward it by responding to it, you'll likely see a lot more of it. Avoid the reinforcement error. Don't bite.

When does attitude cross the line and become misbehavior that shouldn't be ignored? This is a judgment call every parent has to make at the time. I can offer some guidelines to keep you on track. Mumbling, grumbling, eye rolling, looks of disgust, and even sticking out the tongue are the baits I generally ignore. Profanity, name-calling, insults, hurtful statements, or extreme rude gestures cross the line. I respond to these with a time-out.

WHEN KIDS CROSS THE LINE, HOLD FIRM

Does your child try to evade your consequences by pleading for a second chance or by promising not to do it again? Do you go along with it? Parents who do set themselves up for further testing and power struggles. When children give us the right words but the wrong behavior, hold firm and stay focused on the behavior. Let's look at how Dean's mother does this.

Dean, age eight, walks by his younger sister and gives her a kick. She screams, and their mom arrives on the scene.

"Dean kicked me," his sister complains. The red spot on her leg is still visible.

"I barely touched her," says Dean. "It didn't hurt."

"It's not okay to kick others," says his mother, matter-of-factly. "I'll see you in fifteen minutes." She sends him for a time-out.

"I won't do it again," Dean says contritely. "Can I have another chance?"

His mother holds firm. "That's a good choice for next time," she says, "but this time you need to head to your room."

Twelve-year-old Brenda had a similar experience when she tried to take her mother's cell phone to school without permission.

> When children give us the right words but the wrong behavior, hold firm and stay focused on the behavior.

"Brenda, is that my cell phone in your backpack?" asks her mother. "You know you're not supposed to use it without asking. May I have it back, please?"

"Come on, Mom," Brenda says contritely. "I forgot. I won't do it again. I promise. May I use it, please?"

Her mother holds firm. "Not this time," she replies. "Maybe next time if you ask for permission first." No second chances and no dances. Brenda will probably think carefully before she tries this one again.

WHEN KIDS GET HOT, COOL THEM DOWN

Effective problem solving is difficult for anyone to do, parents or children, in an atmosphere of anger or strong emotion. The cooldown keeps both sides off the dance floor until the time is right for problem solving. In situations of anger or upset, separate yourself from your child by saying something like the following:

> (When both sides are upset) "I think we both need a little time to cool down. Wait for me in your room (or living room, den, etc.) and we'll talk in about five minutes or however much time you need to cool down."
>
> (When the parent is upset) "I'm feeling angry, and I need some time to cool down."

The technique works best when parents and children are in separate rooms during the cool-down period. People recover at different rates. Don't assume your child is ready to talk just because you are. Allow sufficient time for all parties to restore control before problem solving. You may want to preface your problem solving with a question such as, "Are you ready to talk?" If things get

hot a second time, use the procedure again. Use it as often as you need it. Consider the following.

When I first met nine-year-old Sam and his dad, they were stuck in an angry dance. Whenever Sam misbehaved, his dad began yelling; and before he knew it, he was saying hurtful things he later regretted.

Sam felt hurt by his father's comments and was becoming skillful at hurting back. They both needed some way to interrupt their dance. I suggested the cool-down method and showed them how it worked. They agreed to give it a try.

Shortly after our appointment, Sam was in the garage building something with nails. When he finished his project, he left a number of nails scattered on the garage floor. When his father saw the nails, he exploded.

"Sam! Get in here!" he shouted, but as soon as the words left his mouth, he remembered what we discussed.

> The cooldown keeps both sides off the dance floor
> until the time is right for problem solving.

Sam arrived, expecting the worst; but to his astonishment, his father said, "I need a few minutes by myself to cool down. Wait for me in your room, please."

It took about five minutes for Sam's dad to cool down. Then, he went to Sam's room and calmly asked him to pick up the nails. No yelling, no insults, and no injured feelings! It felt strange to be treated respectfully, but Sam was more than happy to comply.

By using the cooldown, Sam's father role modeled anger management and respectful problem solving. Both had taken a big step toward ending their angry dance.

WHEN PARENTS CROSS THE LINE, APOLOGIZE

Five-year-old Jaime is having a rough day. She woke up grumpy and didn't like any of the outfits her mother picked out for her. She complained all through breakfast. When her sister smirked at her, Jamie poured syrup in her sister's orange juice and got a time-out. When it was time to leave for school, Jamie stormed out the door and forgot the permission slip she needed to go on a field trip. Her mother had to make an extra trip.

When Jamie returns home from school, she picks up from where she left off in the morning. She pesters her sister, fusses and complains all through homework, and sticks out her tongue when her mother asks her to put away her books and backpack. That's when her mother loses her patience.

"Damn it, Jamie!" her mother shouts. "What's wrong with you? I'm sick and tired of your bratty attitude! You're behaving like a two-year-old." Her mother is about to say something even more hurtful when she realizes what she's doing and stops herself.

"Please go to your room and wait for me," she says. "I need some time to cool down."

After the cooldown, she goes to Jamie's room to apologize.

"I'm sorry for the hurtful things I said," her mother begins. "I lost my temper. I think you're a wonderful nine-year-old who's having a rough day, and I love you very much. Will you accept my apology?" Jamie nods and gives her mother a big hug. No retaliation or power struggles after this incident.

Raising a strong-willed child is a challenging and exhausting job. From time to time, we all lose our patience, react in frustration, and say or do things we later regret. How should we handle this when it happens?

> An apology from a caring adult gives children per-
> mission to be human and imperfect and the courage
> to try harder.

An apology is the best way to begin. The gesture conveys all the right messages. It shows children how to be respectful of others' feelings. It teaches them how to heal the little hurts in relationships that often lead to resentment and power struggles. Most important, an apology from a caring adult gives children permission to be human and imperfect and the courage to try harder.

Some parents believe that apologizing to a child is a sign of weakness that diminishes the child's respect for the adult. My years of family counseling have shown that just the opposite is true. To children, an apology is not a sign of weakness. It's a sign of strength that inspires them to try harder. Children respect adults who have the courage to be human and take responsibility for their own imperfections and mistakes.

DON'T PERSONALIZE THE MISBEHAVIOR

When your child misbehaves, do you sometimes ask yourself, *Why is he doing this to me?* If so, you're probably personalizing your child's testing and setting both of you up for power struggles in the process. Aggressive research is wearing, but it's not intended to be a personal attack. Sid, age ten, is a good example.

Sid's mom has asked him repeatedly not to wear his Rollerblades in the house because the wheels leave marks on the floor. But Sid has been playing hard and he's really thirsty. When he thinks his mother isn't looking, he sneaks into the kitchen with his Rollerblades on. She catches him.

"Sid! Why are you deliberately disobeying me?" she asks in an irritated voice. "You know I don't allow Rollerblades in the house. They leave marks that are hard to clean up."

> If you tend to personalize your child's testing, try to hold on to the bigger picture. Aggressive research is a normal learning process for strong-willed children.

"I was being careful," Sid replies. "I didn't think you'd mind if I only went into the kitchen."

"Well, I do mind," says his mother. "It's not considerate. I have enough work to do without cleaning up any more of your messes. Do you understand? Now take them off and put them up for the afternoon."

"That's not fair!" protests Sid. "I won't do it again. I promise. Can I have one more chance?" he pleads.

"You can tomorrow," replies his mother. "Put them away, please."

"You're mean!" grumbles Sid as he takes off his Rollerblades.

Sid's persistent testing is not intended to be a personal attack upon his mother's authority. In fact, his testing is not about her at all. It's about him and how he learns. He needs to collect a lot of evidence in the form of experience before he's convinced that her rules are mandatory, not optional. Persistent testing is part of his normal learning process.

His mother was on the right track when she took away his Rollerblades for violating her rule, but she turned an instructive guidance lesson into a power struggle by personalizing his testing. If you tend to personalize your child's testing, try to hold on to the bigger picture. Aggressive research is a normal learning process for strong-willed children. Parents set themselves up for power struggles when they take their child's testing personally.

CHAPTER SUMMARY

Let's reflect upon the new tools you've added to your toolbox thus far. In Chapter 6, you learned how to be clear with your words. In Chapter 7, you learned how to stop power struggles by not allowing them to begin. You're as prepared as you can be with your words, but your words are only the first part of your overall message. If your child continues to test, then it's time to act. Consequences are the second part of your overall message. They speak louder than your words. It's time to get acquainted with your next set of tools.

8

Supporting Your Rules with Logical Consequences

Strong-willed children and many fence-sitters need more than words to be convinced that following your rules is required, not optional. They need to experience what you say before they'll believe it. This doesn't mean that your words are less important than your actions. It simply means that your words are only the first part of your total message.

Your child may decide to test even your clearest message, and, when this happens, the time for talking is over. It's time to act and help your child learn the lesson the hard way. Logical consequences are the second part of your limit-setting message. They speak louder than your words.

This chapter will show you how to use these instructive guidance tools in the clearest and most understandable way. Get to know them. Make friends with them. You'll need to use them frequently and in generous helpings with your strong-willed child. They are your ticket to credibility.

WHY CONSEQUENCES ARE IMPORTANT

Consequences are like walls. They stop misbehavior. They provide clear and definitive answers to children's research questions, and they help strong-willed children learn rules the way they learn best—the hard way. Consequences are the hard way.

> Consequences are the second part of your limit-setting message. They speak louder than your words.

The consequences you'll learn in this chapter will teach your strong-willed child to tune back in to your words, take them seriously, and cooperate more often. If you've relied on permissiveness in the past, the consequences you learn will help you regain cred-

ibility and authority. If you've relied on punishment in the past, the consequences you learn will help you rebuild a cooperative relationship based on mutual respect rather than fear and intimidation. If you've used the mixed approach, the consequences you learn will help you develop consistency. For anyone recovering from a bad case of soft limits, the consequences in this chapter will be a big step in the right direction.

WHAT MAKES CONSEQUENCES EFFECTIVE?

Consequences can be highly instructive tools, but their effectiveness depends largely upon how you use them. If you apply them in a punitive, permissive, or inconsistent manner, your consequences will have limited training value and may teach lessons other than the ones you intend. If you apply them in a logical and respectful manner and incorporate the following characteristics, your consequences will have their greatest instructive value. Let's look at some of the characteristics that make consequences effective.

Immediate

Four-year-old Tracy decides to give herself a milk mustache by taking big gulps out of her glass. It's funny the first time, but she does it again and again. Her father asks her to stop. She does so initially, but after a few minutes, she decides to test and do it some more. Without any further words, her father applies a logical consequence. He removes her cup from the table.

Consequences are most effective when they are applied as

immediately after the unacceptable behavior as possible. In the preceding example, the immediate consequence helped Tracy make the cause-and-effect connection between her misbehavior and the loss of the cup. If Tracy's father had chosen instead to remove her cup at the next meal, the consequence would have had far less impact.

Consistent

Twelve-year-old Trenton knows he's not supposed to leave the house after dinner on school nights, but he really wants to show something to his buddy, Kevin, down the street.

"May I go to Kevin's house for a few minutes?" he asks his mother. "I have something I want to show him." Trenton hopes she'll make an exception this time and let him go, but she holds firm.

"You can share it with him tomorrow," she says.

Rats! Trenton says to himself. He decides to plead his case to his father, who also holds firm.

Trenton remembers what happened the last time he decided to violate his parents' rule by sneaking out after dinner. He lost his after-school play privileges for the next three days. *I'll only be gone for few minutes,* he says to himself. *They'll never know.* He sneaks out and gets caught. Once again, he loses his after-school play privileges for another three days. Chalk up another hard-way learning experience for Trenton.

> Inconsistency is an invitation to limit testing for strong-willed children.

Consistent consequences are vital to effective child training, but consistency has many dimensions. There's consistency between what we say and what we do, between one parent and another, and from one time to the next. All are important. Training can break down when we are inconsistent in any of these areas.

Trenton's parents were consistent in all these areas. Trenton receives the clearest possible signal from his parents about their rule and expectations. Compliance is expected and required.

What do you think would happen if Trenton's parents were only 50 percent consistent in enforcing their rule about leaving the house on school nights? More testing? Of course. In reality, the rule is only in effect 50 percent of the time. How does Trenton know when it is and when it isn't in effect? He doesn't. He has to test to find out. Inconsistency is an invitation to limit testing for strong-willed children.

Logically Related

When we fail to pay for our phone bills for several months at a time, does the phone company respond by shutting off our water? No. That would not stop us from using the phone without paying. Instead, the phone company does something meaningful. It applies a logical consequence. It shuts off the phone service. This consequence sends the right message about responsibility: Pay for the service if you want to use the phone.

Consequences are most instructive when they're logically related to the behavior.

It makes little sense to withhold a child's favorite dessert or TV show because that child failed to put away his bicycle in the evening. What do desserts and TV shows have to do with putting away bicycles? Nothing. The consequences are not related to the behavior.

Consequences are most instructive when they're logically related to the behavior. What is a logical consequence for a child who fails to put his bicycle away? Loss of the bicycle for a day or so. The message is clear: Take care of your bike or you'll lose the privilege of using it for a while.

Punitive consequences are not logical nor is the thinking that accompanies them. Punitive thinking goes something like this: *What do they like? What do they care about? I'll show them. I'm going to take it away.* The goal is to hurt and force compliance. Instead of teaching responsibility, punitive consequences inspire anger, resentment, and retaliation.

> Instead of teaching responsibility, punitive consequences inspire anger, resentment, and retaliation.

Consequences applied in a permissive manner are even less effective. They lack firmness and clarity, and encourage testing, not cooperation. Justin, age nine, is a good example.

Justin knows he's not supposed to invite his friends to swim at his home without first asking his parents for permission, but two of his friends arrive at the door with their swimsuits on and towels in hand.

"Is Justin here?" asks Tommy. "He invited us to swim in your pool." She invites them in, then goes to find Justin.

"Did you invite friends to swim in our pool without asking again?" she asks. "You know how I feel about that. It's very inconsiderate. Did you ever consider that I might have something else to do besides supervise your friends? I really don't appreciate it."

"I'm sorry," says Justin, contritely. "Can they swim, please?"

"Okay," concedes his mother, "but this is the last time. Do you understand? If happens again, I'm going to send them home. I really mean it."

Sure you do, Mom, Justin says to himself with a smile. He grabs his towel and heads off to join his friends.

How many times do you think Justin has heard this lecture?

Has she ever followed through before? Why then should he take her any more seriously this time? Do you think this is the last time Justin will invite his friends to swim without asking?

Proportional

Consequences are most effective when they are proportional to the behavior, that is, not too much, not too little, not too long, and not too short. This concept is difficult to grasp for those who use the punitive and permissive models. Consider the following.

Toby, age eight, arrives home from the park twenty minutes late. His father goes ballistic.

> Consequences are most effective when they are
> proportional to the behavior, that is, not too much,
> not too little, not too long, and not too short.

"I told you to be home by 5 P.M.!" his father shouts. "It's 5:20. You're grounded to the house for the next three weeks."

"But, Dad, that's not fair," complains Toby. "I was only twenty minutes late."

"Don't argue with me," says his father, sternly. "I can make it a month if you'd prefer."

Toby's father is a good example of punitive thinking. He sincerely believes that if a little is good, then a lot must be wonderful. So he tends to go overboard with his consequences.

Long, drawn-out consequences are almost always harder on parents than on children. Why? Because parents have to live with an angry and resentful child for the duration of the consequence. A proportional logical consequence, such as removing Toby's play privileges for the next day, would have taught the lesson just fine.

Consequences applied in a permissive manner are often "too brief" or "too little" to be effective. Kids don't take them seriously. Seven-year-old Claire is a good example.

Claire has been asked repeatedly not to ride her bike in the street but continues to do it anyway. Her mother intervenes.

"Claire, I've asked you repeatedly not to ride your bike in the street, but you continue to disobey me. You need to put your bike away and come in the house for the next ten minutes," says her mother.

Ten minutes! What a joke! Claire says to herself. *I was ready for a snack anyway.*

Do you think ten minutes away from her bicycle will keep Claire from riding it in the street again? Not likely. Removing her bicycle for the rest of the day would have been much more instructive.

Followed by a Clean Slate

When a consequence is over, it should really be over. No debriefings. No lectures or inquisitions. No rubbing their noses in it or adding "I told you so" words. If your child lacks the skills to behave acceptably, then teach the appropriate skill. Otherwise, allow the experience to teach the lesson. You're not likely to achieve much more with your words. In fact, saying or doing more may diminish the effectiveness of your consequence. If your child has more learning to do and chooses to misbehave again, then provide another piece of hard data, and repeat the experience. But when the consequence is over, it should be followed with a clean slate and forgiveness.

For example, six-year-old Tommy knows he's not allowed to watch TV before dinner, but he decides to take his chances and turn it on anyway. He gets caught. When his mother turns it off, he tries to argue with her.

"We're done talking about it, Tommy," says his mother. "If you bring it up again, you'll have to spend the next five minutes by yourself in your room."

"You're not fair!" Tommy complains, hoping to hook her into negotiating. "I don't see why I have to follow this stupid rule." His mother follows through and sends Tommy to his room. He returns five minutes later, ready to cooperate.

> When the consequence is over, it should be followed with a clean slate and forgiveness.

"What did you learn from this?" asks his annoyed mother. "Wouldn't it have been easier if you had done what I asked the first time? I'm sick and tired of having to go over these same lessons again and again. When will you ever learn?"

Tommy's mother can't seem to let go. Her focus is stuck on stopping the unacceptable behavior when it should be focused on encouraging Tommy's present cooperation. Tommy needs a clean slate and a fresh opportunity to show that he can cooperate.

Now that you have a better understanding about what makes consequences effective, let's look at different types of consequences you can use for handling a wide range of misbehavior. We'll begin with the consequence that requires the least amount of time, energy, and involvement from parents.

NATURAL CONSEQUENCES

Kellen and his buddy, Craig, both eight-year-olds, have been playing hard. They enter Kellen's house, tired and thirsty.

"May we have a couple of cold box drinks?" Kellen asks. Kellen loves punch-flavored box drinks on hot days.

"Sure," says his mom. She takes two drinks out of the refrigerator, pokes holes in the tops, and puts the straws in. "Here you go, guys," she says. They thank her and head out the door.

When she looks out the window, she sees Kellen squirting his box drink at Craig like a squirt gun. Then Craig squirts Kellen, and Kellen squirts back.

The drinks won't last long like that, Kellen's mom thinks to herself. She's right. Within minutes, the two boys return to the house with empty boxes.

"May we each have another one?" asks Kellen. "Ours are empty." Kellen's mom recognizes her opportunity to teach a lesson with a natural consequence.

"One is all you get," she says, matter-of-factly.

"But, Mom, we're really thirsty!" pleads Kellen.

> Natural consequences, as the name implies, follow naturally from an event or situation. They are nature's version of the "hard way."

"When you squirt your box drinks all over each other, it doesn't leave much for drinking," she replies. "If you're still thirsty, you can have all the water you can drink."

Kellen's mom is letting the natural consequence of squirting the box drink teach the lesson her hard-way learner needs to learn. Like many parents, she was probably tempted to say "I told you so" or give a lecture on the poor choice of using box drinks as squirt guns, but she realizes any further words on her part might sabotage the effectiveness of the real-life consequence Kellen experienced. He will probably think twice before he decides to use his box drink as a squirt gun again.

Natural consequences, as the name implies, follow naturally from an event or situation. They are nature's version of the "hard way." Natural consequences require little or no involvement from parents. A lecture, an "I told you so," fixing the problem, or adding additional consequences can undermine the instructional value of the natural lesson. This is one lesson that teaches itself.

Some parents find natural consequences easy to use and welcome opportunities to allow their children to learn from their poor choices and mistakes. For other parents, natural consequences are not easy to use. When something happens, they find themselves fighting the urge to take charge and do more than is needed. If this happens to you, practice limiting your involvement by restating the obvious facts of the situation, such as when the toy is broken, we can't play with it. Let's look at some of the many situations in which you can use natural consequences.

Situations for Using Natural Consequences

Natural consequences can be instructive guidance tools in situations when an item is lost, damaged, or stolen due to carelessness; when children make a habit of forgetting; when children dawdle and procrastinate; and when children fail to do their part.

When an Item Is Lost, Damaged, or Stolen Due to Carelessness
Natural Consequence: Don't replace or repair the lost or damaged item until enough time has passed for the child to experience the loss.

Jordan, age twelve, received an expensive pocket-size video game from his parents for his birthday. Within a few days of receiving the gift, he left it at a neighborhood swim club. When he remembered and returned for it, it was gone. He cried, and his parents promptly went out and bought him another one.

The second video game lasted almost two weeks before Jordan left it on the car seat on a very hot day. The plastic case melted. The second one was ruined. Once again, Jordan cried and pleaded for another one.

His parents had learned their lesson, but not Jordan. When he begged for a new one, his parents announced a different plan.

"We'll contribute half toward the purchase of a new one if you save your money, pay the rest, and present us with a good plan for taking care of it," said his father. Reluctantly, Jordan agreed. This time, Jordan also will do the learning.

When Children Make a Habit of Forgetting

Natural consequence: Don't remind them or take away responsibility by doing for them what they should be doing for themselves.

Nine-year-old Kendra has a habit of forgetting her homework and lunch money in the morning. Each time this occurs, one of her parents makes a dutiful trip to school to drop off the forgotten item. Noticing this had become a pattern, Kendra's teacher suggested they use a natural consequence to handle the problem. She recommended that they not make any trips to school for a two-week period. Kendra was a good student. If she missed one or two lunches or assignments, it wouldn't hurt her. Kendra's parents agreed.

On Tuesday of the first week, Kendra forgot her lunch money. When lunchtime arrived, she asked her teacher if her parents had dropped off her lunch money. "Not yet," her teacher replied.

That night, Kendra complained to her parents, "You forgot my lunch money! I couldn't eat lunch today."

"I'm sure you'll remember it tomorrow," said her father, matter-of-factly. Nothing further was said.

Kendra did remember her lunch money, but on Thursday she left home without her homework. As before, she asked her teacher if her parents had dropped it off. "Not yet," said her teacher. Kendra got a zero on the assignment.

Once again, Kendra complained to her parents. "You forgot to bring my homework. I got a zero on that assignment!"

"You're a very good student," said her mother. "I'm sure you'll remember it tomorrow." She did.

When Children Dawdle or Procrastinate

Natural consequence: Let them experience the outcome of their dawdling and procrastination.

Five-year-old Alex knows how to get maximum attention from his morning dawdle routine while getting dressed. His parents have tried reminding, cajoling, reasoning, explaining, bribing, bargaining, and threatening loss of privilege and toys. Nothing helped. Desperate, they decided to use a natural consequence.

One morning as he begins his usual stall, his mother announces, "Alex, you have fifteen minutes to finish dressing, then you're out the door, ready or not. I'll set the timer."

She doesn't mean it, Alex thinks to himself. *She'll remind me a few more times, then come over and help me finish up.* He continues to dawdle. Fifteen minutes go by, and he has only his socks, underwear, and T-shirt on. The buzzer goes off.

"Time to go," his mother says, matter-of-factly. She puts his remaining clothes in a shopping bag and escorts him out the door. The commotion catches the attention of other children heading off to school.

Oh no! Alex says to himself. His theatrics are not intended for them. They know he's capable of getting dressed and out the door on time. He sprints for the car.

"Here's the bag," says his mother as they get into the car. With tears streaming down his face, Alex scrambles to finish dressing. His pants, shirt, and shoes are on before they even back out of the driveway. Nothing further is said. The next morning, Alex is dressed on time.

When Children Fail to Do Their Part

Natural consequence: Let them experience the result.

Serena, age ten, knows she's supposed to put her dirty clothes in her bedroom hamper and bring them downstairs on Saturdays to be washed, but that's not what really happens. Instead, Serena leaves them lying all over her bedroom floor, and her frustrated parents pick them up for her and wash them anyway.

Her parents decide it's time for Serena to handle the complete job on her own. The parents agree not to pick up any more of Serena's dirty clothing. If she wants them washed, she'll have to put them in the hamper herself and bring them downstairs on Saturdays.

Two weeks pass before Serena discovers that she's out of clean socks and nearly out of underwear.

"Mom, I'm out of socks," Serena complains.

"I didn't see any in the hamper on Saturday," says her mother. "If they're not downstairs in the hamper, they can't be washed. I guess you'll have to wear a dirty pair today." She did, and she didn't like it. The next weekend the socks were in the hamper and waiting to be washed.

LOGICAL CONSEQUENCES: THE GOLD STANDARD FOR DISCIPLINE

Meredith, age nine, knows she's not supposed to ride her bike without a bike helmet. The last time she was caught, her mother took the bike away for the rest of the day. But Meredith is an aggressive researcher. She decides to try it again and gets caught.

"Put the bike in the garage, Meredith," says her mother.

"But, Mom, I told Cindy I'd be at her house in five minutes," Meredith complains. "May I have another chance? Please?" Her mother holds firm.

"You can tomorrow," says her mother. "Today, you'll have to walk."

> Logical consequences are structured learning opportunities. They are arranged by the adult, experienced by the child, and are logically related to the situation or behavior.

Meredith's mother is using a logical consequence to support her rule about wearing a bike helmet when using the bike. Unlike natural consequences, which follow naturally from a behavior, logical consequences are structured learning opportunities. They are arranged by the adult, experienced by the child, and are logically related to the situation or behavior.

Meredith temporarily lost the privilege of using her bike because she chose not to abide by her parents' rule for wearing a bike helmet. No yelling or threatening. No warnings, lectures, or second chances. No loss of unrelated toys or privileges. Her mother's message is clear: Use a helmet or you can't ride the bike. In effect, Meredith chose the consequence she experienced.

Logical consequences are ideal training tools for strong-willed children. They stop misbehavior. They teach responsibility, and they promote hard-way learning in the clearest and most understandable way. When used consistently, they are your ticket to credibility.

Some parents have difficulty using logical consequences, but those who do usually encounter two types of problems. They think too hard and try to come up with the perfect consequence for each situation; or they don't think enough, react emotionally, and apply consequences in a permissive or punitive manner.

Guidelines for Using Logical Consequences

If you're willing to take a little time and get to know these tools, you'll discover that logical consequences are easy to use. Almost anyone can use them. You don't have to think on your feet like a courtroom attorney, and you don't have to rack your brain to come up with the perfect consequence for each situation. All you have to do is think logically and follow a few simple guidelines.

> Anger, drama, or strong emotion convey overinvolvement on your part and sabotage the instructive value of your consequence.

Use Your Normal Voice

Logical consequences are most effective when carried out in a matter-of-fact manner. Anger, drama, or strong emotion convey overinvolvement on your part and sabotage the instructive value of your consequence. Remember, logical consequences are intended to stop misbehavior, not shame, blame, humiliate, or discourage your child.

Think Logically

When you think in simple, logical terms, an appropriate logical consequence usually jumps out at you. For example, most misbehavior involves the following situations: children with other children, children with adults, children with objects, children with activities, or children with privileges. In most cases, you can apply a logical consequence by temporarily separating one child from another, a child from an adult, a child from an object such as a toy or bicycle, a child from an activity such as a video game, or a child from a privilege such as an after-school play privilege.

Use a Timer When Children Dawdle

Timers are useful in situations when children test and resist our rules by dawdling or procrastinating. Carrie, age twelve, is a good example. It's 8:30 in the evening, and Carrie has been on the phone for nearly an hour.

"It's time to finish your conversation and get ready for bed," says her mother.

Logical consequences provide instructive data in the form of real-life experience that aggressive researchers need to be convinced that your rules are mandatory, not optional.

"I will," says Carrie, but another five minutes go by, and Carrie is still talking. Her mother asks again.

"I will," says Carrie insistently, but makes no move to end her conversation. This time her mother decides to support her request with a logical consequence.

"You have one minute to finish your conversation," says her mother. "If you're not off the phone when the timer goes off, the phone will be off-limits for the next two days." This time Carrie takes her seriously and hangs up.

Use Logical Consequences As Often As Needed

Logical consequences are training tools. They provide instructive data in the form of real-life experience that aggressive researchers need to be convinced that your rules are mandatory, not optional. Don't assume that a logical consequence is ineffective simply because your child needs to experience that consequence many times for the same misbehavior. More likely, your child has more learning to do. Hard-way learning takes time.

Punitive Thinking Is Not Logical Thinking

If you've relied upon punitive guidance practices in the past, you will have to guard against using logical consequences in a punitive manner. Punitive consequences may stop misbehavior, but they seldom teach or inspire acceptable behavior. Why? Because children often perceive punitive consequences as a personal attack, and that is where the lesson ends. Punitive consequences do not inspire cooperative, respectful relationships between parents and children.

If you have punitive tendencies, check your thinking. Remember, punitive thinking is not logical thinking. When your children misbehave, do you ask yourself, *What do they like? I'll show them! I'll take it away!?* If the answer is yes, you probably have punitive tendencies, and your guidance lessons are likely to break down.

If you're still in doubt, examine the types of consequences you use. Are they logically related to the misbehavior or situation? Is your consequence intended to teach your children acceptable choices or behavior? Or is it intended to hurt and show them who's boss? If the answer to the last question is yes, you're probably using a punitive consequence. Think it through, and try it again.

When to Use Logical Consequences

Logical consequences can be used in a wide variety of situations. The following are just a few of the many possibilities.

When Kids Don't Cooperate with Other Kids

Logical consequence: Separate the kids temporarily.

Seth, age seven, and his brother, Paul, age five, are playing checkers when Seth tries to take advantage of his brother's inexperience and gets caught in the act.

"You cheated!" Paul shouts. "You can't move two spaces in the same move. I'm gonna tell Mom."

"No, I didn't," says Seth. "You're such a baby!"

"Oh yeah," Paul replies. "You're a cheater!" Seth pushes Paul, and Paul pushes back. When their mother arrives, the two boys are shouting and calling each other names.

"Guys, you're going to have to play apart for the next thirty minutes," says their mother. "I'll set the timer. Paul can play in the living room, and Seth can play in the den."

Misuse of Toys or Possessions

Logical consequence: Temporary loss of the item.

Three-year-old Kate knows she's not supposed to use her tricycle like a bumper car, but when she sees her friend sitting in a wagon, Kate decides to ram into her. Her mother intervenes.

"That's not how we use tricycles," says her mother, matter-of-factly. "We need to put it away for the rest of the afternoon."

Making a Mess

Logical consequence: Clean it up.

Kramer, age eight, leaves his construction set spread out all over the living room floor and tries to sneak out the door without cleaning it up. He gets caught.

"Kramer, you need to put away your construction set before you go outside to play," says his father.

"I'll do it later," says Kramer. "I promise."

His father holds firm. "There won't be any playing until it's done," says his father. He stays in the room to ensure compliance. Reluctantly, Kramer cleans up his mess.

When Kids Aren't Responsible for Their Toys

Logical consequence: Separate the child from the item temporarily.

Shana, age seven, refuses to put away her toys, which are scattered throughout the house.

"You have fifteen minutes to pick them up," says her mother. "If you don't, I'll have to put them in the Saturday basket, and you can have them back on Saturday." Shana doesn't budge.

When the timer rings, her mother collects the remaining play items and puts them in the Saturday basket, which she keeps on a high shelf in the garage. Shana will get them back on Saturday. If she fails to pick up the same items repeatedly, Shana's mother will probably slip those items into the Goodwill basket, and Shana will probably never miss them.

Saturday baskets are an instructive logical consequence for helping children learn to be responsible for taking care of their toys and play items. Parents who use this method quickly discover which toys their kids do and do not care about. Kids pick up the toys they value, and they avoid picking up the ones they don't.

When Kids Don't Take Turns

Logical consequence: Separate the child from the activity temporarily.

Chuck, age ten, is a master at video games, but he's not a master at sharing. When his friends come over to play video games, they frequently complain that Chuck won't take turns. Chuck's father confronts this familiar scene once again.

"You just had a turn," says one friend. "It's Jake's turn now."

"It's my house," says Chuck. "I decide whose turn it is."

His father intervenes. "Chuck, I'm going to set the timer for thirty minutes," says his father. "Your friends are going to have to play without you for a while. You can join them again in thirty minutes when the timer goes off if you're willing to take turns. If not, I'll have to put the game away until tomorrow."

Destructive Behavior

Logical consequence: Repair, replace, or pay for the damaged item.

Eleven-year-old Maria is annoyed with her five-year-old sister, who continues to walk into Maria's room without permission.

"If you come into my room again, I'm going to break all your crayons," Maria threatens.

"I'll tell Mom," says her sister.

"Go ahead," replies Maria. "I don't care." Within minutes, her sister enters Maria's room, and Maria follows through with her threat.

Their mother comes to investigate all the screaming.

"She broke all my crayons," Maria's sister says.

"But she was bugging me all morning," says Maria. "I told her what would happen if she didn't stop."

"Breaking all your sister's crayons was not the best way to handle this problem," says Maria's mother. "You're going to have to pay for a new box of crayons with your allowance."

Misuse or Abuse of Privileges

Logical consequence: Temporary loss or modification of the privilege.

Sandra, age eight, knows she's supposed to keep her mother informed before going anywhere after school, but she heads off to a park with some friends and doesn't return until just before dinner.

"Where were you?" asks her worried mother. "We saw your backpack, but there was no message or phone call. We thought something might have happened to you. Your father and I were about to call the police."

"Sorry, Mom," says Sandra. "I just forgot."

"Then we'll give you some time to practice remembering," says her mother. "Your after-school play privileges are suspended for the rest of the week. We'll start off fresh again on Monday."

Failure to Complete Chores or Homework

Logical consequence: Temporarily withhold the fun activities that normally follow completion of the task.

Eleven-year-old Jordi has had the same after-school routine for years. First, he's supposed to unload the dishwasher, then he's supposed to do his homework. When these jobs are done, he's free to watch TV, play video games, or play with his friends in the neighborhood.

His friends planned a baseball game that begins immediately after school. Jordi really wants to join them. When he arrives home, he grabs a quick snack, changes into his play clothes, then heads out the door with his baseball glove.

"Aren't you forgetting something?" asks his mom.

"I'll do my chores and homework when I get back," says Jordi. "My friends are playing baseball, and I really want to join them."

"I know you do," says his mom, "but you know the rule—chores and homework first, playing second. I suggest you hurry and get them done so you can join your friends."

"But Mom!" protests Jordi. "I'll be late."

She holds firm, so Jordi tries to strengthen his case with a threat. "If you don't let me go now, I'm not going to do them at all tonight," he says. She doesn't take the bait.

"That's up to you," says his mom, matter-of-factly.

Rats! Jordi says to himself. No way out of it. He considers his options for a few minutes, then scrambles to finish his jobs so he can join his friends.

Jordi's mom is using "grandma's rule," work-before-play, to arrange a logical consequence and teach an important lesson in good work habits and responsibility. The message is clear: Do your job and collect the paycheck. If you don't do your job, then you don't get a paycheck. The paycheck in this case is the "fun stuff" that normally follows successful completion of Jordi's jobs.

Whining, Fussing, Nagging, or Badgering

Logical consequence: Separate the child from the parent temporarily.

Carly, age four, knows she's not allowed to have cookies before dinner; but when her mother isn't looking, Carly sneaks into the cookie jar and grabs a handful. She gets caught.

"Put them back, Carly," says her mother.

Carly complies but starts to whine and fuss. "I'm really hungry," she complains.

"You can have a yogurt snack or some string cheese," offers her mother, "but cookies are for after meals."

"But I only want cookies," Carly moans. She continues to fuss and complain in the hope that her mother will wear down and give in. No luck. Her mother holds firm.

"If you bring it up again, Carly, you're going to have to spend the next five minutes by yourself," says her mother. Carly continues fussing so her mother follows through. She leads Carly back to her room and sets the timer. Now the message is very clear. Carly hears "stop" and experiences stopping.

Hurting Others

Logical consequence: Separate the child from others temporarily.

Chandler, age nine, becomes upset when his sister borrows his scooter. He gives her a kick. She screams and their father intervenes.

"We don't kick," says his father. "I'll set the timer for ten minutes. You need to go to your room now." Chandler heads to his room for a time-out.

Common Questions About Logical Consequences

Q: When I take away toys that my child refuses to pick up, he often responds, "I don't care." This really annoys me. How should I handle this?

A: Two things are likely going on. First, there is the possibility that your son really doesn't care about the toys you take away, and this is why he refuses to be responsible for them. If this is the case, both of you will be better off without these items. I suggest you try using a "Saturday basket" to determine whether the same items end up in the basket on a regular basis. If so, you may want to put them into the Goodwill basket, and nobody will miss them.

The second and more likely possibility is that your child is trying to hook you into a dance with the comment, "I don't care." Don't take the bait. If you act unconcerned and follow through matter-of-factly the way you said you would, the "hot potato" of responsibility sits in his lap, not yours. Temporary loss of the item will hold him accountable for his unacceptable choice not to pick it up.

Q: When I remove a play item or privilege temporarily, my daughter becomes argumentative and disrespectful. What should I do when this happens?

A: Most likely, your daughter is trying to hook you into a dance with the goal of wearing you down so you'll give in. Don't take the bait. Remain firm. Use the cutoff or cool-down procedures you learned in the last chapter. If she persists with her testing, follow through with a time-out. The time for discussion is not when your rules are being tested or violated.

Q: I'm beginning to think logical consequences are ineffective. When I remove a toy or privilege, my child will repeat the same misbehavior a few days later. What's going on?

A: Applying consequences is part of a teaching-and-learning process. The fact that your aggressive researcher needs to repeat the lesson many times does not mean that your consequences are ineffective. More likely, it means that your child needs to collect more data and do more learning before he or she is convinced that following your rules is required, not optional. Your consistent follow-through will earn you credibility. Let your child collect all the data he or she needs to learn the rule you're trying to teach.

THE TIME-OUT PROCEDURE

Five-year-old Allie and her younger brother are pasting animal stickers into their sticker books. When her brother reaches for a sticker Allie wants, she hits him in the face with her book and wrestles the sticker away from him. He screams and their father intervenes.

"Allie hit me," sobs her younger brother.

"But he had a sticker I wanted," says Allie.

"Hitting is not okay, Allie," says her father, matter-of-factly. "You need to spend the next five minutes by yourself in your room. I'll set the timer. When you come out, we'll talk about better ways to share stickers with your brother." Allie heads to her room for a time-out.

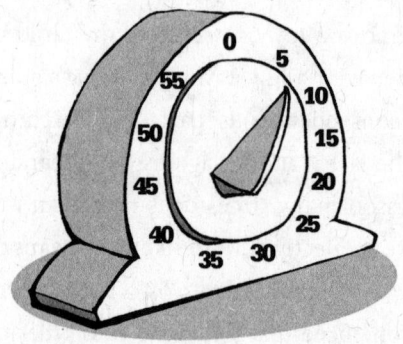

Time-out is a highly effective guidance procedure when used as it was intended—as a logical consequence. Time-out sends all the right messages to children about our rules and expectations. It stops misbehavior, prevents dances, and provides them with the time they need to restore self-control. When used consistently, time-out teaches children important skills in anger management and nonviolent problem solving.

Unfortunately, time-out has been widely misused and misunderstood as a guidance procedure. Punitive parents use it as a jail sentence to force and humiliate children into compliance. The punitive version of time-out sounds something like this (parent shouting): "Go to your room, sit in the corner, and don't come out until I tell you to. If I hear a peep out of you, you'll stay there all day!" Punitive time-outs tend to be lengthy (several hours or an entire evening), adversarial, and carried out with a lot of anger, drama, and strong emotion. Children often perceive them as a personal attack and respond with anger, resentment, and revenge. The procedure is more than firm. It's harsh.

Permissive parents, on the other hand, view time-out as a tool for the child to use at his or her discretion. The child decides when it starts, when it ends, or whether it even happens at all. The permissive version of time-out sounds something like this (parent suggesting): "I think it would be a good idea if you went to your room for a while. Okay? You can come back when you feel ready." The child decides the time, which is usually quite brief.

Permissive time-outs have little meaning to strong-willed children. Why? Because the child, not the adult, controls the action step and whatever learning results from the experience. The procedure lacks firmness. Compliance is optional, not required.

In actuality, neither the punitive nor the permissive versions of time-out are really time-out. The procedure is not supposed to be jail or Siberia, nor is it an optional consequence that children use at their discretion. When used in either of these ways, responsibility shifts in the wrong direction, and most of the training value of the consequence is lost.

> Time-out sends all the right messages to children about our rules and expectations. It stops misbehavior, prevents dances, and provides them with the time they need to restore self-control.

Time-out is really time away from the good stuff or what helping professionals call "reinforcement." In most families, the good stuff is the many rewards of daily living: time spent with family, friends, privileges, pleasurable activities, or just enjoying free time. Time-out separates kids temporarily from the good stuff.

Does time-out still sound like jail? The two are similar to the extent that they both provide a solid set of walls that stop misbehavior and separate the misbehaving person from the rewards of daily life. There are also some major differences.

> Strong-willed children need to collect a lot of data before they're convinced that following our rules is required, not optional. The more data they collect, the quicker they learn.

Time-outs are generally brief (five to twenty minutes) and can be used repeatedly. Why is this helpful? Because repeated guidance experiences provide more opportunities for learning. Remember, strong-willed children need to collect a lot of data before they're convinced that following our rules is required, not optional. The more data they collect, the quicker they learn.

Jail sentences, on the other hand, tend to be lengthy. They provide fewer, not more, opportunities for children to collect data and practice new skills. The less data they collect, the slower they learn. Jail is a slower and less effective learning process.

Guidelines for Using Time-Out

The time-out procedure is quick, simple, and easy to carry out. It can be used with children of nearly all ages (age three through teens) and in many different settings. Here's what you need to know to get started.

Introduce Time-Out Before Using It

If you haven't used time-out before or if you've used it in a punitive or permissive manner, be sure to explain to your children how it's supposed to work before using it. A sample introduction might be: "I have a plan for helping you cooperate and learn my rules. I think it will help us get along better, too. Here's how it works: When you refuse to cooperate with my rules or you do certain things that are not okay, I will ask you to go to your room for five or ten minutes, or however much time it takes for you to get under control.

> If your child's room is a high-tech recreation center, or if it's shared with another sibling, then it's not a suitable place for time-out.

"Each time, I'll set the timer, and I'll let you know when the time is over. You can look at a book, draw, or do some quiet activity. If you come out before the timer goes off, then you'll go back and the time will start over. We'll just use this procedure as often as we need to. Do you understand? Tell me in your words how you think it works."

Select an Appropriate Place

Selecting an appropriate place for time-out is critical to the effectiveness of the procedure. At home, your child's bedroom is preferable as long as it has four walls, a door, and is not loaded with entertainment items such as a TV, videocassette recorder, or electronic games. Remember, time-out is "time away from the good stuff." If your child's room is a high-tech recreation center, or if it's shared with another sibling, then it's not a suitable place for time-out. Select another room such as the den or bathroom. The quietest room with the least amount of traffic is best.

Always Use a Timer

If you're not using a timer, then you're not doing time-out. You're doing something different. It won't take long for your children to pick up on the inconsistency of the procedure. They'll begin to resent it as arbitrary and unfair.

Kitchen timers work fine. You can also use an inexpensive egg timer or a watch with an audible beeper or alarm. The time should not begin until your child is actually in the room. If your child decides to leave before the timer goes off, send your child back and start the full time over again. Once you set the timer, you effectively take yourself out of the picture. The rest is between your child and the timer.

I don't recommend permitting children to set the timer themselves or keep the timer in their rooms during the time-out. Parents who adhere to this practice encounter some of the world's shortest time-outs.

> How much time should your child spend in time-out? One minute per year of age and don't begin before age three is a good rule of thumb.

How much time should your child spend in time-out? One minute per year of age and don't begin before age three is a good rule of thumb (five minutes for a five-year-old) with one proviso. The child should not be permitted to leave the time-out area until he or she is under control. One of the goals of time-out is to help the child restore self-control. If a child throws a tantrum during a ten-minute time-out and remains out of control well after the timer goes off, then he or she should remain in time-out until the tantrum is over.

For more serious misbehaviors, such as hitting, kicking, biting, or destructive behavior, doubling or tripling the time is recommended, but not more. This will appeal to those who have used punishment in the past, but I encourage you to guard against making longer time-outs a routine practice. For less serious misbehavior, a minute per year of age will get your message across.

A Clean Slate

When the timer goes off, the consequence should be over, provided your child has stopped misbehaving and has restored self-control. If not, your child is not ready to come out. You can say, "The timer went off. You can come out when you're calmed down, but not before that time."

When your child is ready to come out, invite him or her back in a friendly voice. No debriefings, inquisitions, or lectures on cooperation. An "I told you so" or lecture personalizes the lesson, creates resentment, and sabotages the effectiveness of the consequence. When you are friendly and accepting, you communicate confidence in your child's ability to cooperate and make better choices.

> Time-out is a powerful training tool when used appropriately and consistently.

Use As Often As Needed

Time-out is a powerful training tool when used appropriately and consistently. Don't assume the procedure is ineffective because your child continues to test your rules and authority and requires lots of time-outs. Let your aggressive researcher collect all the data he or she needs. Consistent repeated exposure to your consequences will lead to the learning you desire.

When to Use Time-Out

Time-out should be used to handle more extreme misbehaviors such as testing that becomes defiance, extreme disrespectful behavior, defiant behavior, antagonistic or hurtful behavior, and tantrums. Consider the following examples.

Limit-Testing Behavior

Casey, age eleven, is told she can't go to the park with her friends until her room is clean, but she tries her best to wear her mom down and turn a no into a yes.

"Come on, Mom," pleads Casey. "It's not fair! I don't see why I can't clean my room after I return." Her mother holds firm.

"We're done talking about it," says her mother. "If you bring it up again, you'll spend the next ten minutes in your room. It's up to you."

"But Mom!" Casey protests. "You're not being fair!" Her mother doesn't take the bait.

"I'll set the timer, Casey," she says. "See you in ten minutes." Reluctantly, Casey marches off to her room. Her mother's message is very clear.

Disrespectful Behavior

C.J., age five, is upset because his father won't allow him to practice doing cartwheels in the house. "You're the meanest," shouts C.J. "I hate you! I really hate you!"

"You look pretty angry," says his father. "Do you need a few minutes to cool off?"

C.J. glares at his father and continues to shout. "I don't need anything from you, you poo-poo head!" says C.J.

"I'm setting the timer," says his father. "I'll see you in five minutes."

C.J. heads off to his room.

Defiant Behavior

Chuck, age three, leaves his collection of plastic dinosaurs spread out all over the dining room floor. "Are you finished playing with your dinosaurs?" asks his mother. Chuck nods. "Then it's time to pick them up," she says.

"I don't want to," says Chuck. "You pick them up." He sits down defiantly with his arms crossed.

"You can do what I asked, or you can spend the next three minutes in your room getting ready to do it," his mother replies, calmly. "What would you like to do?"

"I won't do it!" he shouts.

"I'll see you in three minutes," says his mother. She sets the timer, and Chuck heads off to his room. When the timer goes off, she invites him back.

"I'm still not doing it!" says Chuck, insistently.

"That's up to you," replies his mother. "I'll set the timer again."

Suddenly, Chuck has a change of heart. "Okay, I'll pick them up," he says, realizing the firmness of his mother's resolve.

Antagonistic or Hurtful Behavior

Mel, age nine, wants to take his evening shower before watching his favorite TV show, but his teenage sister is using the bathroom. "Come on, hurry up!" he yells outside the door. "If you weren't such a dirty zit-face, you wouldn't need to be in there so long."

His father overhears the comments and intervenes. "Calling your sister names is not okay, Mel. I'll set the timer. See you in ten minutes."

Mel heads to his room for a time-out.

Violent or Aggressive Behavior

Lizzy, age five, and her playmate, Robin, are building castles in the sandbox when a dispute breaks out. "It's my turn to use the bucket," says Lizzy.

"No. You just had it," says Robin. "It's my turn."

Lizzy tries to grab the bucket out of Robin's hands. When Robin resists, Lizzy kicks her in the stomach. Robin lets out a scream, and Lizzy's mother investigates.

"She kicked me in the stomach," moans Robin.

"But she wouldn't give my bucket back," says Lizzy.

"We don't kick," says Lizzy's mother, matter-of-factly. "I'll set the timer for ten minutes. You need to go to your room. When you return, we'll talk about other ways to share the bucket."

Lizzy goes for a time-out.

Tantrums

Gavin, age six, knows he's not supposed to swing his plastic whiffle-ball bat in the house, but when he thinks his parents aren't looking, he decides to take a few practice swings. His father asks him to stop. Gavin does, for the moment; but when his father looks away, Gavin does it again. His father sees what's happening and applies a logical consequence. He takes the bat away for the afternoon.

Gavin complains and protests, but his father holds firm. So Gavin decides to play his drama card. He throws himself on the floor and does a full-blown wailing and screaming tantrum.

I'm not giving in to this, his father says to himself. He picks up Gavin, carries him to his bedroom, and makes an announcement. "I'll set the timer for twelve minutes. If you're calmed down when the timer goes off, you can come out. If not, you'll stay here until you are calmed down." No payoffs for this tantrum.

Using Time-Out Outside of the Home

How many times have you seen children plead for toys or treats at the checkout counter, then fuss or throw a tantrum when the parent says no? Children know we're vulnerable when we're away from home. They wonder if the rules still apply and what will happen if they decide to test. Fortunately, the time-out can be used effectively outside the home, but you'll have to make some modifications in how you carry out the procedure. Let's look at how to handle some challenging situations.

> Children know we're vulnerable when we're away
> from home. They wonder if the rules still apply and
> what will happen if they decide to test.

At the Mall or Shopping Center

Dana's mom dreads trips to the mall because her four-year-old frequently bolts away from the shopping cart and runs down the aisles. Dana's mom decides to handle these situations with time-outs. She explains the plan to Dana in the car on the way to the mall.

"Dana, when we're in the mall, you need to stay next to me the whole time. It's not okay to run down the aisles or hide behind the clothing racks. If you do, you'll do a five-minute time-out."

A time-out in the mall? *How's she going to do that?* Dana wonders.

She knows the best way to find out. She's in the mall less than five minutes before she decides to test out her mom's plan. When her mom is busy talking to a sales clerk, Dana bolts down the aisles.

"Excuse me," Dana's mom says to the salesperson. "Is there a quiet place where I can sit with my daughter for about five minutes?" The salesperson points to a lounge area near the restrooms.

When Dana and her mom arrive at the lounge area, her mom says, "You need to sit here quietly for the next five minutes." No

angry lectures. No threats. No scoldings. Her mom doesn't answer
or respond to any of Dana's questions or comments.

Hey, this is no fun, Dana thinks to herself. *I liked it better the old way
when Mom ran after me and got upset.* Five minutes pass.

"Are you ready to stay next to me now?" her mom asks.

"Okay," says Dana, and she does.

Dana and her mother may need to repeat this procedure a number of times before Dana is convinced that her mother's rule is
firm, but Dana will surely get the point. Her mother has a new tool
for making shopping more bearable.

At the Supermarket

Three-year-old Bernie is a pistol. He loves going to the supermarket
with his mother. When she pushes the shopping cart by anything
he likes, he grabs it and throws it into the cart. This is great fun
for Bernie, but no fun at all for his mother. She decides to take a
new approach.

As they're driving to the store, she makes an announcement.

"You may not grab things off the shelf unless I ask you to do
so," she says. "If you grab things without permission, you will take
a time-out."

Bernie hears the words, but he doesn't believe them. *How's she
going to do that?* he wonders. As they're heading down the cereal aisle,
he decides to find out. He grabs a box of his favorite cereal and
throws it in the cart.

"Excuse me," Bernie's mother says to a clerk. "May I leave my
cart here for a few minutes? I'll be back soon."

"Sure," says the clerk.

Bernie's mother lifts him out of the cart and takes him to a bench outside the market. "We're going to sit here for the next few minutes," she says. "It's not okay to grab things off the shelves," she repeats. She doesn't say anything more for the full three minutes. Bernie gets the answer he's looking for.

Three minutes may not seem long to most adults, but to a strong-willed three-year-old, it feels like an eternity. He can't wait to get back to the supermarket, but this time he points and asks before grabbing any items.

"Thanks for doing it the right way," says his appreciative mother.

Bernie and his mother may need to repeat this drill a number of times before he's convinced to follow her rule without testing, but the training method will lead to the desired outcome.

At a Restaurant

Lynn, age seven, enjoys going to restaurants with her parents but sometimes tries to get away with things she can't get away with at home. On one occasion, she tries to get attention by talking in a very loud voice. People at other tables look at her.

"Lynn, use an indoor voice, please," requests her mother, but Lynn keeps it up.

What's she going to do? Lynn asks herself. *We can't leave. We've already ordered the food.* Her father gives her some choices.

"Lynn, you can use an indoor voice or you can take a time-out in the car. What would you like to do?" he asks.

A time-out in the car? How's he going to do that? Lynn wonders. She decides to find out by talking loudly again. Without saying anything further, Lynn's father takes her by the hand and walks her out to the car.

"Have a seat," he says, as he opens the door. Then he gets in the car too. "I'll let you know when the time-out is over," he says, then sits back as though taking a nap. No glaring looks of disapproval. No threats to withhold dessert. Nothing but silence.

This is no fun, Lynn thinks to herself. When the seven minutes is over, her father asks if she's ready to return to the restaurant and cooperate. She nods. He's ready to repeat the procedure if Lynn decides to test again.

In the Car

Kara and Daniel, ages seven and nine, grab and tickle each other in the backseat while their mother is trying to drive. They squeal and giggle, then Kara lets out a scream. Their mother pulls over and stops.

"You may not play that game in the car," says their mother. "If you do it again, you'll have to do a time-out."

In the car? Daniel thinks to himself. *How's she going to do that?*

The two kids cooperate for a while, then Daniel pinches Kara, and she screams again. Their mother pulls the car over a second time.

"We're not going any farther until you both cooperate," says their mother. "I'll set my watch for ten minutes." The two kids stare at each other in disbelief.

Wow! She really did it, Daniel says to himself. Suddenly, his mother's authority comes into perspective. She makes the car go and stop. She's truly in control. Ten quiet minutes pass.

"Are you guys ready to cooperate?" asks their mother. They nod, and off they go.

Common Questions About Time-Out

Q: What should I do when my child refuses to go to the time-out area?

A: This is aggressive research in action. Give your child a choice. Tell him he can go to his room on his own or you will take him back there for twice the time. Give him twenty to thirty seconds to think it over. If he doesn't budge, usher or carry him back there for twice the time. Your child will quickly figure out the advantages of going to his room unassisted.

Q: What should I do when my children leave the time-out area before the timer goes off?

A: Return them to their rooms and start the time over again.

Q: What should I do if they leave a second time?

A: Your children are trying to determine whether your saying stop really requires their stopping. Your job is to make stop happen. If they refuse to stay in their rooms, return them to their rooms for twice the time, and tell them you have no choice but to hold the door shut during the time-out. No, this isn't cruel or unusual, and it won't injure their feelings or bodies. No one is being hit or humiliated. Their rooms are safe places, and you are simply supporting your words with effective action. After you go through the drill enough times, your children will accept the boundary and stay when asked to.

Q: What should I do if my child yells and screams during time-out?

A: This is usually drama for the parent's benefit, or your child may be discharging pent-up frustration. Do not reward the drama by giving in to it or by returning to the room with threats or lectures. The drama will pass. Wait it out. When it's over, welcome your child out.

> After you go through the drill enough times, your children will accept the boundary and stay when asked to.

Q: What should I do when my children throw their toys around or make a mess of their room?

A: Inform them that they can't come out until they pick up all their stuff and put it away. Then, set the timer for twenty minutes to give them time to get the job done. If they still refuse to pick things up when the timer goes off, don't let them turn the issue into a power struggle. Calmly inform them that if they're not willing to take care of their stuff, then they can't keep their stuff in their room. Then box up the items your children refuse to pick up and store them away for safekeeping. Tell your children that you'll be ready to return the items when they're ready to take care of them. They'll probably want the items back right away, but I recommend withholding them for at least a week to get the message across.

Q: What does it mean when my child returns from a time-out and does the same misbehavior all over again?

A: Most likely, it means your aggressive researcher has more data to collect before he or she is convinced that you mean what you say. Repeat the procedure as often as needed.

Q: When I ask my child to go to time-out, sometimes he yells, calls me names, or talks disrespectfully while he goes there. Should I add five more minutes each time he does this?

A: No. Your child is trying to hook you back out on the dance floor with these gestures. As tempting as it is to take the bait and respond, ignore it. If your child goes to his room and stays there the whole time, then the procedure is working just fine.

Q: I read a parenting magazine that said children will associate their bedrooms as a place of punishment if you use their bedrooms as a time-out area. Is this true? If so, how can I avoid this?

A: Your child's response to time-out depends largely upon how you apply it. If you apply it in a punitive manner with lots of anger, yelling, and hurt feelings then sure, your child will associate his bedroom or any other room you use as a place of punishment. If you apply the time-out procedure as recommended in this book, in a firm but respectful manner, your child shouldn't associate any room you use as a time-out area as a place for punishment.

ASSERTING PHYSICAL CONTROL: A LAST RESORT

What is physical control and how do you do it? Physical control, as it's being presented here, is a nonviolent method of stopping misbehavior by not allowing it to continue. It should not be confused with hitting, spanking, or inflicting pain on children.

When should parents use physical control? Imagine a line that separates these two types of misbehavior:

1. Misbehavior that stops without the need for physical restraint
2. Misbehavior that will only stop when you assert your physical control

> If you apply the time-out procedure in a firm but respectful manner, your child shouldn't associate any room you use as a time-out area as a place for punishment.

How do parents know when behavior has crossed the line? If your children are misbehaving and refuse to go to time-out, then their behavior has crossed the line. If they don't comply when you request them to stop behavior that is violent, destructive, or dangerous to themselves or others, then that behavior also crosses the line. In these situations, children need help restoring lost control.

Strong-willed children are the most likely to push things to this extent. Jill, age seven, is a good example. Her mother arrived at my office feeling very discouraged. For years, she had given in to her daughter's defiant and disrespectful behavior. Her mother thought it was just a phase that would disappear with time, but Jill continued to get bolder and bolder. Their conflicts were getting closer to what Jill's mother feared most—physical confrontation.

Intuitively, Jill sensed that her mother feared physical confrontation and used it as a threat to intimidate her mother into giving in. It worked! Jill's younger brother was beginning to try some of the same tactics.

We completed temperament profiles for each family member, then examined her limit-setting practices. As expected, Jill profiled as a strong-willed child who was also reactive and intense. Her soft-spoken mother, on the other hand, was compliant and permissive. We discussed the bad match and what Jill's mother could do to improve things. She was ready to learn new skills.

I showed her how to state a clear message with her words and how to use the check-in to avoid the old repeating and reminding routine. Next, Jill needed walls to guide her testing and stop her misbehavior. I introduced the time-out procedure and explained how it works.

One important step remained. Jill's mother needed to be prepared to handle the inevitable confrontation that would take place when Jill would respond to her mother's time-out with, "You can't make me!" We discussed physical restraint and how to use it. Jill's mother was ready to carry her daughter to her bedroom if necessary.

The confrontation came the next day after school. Jill arrives home wearing a new outfit she had received as a gift from her grandparents. "I'm going out to play," Jill announces.

"Not in those clothes," says her mother. "You need to change into your play clothes, please."

"Come on, Mom," Jill protests.

Her mom holds firm. "You know the rules, Jill," her mother says, matter-of-factly. "School clothes are for school, and play clothes are for playing."

Jill ignores her mother's words and heads for the door.

Her mother uses the check-in. "Did you understand what I asked you to do?" her mother inquires.

Jill stands there, hands on hips, and glares back at her mother defiantly. "I hate you and your stupid rules," she explodes. "I'm not going to change, and you can't make me!" She struggles to get out the door, but her mother remains firm.

"It looks like you need some quiet time by yourself," says her mother. "I'll set the timer for ten minutes."

"You can set it for two hours for all I care," Jill shouts, defiantly. "I'm not going anywhere, and you can't make me." To Jill's astonishment, her mother picks her up and carries her to her room. Jill screams and struggles the whole way.

When they arrive, her mother sits Jill down on the bed. Jill bolts for the door. Catching her by the arm, her mother says, "You can come out in ten minutes or as long as you need to get yourself under control."

Jill screams defiantly. As soon as her mother walks out the door, once again, Jill bolts.

"I'll hold the door shut for the full ten minutes, or as long as it takes you to get under control if I need to," says her mother.

Jill screams insults and defiance for the next twenty minutes and checks the door intermittently to see whether her mother is still holding it shut. She is. After five minutes of silence, Jill's mother opens the door and invites her daughter to come out if she's ready to change into her play clothes. To her mother's surprise, Jill has already changed and is ready to go outside. Nothing more is said.

Jill and her mother had taken a big step toward ending their ugly dances and redefining the balance of power and authority in their relationship. They still had a ways to go. It took three more confrontations that first week before Jill realized that intimidation and defiance no longer worked. By the end of the first week, Jill was going to time-outs on her own and staying there the full time without leaving.

CHAPTER SUMMARY

Consequences are essential training tools for strong-willed children. They stop misbehavior. They send clear signals about our rules and expectations, and they provide firm boundaries to keep children on the path of acceptable behavior. When applied in a firm, consistent, and respectful manner, consequences teach children to take your words seriously and cooperate more often.

The key to using consequences effectively is the manner in which they are applied. When applied in a punitive or permissive manner, consequences have limited instructive value with strong-willed children and inspire their testing and power struggles. When applied in a democratic manner with firmness and respect, consequences teach cooperation and responsibility by holding children accountable for their choices and behavior. Logical consequences are the gold standard for effective teaching and learning.

9

Managing the Resistance You'll Likely Encounter

What parent doesn't want their limit-setting efforts to go as smoothly as possible with as few hurt feelings as possible for both parents and child? Learning the "easy way" is very appealing, but this isn't the way most strong-willed children and many fence-sitters learn. As you know, they do much of their learning the "hard way." They need to repeatedly experience the consequences of their poor choices and behavior before they learn to accept our limits, respect our authority, make better choices, and cooperate for the asking.

Hard-way learning is still good learning, but no matter how you cut it, the "hard way" is hard on both kids and parents.

When you're effective, you're not likely to hear comments such as, "Gee, Mom, you handled that really well!" or "Good job, Dad! You gave me some great choices." Instead, you'll probably hear complaints such as, "You're mean!" or "You're not fair!" or "I liked you better the other way." Don't expect it to be easy and don't expect them to like it. What should you expect instead? Resistance.

The resistance you'll likely encounter may take many forms and comes from many sources: from your strong-willed child, from siblings, from your spouse and other family members, and from within yourself. This chapter will help you recognize the different forms of resistance you'll likely encounter, respond to it effectively, and move forward without collecting all the hurts and baggage that accumulate with unresolved conflict.

WHAT IS RESISTANCE?

Frustration and hurt feelings are normal reactions in the learning and behavior change process, but strong-willed children take these reactions to extreme levels. They can mount considerable protests and resistance when things don't work out the way they want. You should expect them to turn up the volume and intensity level—more yelling, more screaming, more drama, longer tantrums, hurtful statements, even physical confrontation. All these are normal and expected forms of resistance from strong-willed children.

Their tactics may appear dramatic and extreme, but don't be misled by the heightened emotion and drama. What appears to be a new layer of conflict and obstacles is simply an extension of the limit-testing process you learned about in Chapter 2. This is still research. The basic research questions haven't changed. Children still want answers to their basic questions: What's okay and not okay? Who's in charge? How far can I go? What happens when I go too far?

Their goal is to wear you down and get you to give in. That's why they're turning up the intensity and drama in their protests. They want you to react on an emotional level. What feels like emotional manipulation, in most cases, is not conscious or malicious on their part. They do it because it works. Their tactics are simply a means to an end, and the end goal is to get you to give in.

But the process can be confusing for parents. On an intellectual level, we recognize that extreme limit testing is normal for strong-willed children, but does resistance feel normal when you confront it? No. It seems extreme, and often, it brings out extreme emotional reactions in us. If we act on these feelings, we're right back into the dance. Reacting doesn't require much emotional maturity, thoughtfulness, or impulse control on our part. Reacting works for kids, not for parents.

Reacting Versus Responding

Parents can't control our children's reactions to the consequences we use, but we can control how we respond to our children's reactions. Reacting and responding are very different processes. One leads predictably to conflict, power struggles, and loss of control. The other diffuses conflict and keeps us in control. Learning to respond, rather than react, to your child's resistance, is the key to managing that resistance effectively.

Let's begin by defining terms. What is reacting? Reacting is a natural, automatic, and nearly reflexive process that is not always within an individual's conscious control. Anyone can react. It just happens—the first thoughts you think, the first feelings you feel when something happens to you. That's a reaction. Children do it naturally in response to their parents' limit-setting efforts. Compliant children show milder reactions. Strong-willed children show more intense and extreme reactions. Fence-sitters do a little of both. Reacting doesn't require emotional maturity, impulse control, or thoughtfulness.

Responding, on the other hand, is a more thoughtful process that involves observing and being aware of how we react, then choosing how to respond. Responding requires patience, thoughtfulness, and emotional maturity on our part. As adults, we're better equipped with the emotional and intellectual tools to do it. Responding allows us to stay in control.

Sure, responding sounds great on a theoretical level, but how do we actually do it on a real-life level? How do we respond like mature adults when our children try to get us to react like children? We need patience to pull this off.

I'm certainly no expert on patience. I have always considered my efforts to be a work in progress, but I'm happy to share what has worked for me and thousands of other parents. The process begins with awareness. First, we need to be aware of what resistance looks like before we confront it so we're not taken by surprise or caught off guard. This chapter provides lots of examples to help you do that. Second, we need to be prepared to respond by giving ourselves a "thoughtful moment." We'll lay the groundwork for responding in this chapter and finish the process in Chapter 12.

When Ian was young, my "thoughtful moments" were simply attempts to buy myself a little time to cool down and put things into perspective. I'd begin by saying to myself, *I'm the adult. He's the kid.* This always seemed to help. Then, I'd ask myself three questions: *What am I feeling? What's going on? What am I going to do about it?*

The first two questions were easy to answer. Usually, I was feeling angry, and usually, Ian was testing me in some extreme way. The third question helped me follow through with the appropriate logical consequence. As Ian got older and I became more patient, I condensed my thoughtful moment to saying my mantra—*I'm the adult, he's the kid*, then going directly to question number three—*What am I going to do about it?* That's when I realized I was responding on a routine basis, but the process took time and a lot of practice. I've taught this procedure to thousands of parents in my workshops and family counseling work. Let's see how Hunter's dad handles a typical situation with his strong-willed son both before and after he learned to take a thoughtful moment.

Hunter, age eleven, finishes his snack in the kitchen and leaves an empty cereal box, carton of milk, bowl, utensils, and crumpled napkins strewn all over the counter. Then, he returns to the living room to watch his favorite show. When Hunter's dad enters the kitchen, he sees the mess and reacts.

"Damn it, Hunter!" he shouts. "You are so inconsiderate! What's wrong with you? You're always leaving messes for others to clean up, and I'm sick of it. Get your butt in here and clean up."

"I'll do it later," Hunter replies.

"No, you'll do it now or you'll be sorry," says his dad, pointing a threatening finger.

"Oh, I'm real scared," says Hunter, sarcastically. "What are you going to do? Take away my cereal privileges?" He rolls his eyes, gives his dad a look of disgust, and makes no effort to get up from the couch. His dad becomes even more enraged.

"You don't talk to me like that, young man!" says his dad. "If you don't clean up this mess this instant, I'll turn the TV off, and you won't be watching it again the rest of the evening." Hunter doesn't like the sound of that. Reluctantly, he walks back to the kitchen to clean up his mess.

What convinced Hunter to cooperate? It wasn't his dad's anger or drama. Hunter chose to cooperate because he didn't want to lose his TV privileges for the rest of the evening. His dad's intense reaction just fueled their angry power struggle and made things worse.

Now, let's replay the scene, but this time, Hunter's dad exercises a different choice. He expects his son to resist and chooses to respond, rather than react. When Hunter's dad enters the kitchen and sees the mess, his initial reaction is the same. He feels angry, but rather than explode at his son, Hunter's dad takes a moment to put things into perspective.

It's just a mess, not the end of the world, he tells himself. Then, he approaches his son in a more thoughtful and respectful manner.

"Hunter, you need to clean up your mess in the kitchen before you do anything else," says his dad says, matter-of-factly. No blaming. No anger. No drama.

"I'll do it later," replies Hunter. He shoots his dad an irritated look and makes no effort to comply with the request. This is the resistance Hunter's dad expects. He remains calm and doesn't take the bait.

"You can do it now or in a few minutes," says his dad, "but the TV will stay off until it's done." He walks over and turns the TV off.

"Okay," says Hunter, reluctantly, "but I don't see what the big deal is." He gets up to clean up his mess so he can return to his show.

"Thank you," says his dad with an appreciative smile.

Isn't responding more effective and less stressful than reacting? Hunter's dad accomplished all his goals with much less energy.

He modeled respectful communication and problem solving. He gained respect for his rules and authority, and he managed Hunter's resistance without getting hooked into a power struggle.

Forgiveness Versus Reconciliation

Most of us can agree that resistance is hard on parents, but how do parents avoid collecting all the baggage, the many hurts and disappointments, that accompany the repeated resistance we encounter from our children? How do we move past each encounter without harboring negative feelings toward our children? The answer is forgiveness. Forgiveness is liberating, and it's solidly within your control.

But let's be clear about what we're forgiving. Are we forgiving unacceptable behavior? No. Unacceptable behavior shouldn't be tolerated. That's why we're setting limits on it and providing instructive guidance. What we should forgive is the child doing the behavior. We need to separate the deed from the doer. This is an important distinction that makes forgiveness possible. We're rejecting unacceptable behavior, not the child doing the behavior.

The message to the child is this—*You're a good kid, and I love you, but what you're doing is not okay.* This message puts the focus where it belongs, on the child's behavior, not on the value of the child. When we forgive the child, we can move forward without harboring the burdens of anger and resentment that we would otherwise carry around with us.

Forgiveness is a one-way process that is entirely within your control. It doesn't require your child's agreement or acceptance or anything else from your child. It's a choice, and a very powerful one, that is liberating for you and your child every time you choose to exercise it. Just write an imaginary forgiveness slip and let it go. No baggage.

Many parents I see in my family counseling work are more concerned about reconciliation than forgiveness. That is, they want their children to understand, accept, and agree with the parents' limits and guidance methods, and many parents feel upset when this doesn't happen.

Reconciliation is a two-way process, one that parents can't control. We can only control what we say or do, not how our children react to it. Reconciliation is not a realistic outcome of your limit-setting efforts with strong-willed children.

What reaction do you really expect from strong-willed children when you set firm limits? Do you want them to agree with you? Do you want them to understand that what you're doing is a gesture of love and caring? Do you want them to like it? Or are you ready to forgive their behavior and move forward? The choice is yours. You can collect baggage that interferes with your relationship, or you can drop that burden and preserve a positive relationship with your child while you set limits on his or her unacceptable behavior.

Typical Forms of Resistance

You're as prepared as you can be to confront and overcome the resistance you're likely to encounter. You understand that resistance is simply an extreme version of the limit testing you learned about in Chapter 2. You recognize that responding thoughtfully, not reacting, will keep you on the right track and out of dances and power struggles. Finally, you know that forgiveness will prevent you from collecting the baggage that wears you down and weakens your resolve. Now, it's time to take a closer look at the typical forms of resistance you're likely to confront.

Resistance takes many forms and comes from many sources. Resistance from your children may range from subtle protests to full-blown tantrums and all points in between. Don't be surprised if you also encounter resistance from unexpected sources such as other family members, and even from within yourself. Whatever form resistance takes, recognize it for what it is, hold the firm line, respond to it thoughtfully, write your child a forgiveness slip, and move forward in a positive direction.

Increasing the Drama

When milder forms of protest and drama are not enough to wear parents down, often strong-willed children will turn up the volume and increase the drama to achieve their goal. Celia, age nine, is a good example.

Celia hates time-outs. She mumbles, grumbles, and complains all the way to her room, and when she arrives, she usually shouts out something hurtful such as, "I hate you!" or "You're the worst parents ever!" then slams the door loudly in protest. Each time, Celia fully expects her parents to take the bait and yell at her for slamming the door, but this has been going on for two weeks, and nothing happens. Her parents know that reacting will only prolong Celia's limit testing.

I'll show them! Celia says to herself. The next time Celia is asked to go to her room for a time-out, she stands in the hallway, slams her bedroom door three times, and shrieks insults at the top of her lungs. Her parents don't respond, but Celia does not give up easily. Like many strong-willed children, she tries this tactic half a dozen times before she finally accepts her time-outs without protest.

Hurtful Statements

Hurtful statements directed at parents can be powerful tools in a child's limit-testing arsenal, especially when parents take these comments personally. In most cases, the child's goal is not to inflict emotional pain on the parent. Rather, the goal is to make the parent feel guilty or sympathetic or to weaken their resolve. Yes, this is a form of emotional manipulation, but most children don't do it maliciously or even consciously. They do it because it works. It's a means to an end. The behavior is their best attempt to control you and get you to do what they want. Consider the following.

Randal, age ten, refuses to pick up his toys in the living room. In a calm, matter-of-fact tone, his mother says, "You won't be going out to play or do anything else until it's done." Randal tries to wear her down with some hurtful statements.

"You don't care about me, anyway," he says. "All you care about is your clean house. You're so mean! I wish I had a nice mother who really cared about her kids." His mother pauses a moment to put things into perspective.

Wait a second, she says to herself. *All I asked him to do is pick up his stuff, and he turns it into an issue about love and caring. This isn't about me, and I'm not going to take the bait.* She holds firm.

"I'm sorry you feel that way," says his mother, "but I love you too much to allow you to do less than your part. You still have to do what I asked, and you won't be doing anything else until it's done." She leaves the room. Randal is too smart to waste his precious playtime. Reluctantly, he picks up his mess.

Repeating the Misbehavior

When your children repeatedly test you, how far are you willing to go before you give up in frustration? That's what strong-willed children are trying to figure out when they repeat their misbehavior. This is aggressive research, and it can be so exhausting that parents begin to ask themselves, *Is this normal? Is this worth all the hassle? Maybe I'm doing something wrong?* I know. I've been there. Strong-willed children require a lot of data.

In Chapter 2, I shared a personal example about my strong-willed son Ian and our morning routine with cartoons and the TV to illustrate how far strong-willed children are willing to go before they accept our rules. How many times do you think I had to turn off the TV each time Ian refused to turn it down? Five? Ten? More? Yes, I had to turn the TV off more than a dozen times before Ian finally accepted my rules and stopped testing!

His compliant brother, Scott, even tried to help Ian with his research by saying, "Mom and Dad really mean it. They'll turn it off." Ian just ignored his brother. This was his research, not Scott's.

Does twelve times seem like a lot to you? It did to me. That's a lot of forgiveness slips! I felt the same confusion and doubt many parents feel when they are tested further than they ever imagined. I even began to wonder if his behavior was normal or if I was doing something wrong. His testing seemed so excessive.

But I held firm and trusted in the process. Sure enough, eventually Ian did the learning I wanted him to do, but I never would have imagined pushing my parents as far as he pushed me. I've heard this same comment from hundreds of parents.

Escalating Misbehaviors

Strong-willed children are very skillful at wearing parents down. If one misbehavior doesn't work, they try another and another until they achieve their goal. Escalating misbehavior is a common form of resistance you need to watch for on your radar screen. Molly, age seven, is a good example.

"May I go to Serena's house to play before dinner?" asks Molly.

"You can if all your homework is done," her mom replies. "Is it done?" Molly nods. "May I see it, please?" asks her mom, expecting some testing.

"Well, most of it is done," says Molly. "I can finish it after dinner."

"You know the rule, Molly," says her mom. "No playing until all your homework is done, and I want to look it over before you leave the house." Molly has tried to sneak out before on many occasions.

"But that's not fair!" protests Molly. "I won't have any time to play if I finish it all. Serena's mom lets her play before she does homework. Why can't I?" Molly's mom can see where this is heading and cuts it off.

"We're done talking about it," says her mom, matter-of-factly. "If you bring it up again, you're going to spend the next five minutes by yourself."

"You're so mean!" Molly shouts. "What a witch!"

"I'll set the timer," says her mom. "I'll see you in five minutes after your time-out." Molly digs in her heels and won't budge.

"You can go on your own for five minutes, or I can take you there for ten, Molly. What would you like to do?" her mom asks. Molly goes limp on the floor.

So her mom picks Molly up, carries her to her room, and sets the timer for ten minutes. Molly cries and screams for the next five minutes before getting herself under control. When the timer goes off, she returns to her homework.

"May I watch TV after dinner tonight?" Molly asks.

"You can if all your homework is finished," says her mom.

Did Molly mount some serious resistance to her mom's rule about completing homework before playing? You bet. In the space of a few minutes, Molly tried deception, protesting, complaining, arguing, name-calling, defiance, and high-screaming drama to wear her mom down. But Molly's mom expected the resistance, kept her composure, and held firm. So can you.

Acting Unconcerned About Consequences

Strong-willed children will go to great lengths to give parents the impression that logical consequences aren't having the intended effect. Isaiah, age seven, is a good example.

Isaiah and his younger brother are playing Monopoly in the family room when his brother lets out a shout. "Hey! That's cheating!" Isaiah's brother yells. "You're taking money out of the bank." When Isaiah's father hears all the commotion, he comes over to investigate.

"I was just kidding," says Isaiah. He puts the money back. His father doesn't get involved. The game continues for a few minutes, then Isaiah's brother shouts again, louder than before. Their father enters the room a second time.

"He didn't think I was looking, but I saw him that time," Isaiah's brother says to their father, who announces the game is over.

"Okay, I'll put the money back," says Isaiah with a mischievous laugh, but it's too late. His father intervenes.

"You need to find something else to do," says his father. "It's time to put the Monopoly game away."

"I don't care," says Isaiah, acting unconcerned. "It's a stupid game anyway, almost as stupid as you." His father takes a few deep breaths to compose himself.

"It's not okay to talk to me or anybody else that way," says his father. "You need to spend the next ten minutes by yourself." He sends Isaiah to his room for a ten-minute time-out.

"That doesn't bother me," says Isaiah. "I like time-outs." The bait is skillfully presented, but his father doesn't bite. "I'll see you in ten minutes," his father replies, as he heads to the kitchen to set the timer.

Plea Bargaining

Strong-willed children are masters at trying to avoid the consequences for their poor choices. Six-year-old Arnie shows how it's done.

Arnie and his four-year-old brother, Simon, are playing with their plastic Transformer toys on the carpet when a squabble breaks out.

"Hey! I want to play with the big one," protests Simon. "It's mine. I got it for my birthday." He tries to wrestle it away from his brother. Arnie refuses to let go. Their mother intervenes.

"Guys, you can share the Transformers, or we're going to have to put them away for now," says their mother, matter-of-factly. "What would you like to do?"

"He's the one who won't share," says Arnie, pointing an accusing finger at his brother.

"Yeah, because it's mine," Simon replies.

"Okay, we need to put the Transformers away for now," says their mother. "You can play with them later when you're both ready to share."

"That's not fair!" exclaims Arnie, who snatches the toy away from his brother and throws it on the floor. Oops! It broke. Simon howls. Their mother takes a deep breath and prepares to ride out the drama.

"It's not okay to break your brother's toys," she says to Arnie. "You need to replace that toy with money from your allowance, and you need to spend the next five minutes in your room."

Arnie pleads for a reduced consequence. "You mean I have to do a time-out and pay for it," says Arnie. "That's not fair! It was an accident. I didn't mean to break it. I won't do it again, I promise." His mother holds firm.

"That's a good choice for next time," his mother replies. No reprieves or second chances this time. She lets the consequence teach the lesson.

Not Responding

Passive resistance can be a powerful form of persuasion for wearing down a worthy adversary. Let's see how five-year-old Sadie uses this strategy to avoid her mother's request. Sadie arrives home from kindergarten, eats a quick snack, and announces that she is going outside to play.

"You need to change your shoes before you go," says her mother. "Those are for school, not play." Sadie pretends not to hear and heads for the door. Her mother intercepts her and checks in.

"What did I ask you to do?" Sadie gives her mother an impatient look, but doesn't say a word or make any effort to comply. So her mom provides some choices.

"You can play inside the house with your school shoes on or outside in your play shoes. What would you like to do?" Sadie glares and doesn't say a thing. Her mother sees where things are headed.

No response is the same as a refusal, her mother says to herself. *I think she's made her choice.* Sadie's mother continues to stand at the door. Sadie recognizes her mother's resolve. Precious time is wasting.

"Okay, I'll change my stupid shoes," says Sadie, reluctantly, as she heads to her room to get her play shoes.

"Good choice," says her mom.

Running Away (The "Chase Me" Game)

The "chase me" game is a popular form of resistance, particularly among preschool-age children. When the game extends outside the home, it becomes a potential safety issue that warrants serious concern. Let's look at how Gavin's mother handles this issue with her four-year-old son.

When Gavin arrives home from preschool each day, his routine is to eat a quick snack, then play hard until dinner. He knows he's supposed to clean up his mess at the table before he goes outside to play, but Gavin is very focused on play.

"I'm going outside to play with my trucks," Gavin announces to his mom.

"That's fine," says his mother, "after you clean up your mess."

"I will," says Gavin as he sneaks out of the kitchen. His mother expects the escape attempt and tries to intercept him, but Gavin is too fast. He reaches the door before his mom.

"You can't catch me," Gavin taunts. His mom knows the game.

"I'm not going to chase you, Gavin," she says, matter-of-factly. "If you don't come back and clean up your mess, you won't be playing outside for the next two days." This is a safety issue, and Gavin's mom wants to impress him with the seriousness of his poor choice. Gavin just laughs and takes off. He hides behind the car in the driveway. Gavin fully expects his mom his mom to chase him. She doesn't.

Gavin waits for the chase game to begin. Two minutes pass, then five, then ten.

What's going on? Gavin says to himself. *This is no fun.* He waits another five minutes. No mom. Gavin reconsiders his choice.

He returns to the house and announces, "I'm back. I wasn't gone long. I'll clean up the mess. Can I still play outside?" His mom holds firm.

"Not for two days," she says, matter-of-factly. "It's never okay to run away from me. You need to spend the next five minutes in your room. When your time-out is over, you need to clean up your mess at the table." This isn't the outcome Gavin had in mind.

Dishonesty and Deception

From time to time, most children are tempted to use dishonesty and deception to avoid taking responsibility for their poor choices and behavior, especially when parents don't witness the actual event. Consider the following.

Taylor, age twelve, and her acrobatic terrier, Tippy, love to play catch with the Frisbee. Her parents insist this is an outdoor game, but when they're not looking, Taylor sometimes takes a few practice throws in the house. This is what her father suspects when he hears a loud crash in the living room. He arrives on the scene; he sees Taylor holding the Frisbee and a family portrait broken on the floor.

"Tippy did it," says Taylor. "We were getting ready to play catch in the backyard, and I guess he got excited." Her dad doubts the story.

"But the picture was on the table," says her dad. "Tippy doesn't usually get up on the table unless he's chasing after something. Are you sure that's what really happened?"

"I swear it," says Taylor, with a sincere look on her face. Her story just doesn't check out.

"I could be wrong," says her dad, "but it looks to me like something else happened. You need to replace the broken frame with your money from your allowance or I can give you some jobs to do to pay it off."

"But that's not fair!" protests Taylor. "Tippy did it, not me." Her dad holds firm.

"We're done discussing it," he says, "and I'm holding on to the Frisbee until you pay for the frame."

Would you give Taylor the benefit of the doubt in her unlikely story? Many parents find themselves in the position of having to make guidance decisions based on incomplete or less than accurate information. In these situations, all we can do is our best. We're parents, not police detectives. We don't need video cameras or surveillance tapes to determine the veracity of our children's stories.

Taylor chose to use dishonesty and deception as a strategy to evade responsibility for violating her parents' rule and for the damage she caused. Did it work? No. Will she try it again? Maybe. This all depends upon how much data she needs to collect before she realizes that deception is a poor strategy for avoiding responsibility. If Taylor's parents continue to use their best judgment in these situations, hold firm, and follow through with the appropriate consequences, Taylor will learn the lessons they're trying to teach.

Rescuing and Enabling

Did you ever imagine that compliant siblings and family members can be a source of resistance? In some families, it happens regularly, and it's done with the best of intentions. Compliant family members have an underlying desire to please and cooperate. They dislike conflict and will go to great lengths to avoid confrontation and upset. When they see aggressive research in action, compliant family members will sometimes step in and try to help out, but the helping is anything but helpful. It actually rewards and encourages strong-willed children to be more persistent in their research.

How do parents handle the well-intended interference? They need to expect it and be prepared to prevent it when they see it happening. Let's follow a typical week in the home of one strong-willed eight-year-old to see how it's done.

Troy is the second of three children and very strong-willed. His younger brother, Max, age six, and older sister, Glenda, are both compliant. Max and Troy share a bedroom.

Each morning before school, the kids are expected to make their beds before they leave the house. Who makes Troy's bed on a semiregular basis? Max. He hates all the commotion that happens when his parents make that last-minute bed check and inform Troy that he's not ready to leave the house until the job is done. Max hates being late to school.

When it's time to get in the car, who gets the coveted spot in the front seat next to mom? Troy. His siblings gladly give it up because Troy antagonizes them when he shares the backseat. Rides to school with Troy in the backseat are not fun.

When the kids arrive home from school, they're expected to do a few chores and finish their homework before playing. Who complains and avoids doing chores and dawdles during homework? Right again. Troy. Who does some of Troy's chores and homework for him when their mom isn't looking? Glenda. She hates to hear Troy's fussing and see how frustrated her mom becomes when he doesn't do his part. Who jumps in and berates Troy when she's had enough of his antics? Glenda.

Sometimes, Glenda's mom catches her helping out and intervenes by saying, "That's Troy's job, not yours. He needs to do it himself," or "You'll be a great parent someday, Glenda, but disciplining Troy is my job." Troy enjoys the drama and thrives on all the negative attention.

Each Wednesday after school, their mom goes to the gym and their grandma helps out with child care. Who doesn't require Troy to do his chores and tolerates his disrespectful behavior? Grandma. Who ignores Troy when he antagonizes Max and Glenda? Grandma.

Troy's mom expects him to do more testing on Wednesdays and encourages her mother to hold firm and use time-outs when Troy misbehaves. But her mother makes excuses for Troy such as, "He'd be in time-outs the whole time I'm here, and I'd never get to see him."

"Maybe that's what he needs to learn, that you won't take it," Troy's mom replies, but Grandma has a soft heart and doesn't want any conflict in her relationships with her grandchildren.

Does any of this sound like your home? Can you see why rescuing and enabling by compliant family members makes the parents' job even more challenging?

Resistance from Other Family Members

Spouses and partners can be a great source of support when they're willing to back you and a source of resistance when they don't. If your spouse or partner is a reluctant supporter, you might have to win him or her over by demonstrating your effectiveness. Role modeling is a powerful tool of persuasion. Give your partner some time to see you in action and getting results.

Two effective parents working together is the best-case scenario, but don't become discouraged if this isn't the case in your home. One effective parent is an improvement upon two ineffective parents. Give your partner time and offer generous helpings of encouragement. The process may feel like taking two steps forward and one step backward, but you will be making forward progress.

Sometimes other family members really do want to support us, but they don't believe their support should include changing their methods, too. This is the dilemma Barbara faced. When I met her, she was a single parent of two children, ages four and seven. Her four-year-old was a handful! Barbara was dependent on her mother and ex-husband for part of her child care.

Barbara became inspired when she attended one of my workshops and decided it was time for a change. She was suffering from a bad case of permissiveness and wearing down. She had been reasoning, explaining, arguing, and negotiating for years without success. Barbara quickly recognized her permissive approach, her drawn-out dances, and the bad match between her methods and her strong-willed four-year-old. She couldn't wait to get started.

In short time, Barbara was stopping misbehavior she couldn't stop before and feeling very good about it. What she hadn't counted on, however, were the influences of her mother, who cared for the children after school each day, and her ex-husband, who had the kids every other weekend. Both disciplined permissively, and neither was willing to do anything different. Her children, particularly, her four-year-old, did more testing after visits. When Barbara realized the change was going to take longer than she expected, she became discouraged.

You may also encounter the conflicting influences of other family members when you begin using your new tools. Some of these influences will be beyond your control, and like Barbara, you may become discouraged. Hang in there. You can work around those who won't support you. Sure, their resistance will slow you down, but it shouldn't deter you from achieving your long-term goals if you persevere. Your persistence will be rewarded.

Resistance from Within Yourself

The biggest obstacle to change for most of us, however, is not our relatives or even our resistant children. The biggest obstacle will come from within ourselves as we struggle against our compelling desire to revert back to our old habits and do things the way we always have. Old beliefs and habits feel comfortable and familiar and are hard to change.

> The biggest obstacle will come from within our-
> selves as we struggle against our compelling desire
> to revert to old habits and do things the way we
> always have.

If you've been permissive in the past, you'll have to resist your urge to talk your child into cooperating, even though those methods haven't worked for you in the past. If you've been punitive or autocratic in the past, you'll have to resist your urge to intimidate, coerce, or force your child into cooperating, even though this hasn't worked for you in the past. If you've used the mixed approach in the past, you'll have to resist the urge to flip-flop back and forth between the two ineffective extremes.

The biggest source of encouragement you'll experience will likely come from the positive results you get from your new methods. If you stay on course, you will experience new levels of cooperation from your children, but they're not going to give it to you for the asking. You'll have to earn it with your consistent efforts.

When Professional Help Is Needed

The vast majority of resistance you encounter should be manageable provided it is in response to your limit-setting practices and not just a symptom of something larger going on. But this is not always an easy thing to determine. What should you do if you've taken the recommended steps in this chapter and your child does not respond positively after six to eight weeks? It's time to consider that something else might be going on that keeps you stuck. You may need assistance from a qualified professional to sort it out.

When parents seek my assistance with their strong-willed children, I routinely begin my family counseling work by taking a thorough history and conducting an evaluation of what's going on. I want to be sure that the primary problem is really limit setting and not something else. I explore a number of factors such as health issues, learning or behavior problems, emotional or relationship problems, developmental disorders, and mental health issues before I conclude that limit-setting practices is the primary focus of our work together. The presence of other issues does not preclude progress with limit setting, but it can certainly slow it down and complicate it.

You may need the same type of evaluation for your child. A licensed child psychologist or educational psychologist can help you collect the information you need and determine the type of help that is needed. Ask your child's school, pediatrician, or your family physician for recommendations.

Developing Support Systems

You should expect resistance, and you should expect to feel discouraged, like most of us do, when resistance slows us down. When the resistance becomes too great, you may need additional support to stay on track.

What kind of support will you need? You'll probably need one or both of two kinds of support:

1. Support for your new limit-setting program.
2. Support for yourself as you cope with resistance.

Support for your program may involve developing consistency between your methods and those of other important adults in your child's life, such as teachers, relatives, and child-care providers. The more consistency you can create, the easier the change process will be for you and your child. Children learn more rapidly when the important adults in their life are teaching the same lesson. Share your guidance tools with other important adults in your child's life.

Mark's parents received a lot of support from their son's preschool teachers, and that support helped Mark get off to a good start in kindergarten. Mark was only four when I first met him, but he had already been expelled from two preschools for his defiant and aggressive behavior. He was enrolled in two part-time programs because no single program was willing to take him for a full day.

Mark's parents were desperate for solutions. Their son was scheduled to start kindergarten in the fall, but they couldn't imagine how that would be possible given his volatile behavior. We got right to work examining temperaments, their guidance approaches, and the angry dance they did to get Mark to cooperate.

Mark's parents used the mixed approach. They started off permissively with lots of repeating and reminding; but when Mark resisted, as he usually did, they got angry, yelled, and spanked.

I showed them how to start off with a clear message, how to stop their angry dances with cooldowns, and how to stop Mark's misbehavior with logical consequences and time-outs rather than spankings. I asked them to record the number of time-outs Mark received each day so I could monitor and chart his improvement.

Next, we tried to accelerate Mark's learning process by developing consistency between home and school. Mark's parents shared their new guidance methods with his teachers, who were more than happy to cooperate. They also agreed to record the number of time-outs Mark received at school so we could monitor his progress.

As expected, Mark tested a lot during the first few weeks, then he began to show gradual improvement. Four months after we started the program, Mark showed a 70 percent reduction in his defiant and aggressive behavior at school and even better progress at home. His behavior continued to improve in the months that followed. His parents began to feel more comfortable about his impending kindergarten experience.

Mark's teacher proved to be an invaluable support system for Mark's parents. Consistency between home and school had a lot to do with Mark's improvement. Although your child's behavior may not be as volatile as Mark's, and you may not be as desperate for change as Mark's parents were, involving other important adults in your child's life may prove very helpful in accelerating the change process.

Support for your program can be very helpful, but sometimes parents need more. Sometimes they need support for themselves as they attempt to cope with all the resistance they encounter. How do you know if you need additional support for yourself? There are a number of factors to consider:

1. The supportiveness of your spouse, partner, or other family members.
2. Your motivation level and commitment to change.

3. The amount of resistance you're encountering from your strong-willed child.
4. The amount of history you and your child have to overcome.
5. How stuck you've become in your dances.

The first two factors fall under the category of support. The last three fall under the category of resistance. If you're high in support and low in resistance, you face the best-case scenario. You'll probably be able to stop your child's misbehavior and your dances without additional personal support. If you're high in support but also high in resistance, additional personal support may be necessary to help you overcome your setbacks and discouragement. If you're low in support and high in resistance, you're the most likely to become discouraged and give up. You need personal support.

> If you're low in support and high in resistance,
> you're the most likely to become discouraged and
> give up. You need personal support.

Where do parents find the additional support they need? Most communities offer a variety of parent support resources. These include support groups, parenting workshops, and family counseling services through church organizations, schools, hospitals, and community mental health agencies.

Where do you fall on the support versus resistance scale? If you're just completing this book, you may need another four to six weeks before you can answer this question. You'll have to put your new tools to the test and observe your child's response before you'll know. If you discover that you're in a high-resistance category, don't lose heart. Your goals are attainable, but you may need personal support from others to reach them.

CHAPTER SUMMARY

Resistance is a normal and expected part of the learning and behavior change process for all of us, but strong-willed children take resistance to new extremes. They can mount considerable protests when things don't work out the way they want. Don't be misled by the heightened drama and emotion. What appears to be a whole new layer of conflict and obstacles is simply an extension of the limit-testing process you learned about in Chapter 2. The basic research questions haven't changed. They still want to know: What's okay and not okay? Who's in charge? How far can I go? What happens when I go too far? Their goal is to wear you down and get you to give in.

Resistance comes in many forms and sometimes from sources other than your strong-willed child. In this chapter, you learned how to recognize various forms of resistance so you won't be taken by surprise. You learned how to respond, rather than react, to resistance and avoid getting hooked back into a dance. You also discovered how to move forward without collecting all the hurts and baggage that accumulate with unresolved conflict. With an understanding of how to manage resistance, you're ready to learn new ways to motivate your child to cooperate and tip the scales in your favor.

10

Motivating Your Child to Cooperate

Limits define the path we want children to stay on, but limits alone may not be enough to motivate strong-willed children to head in the intended direction. Cooperation is still a voluntary act. What more can we do to inspire compliance?

This chapter will show you how to tip the scales in your favor and inspire cooperation through the positive power of encouragement. No shaming. No blaming. No humiliating children into cooperating. No bribes or special rewards for getting them to do the things they should be doing anyway. The methods are quick, effective, easy to use, and a refreshing alternative to motivation by punishment or coercion.

MOTIVATION AND LIMIT SETTING

Imagine two different paths in front of you. On one path, your boss tries to catch you being bad and uses a lot of criticism, shaming, blaming, and coercion to keep you going in the intended direction. On the other path, your boss tries to catch you being good and uses a lot of praise, encouragement, and respectful guidance. Which path would you choose?

> Limits define the path we want children to stay on, but limits alone may not be enough to motivate strong-willed children to head in the intended direction.

The question illustrates a basic truth that applies to all of us, children included. The more positives we see in our path, the more likely we are to travel in that direction. A path with positives is always most inviting.

When it comes to motivating children, most parents head in one of two directions. They take a positive approach and use generous helpings of praise and encouragement to inspire the behavior they want. Or they take a negative approach and try to shame, blame, humiliate, and coerce children into cooperating. There isn't much in between.

The approach parents take has a lot to do with the type of limits they set. Parents who are ineffective in their limit setting are accustomed to seeing lots of testing and resistance. They wear down, get angry and frustrated, and often, they end up saying discouraging things. They assume that the problem is their child's lack of cooperation, not the way cooperation is being requested. Negative messages and ineffective limits go hand in hand.

Parents who use firm limits, on the other hand, expect and require cooperation, but they recognize that children are most likely to cooperate when asked in a respectful manner. Positive messages inspire cooperation. Positive messages and firm limits go hand in hand.

> What we do is what we teach. The methods we use teach a lesson about communication and problem solving.

Positive and negative messages have very different effects on children's behavior. One leads to cooperation. The other leads to resistance. If our goal is to inspire cooperation, then negative messages are one of the surest ways not to achieve our goal.

NEGATIVE MESSAGES INSPIRE RESISTANCE

Randy, age nine, teases his sister Sara and gets the intended response. She screams to the other room for Mom, who has a good idea what's going on.

"Randy, I hope you're not teasing your sister again," says his mother. "You know how I feel about that." Randy continues teasing.

His sister screams again. Randy's mother enters the room upset and unleashes a barrage of negative messages.

"Do you enjoy making other people upset?" she asks. "Do those look like happy tears on Sara's face? I expect that kind of behavior

from a three-year-old. Would you grow up and try to treat your sister nice just once in a while?"

"Do you enjoy being such a crank all the time?" Randy retaliates. Their hurtful dance is off and running.

"That's enough from you!" his mother shouts back. "I'm sick and tired of all your crap!" She hands him a pencil and a piece of stationery and tells him to write one hundred times, "I won't sass my mother." Randy remains defiant.

"You can't make me if I don't want to," he counters.

"You can't play or watch TV for the rest of the week if you don't!" she threatens.

"So what! See if I care," Randy shouts back defiantly. He sits with his arms crossed as his mother leaves the room.

Randy's mother did not start off with the goal of provoking her son into a power struggle. Her intent was to stop his misbehavior and enlist his cooperation, but she was using one of the surest methods not to achieve that goal. Let's take a look at some of the things Randy's mother said in an effort to motivate her son to cooperate.

She begins with a soft limit and becomes angered at the predictable response—more testing. Next, she tries to shame him into cooperating with a series of hurtful comments. The focus is on his worth and capabilities, not on his behavior. The real message is, "You're mean and insensitive, and I don't expect you to cooperate." He doesn't.

How would you respond if someone said these things to you? Would you cooperate? You might if you tend to be compliant, but if you're strong-willed, you'd probably become defensive, resistant, and find ways to retaliate. This is how Randy responds.

Negative messages feel bad. They hurt, humiliate, devalue, and reject, and they are often perceived as a personal attack rather than an attempt to discourage unacceptable behavior. The focus is misdirected, and that's why they backfire.

Let's not overlook another, more subtle, message that accompanies her negative attempts to motivate. What we do is what we teach. The methods we use teach a lesson about communication and problem solving. By role modeling hurtful, coercive methods, Randy's mother is teaching him that hurtful statements are an acceptable way to motivate others to cooperate. Without realizing it, she's teaching the very behavior she's trying to stop.

Examples of Negative Motivational Messages

Negative messages come in a variety of forms. Some are subtle and communicated through our methods. Others are explicit and direct, such as the messages Randy's mother used in the previous example. All negative messages convey little confidence in the child's ability to make good choices and cooperate. All carry an underlying message of shame, blame, and rejection. Let's examine the underlying message in each of the following:

Can you cooperate just once in a while?
The underlying message: "I don't believe you can cooperate." The effect is to single out, shame, blame, diminish, and humiliate.

> Negative messages convey little confidence in the child's ability to make good choices and cooperate, and they carry an underlying message of shame, blame, and rejection.

That's real bright! Show me you have a brain and make a good choice for a change!
The underlying message: "I have little confidence in your ability to make good decisions." The effect is to single out, shame, blame, diminish, and humiliate.

Is it asking too much to get a little respect?
The underlying message: "I don't expect you to treat me respectfully." The effect is to single out, shame, blame, diminish, and humiliate.

Is that the best you can do?

The underlying message: "You're incompetent, and I don't expect you to live up to my expectations." The effect is to single out, shame, blame, diminish, and humiliate.

I don't believe it! You actually did what I asked for a change.
The underlying message: "I don't expect you to cooperate." The effect is to single out, shame, blame, diminish, and humiliate.

Try that again. I dare you.
The underlying message: "Continue misbehaving so I can show you I'm the boss." The effect is to challenge, provoke, shame, blame, single out, and humiliate.

I knew I couldn't count on you!
The underlying message: "You're not capable or trustworthy. I have no confidence in your ability." The effect is to single out, shame, blame, diminish, and humiliate.

POSITIVE MESSAGES INSPIRE COOPERATION

Jacob, age six, enters the kitchen when his four-year-old sister accidentally bumps into him. He gives her a push, and she falls down.

Their mother intervenes. "Jacob, we don't push others when we want them to move out of our way," his mother says, matter-of-factly.

"She bumped into me first," Jacob replies.

"What are you supposed to do when others bump you?" asks his mother.

Jacob just stares at her blankly. "I don't know," he replies.

"You're supposed to say, 'excuse me,' and wait for them to move," says his mother.

"Sometimes they won't move," says Jacob.

"You're right," says his mother. "When that happens, you should ask an adult for help. You have two good choices to use. What are you going to do the next time?"

"I'll say 'excuse me' and wait for them to move," replies Jacob. "If they don't, I'll ask you for help."

"Good!" says his mother. "I'm sure you'll handle it fine. Now, what do you need to say to your sister?"

> Positive messages feel good and motivate us to
> cooperate. They meet our need to belong, reaffirm
> our feelings of competence and self-worth, and give
> us confidence to handle challenging problems on
> our own.

"Sorry, Kristy," says Jacob.

"Thank you, Jacob," says his mother. She gives him a hug and an appreciative smile.

Jacob's mother uses a positive approach to motivating her son's cooperation. Much of her success, however, is due to the way she starts off. She begins with a firm, respectful, limit-setting message. No one is blamed or singled out. In a few brief sentences, she creates a positive atmosphere for problem solving. Now her encouraging words can have their greatest impact.

The focus of her message is on choices and corrective action, not on Jacob's worth or capabilities. She provides the information and skills he needs to behave acceptably, then expresses her confidence in his ability to handle the situation better next time. Her message is positive and inspiring: "You're capable. I have confidence in you. I expect you to cooperate." He does.

How would you feel if someone said these things to you? Would you feel like cooperating? Jacob did, and so would most children. Positive messages feel good and motivate us to cooperate. They meet our need to belong, reaffirm our feelings of competence and self-worth, and give us confidence to handle challenging problems on our own.

GUIDELINES FOR USING POSITIVE MESSAGES

Knowing what to encourage is the key to using positive messages effectively. The focus of our message should address our basic training goals: better choices, improved behavior, cooperation, and independence. All lead to greater responsibility. Consider the following.

Encouraging Better Choices

Sometimes children misbehave because they are unaware that there are other, more effective choices available for handling the situation. Parents are in an ideal position to help children explore their choices and make better ones.

For example, Cole, age eight, runs into the house very upset.

"What's wrong?" asks his father.

"Neal and I were playing pogo in the driveway, and Neal wouldn't stop teasing me. First, he said my haircut looks stupid. Then, he said I was the worst pogo player in the neighborhood. When I beat him, he told me I was lucky. Then, he called me fuzzball after every point and I got mad."

"What did you do then?" asks his father.

"I called him a butthead and threw a dirt clod at him," Cole replies. "I didn't hit him. I was just trying to scare him. He ran home to tell his mom."

> Parents are in an ideal position to help children explore their choices and make better ones.

"Why do you think Neal was teasing you?" asks his father.

"Because he likes to get me upset," Cole replies.

"It sounds like he succeeded, too," says his father. "How could you handle this differently next time Neal teases you?"

"I could try to ignore him," replies Cole, "but he might not stop."

"That's one good choice," says his father, "but he might not stop. What else could you do if he doesn't?"

"I could tell him I'm not going to play with him if he continues teasing me," Cole offers.

"You have two good choices," says his father. "Both of those should work next time. Do you think you owe Neal an apology for throwing a dirt clod at him and calling him a name?"

"I guess so," says Cole, reluctantly.

"I think that's a good choice," says his father. Cole felt supported and encouraged by his father's positive messages. He was aware of his options, and he was prepared to make a different choice next time the situation arose.

Encouraging Better Behavior

Making an acceptable choice is an important first step, but encouraging children to act on that choice is our larger training goal. Penny's mom demonstrates how it's done.

Seven-year-old Penny has been invited to go swimming and runs home to ask her mom. As she blasts into the house, her mom is talking with a neighbor. Penny knows she's not supposed to interrupt, but she's very excited and does it anyway.

"Mom," Penny says, excitedly, "may I go swimming at Paula's house?" She can tell by the look on her mother's face that the interruption was not appreciated.

"Penny, what are you supposed to do when you want to talk to me when I'm in the middle of a conversation?" asks her mom.

"Wait until you're done and say 'excuse me,'" Penny replies.

"Right," says her mom. "Now, go back and try it over again."

Penny leaves and reenters the house. She approaches her mom and waits patiently for a pause in the conversation. "Hi, Penny," says her mom. "What's up?"

> Making an acceptable choice is an important first step, but encouraging children to act on that choice is our larger training goal.

"May I go swimming at Paula's house?" Penny asks. "Her mother said she would watch us."

"Sure," says her mom, "and thank you for asking the right way." She gives Penny an appreciative smile. Penny got the message in a very positive way. If she forgets again, her mother will repeat the lesson in the same positive manner. The positive approach will surely lead to the desired outcome.

Encouraging Cooperation

We don't need misbehavior to cue us to the need for encouragement. Anytime children help out, cooperate, or make a contribution, parents have an opportunity to catch them being good and give an encouraging message. Our encouragement increases the likelihood that cooperation will continue.

For example, Mel, age six, and his two-year-old sister are eating breakfast when the phone rings. Without being asked, Mel helps out with his sister so his mother can get through her phone conversation. His mother appreciates the help and lets him know it.

> Our encouragement increases the likelihood that
> cooperation will continue.

"Thanks for helping with Sarah," says his mother. "I really appreciate it. I can't wait to tell your father what a great helper you were today." She gives him a hug and an appreciative smile. Mel beams with pride. It feels good to have his contribution acknowledged. Next time his mother is on the phone, Mel is likely to pitch in and help out again.

A word or two of encouragement at the right moment can have a big impact. The following are some of the encouraging messages children love to hear.

"I like the way you handled that."
"Your room looks great today."
"Your help really makes a big difference."
"Good job!"
"I knew I could count on you."
"I can't wait to tell your father what a great job you did."

Encouraging Independence

One of our most important jobs as parents is to prepare children to handle challenging tasks and problems on their own. We do this by teaching skills and by limiting our involvement so children have opportunities to practice. Encouragement plays an important role in this process. It gives children the courage and support they need to take risks and act independently. Lee, who's nearly four, is a good example.

Lee sits at the breakfast table and decides to pour some juice from a pitcher into his cup. He looks at his dad first before trying.

"Go ahead, Lee," says his dad encouragingly.

Lee lifts the pitcher with both hands and carefully aims for the cup. He pours, but the pitcher is so big that it obscures his view of the cup. Some juice spills on the table. Lee sets the pitcher down dejectedly. His father encourages him to try again.

"You were very close," he says. "Try it again, but this time let's set the cup off to one side so you can see it more clearly." He moves the cup and hands Lee the pitcher.

Lee looks a little uncertain, but he takes the pitcher, aims, and pours. Bingo! A perfect hit.

"Good job, Lee!" says his father. "I knew you could do it."

Lee beams with pride. He now has the courage to do it independently. His father's support and encouragement gives Lee the confidence he needs to master a challenging skill.

CHAPTER SUMMARY

From a motivational perspective, it's much more powerful to catch children being good and encourage their success than to catch them being bad and point out their failures. In this chapter, we examined two contrasting approaches to motivating children to cooperate. The negative approach, which often accompanies soft limits, backfires more than it succeeds with strong-willed children. It inspires resistance, not cooperation, and discourages the behavior we want to increase.

Positive, encouraging approaches to motivation are highly effective for inspiring cooperation, especially when used with firm limits. Positive, encouraging messages feel good. They meet children's needs for belonging, reaffirm feelings of competence and self-worth, and inspire them to tackle challenging tasks and problems on their own. An encouraging message at the right time can make the difference between cooperation and resistance (see Table 7).

Knowing what to encourage is the key to using encouragement effectively. Encouraging messages have their greatest impact when they focus on better choices, improved behavior, cooperation, and independence.

TABLE 7. Positive Versus Negative Approaches to Motivation

Encouraging Messages	Discouraging Messages
Inspire cooperation	Inspire resistance, retaliation
Motivate and empower	Discourage and humiliate
Convey respect, confidence, support	Diminish, blame, reject
Create cooperative relationships	Create adversarial relationships
Meet needs for belonging, competence, self-worth	Perceived as personal attack
Focus on choices and behavior	Focus on child's worth and capabilities

11

Teaching Skills

SHOWING THEM WORKS BEST

How much time do you spend disciplining your child for the predictable misbehavior your child does repeatedly throughout the week? I'm talking about during trips to the mall, when the phone or doorbell rings, dining out in public, visiting other people's homes, going through the checkout line at the grocery store, during mealtimes, getting ready for school in the morning, and arriving home from school in the afternoon. These are predictable friction points for most strong-willed children and their parents.

Sure, you can stop misbehavior in each of these situations with natural and logical consequences, but consequences alone won't teach your children the skills they need to behave more appropriately. If you want to get off the discipline treadmill, you have to go to the next step in the guidance process. You have to teach children the skills they need to behave in more socially acceptable ways.

This chapter will show you how to do that. You'll learn some simple but highly effective steps for teaching social skills. Then, you'll learn how to apply these steps to the challenging situations you encounter throughout the week. Effective skill training is your ticket off the discipline treadmill.

PROVIDING INFORMATION IS NOT ENOUGH

Often, parents assume that telling children how to handle a challenging situation is equivalent to teaching the skill. For many children, it's not. Providing information is an important first step in the teaching process, but information alone is not enough to help many children master new or unfamiliar skills. They need to be shown what to do, and often they need practice and additional instruction before they can fully master the skills we're trying to teach.

> Effective skill training is your ticket off the discipline treadmill.

I learned this lesson from one of the strangest referrals I've ever received. Kaley, age six, and her mother arrived at my office with a dilemma. Each day, Kaley left for school with a carefully prepared lunch. Her mother packed great sandwiches, fruit roll-ups, box drinks, chips, and delicious dessert items. Unfortunately, the best items in Kaley's lunchbox always seemed to end up in some other child's hands. Kaley arrived home in tears.

"I don't understand it," said her frustrated mother. "She knows what to do. I've told her over and over again to say no to the big kids when they try to talk her out of her lunch items, but she continues to give them away day after day! Her teacher said there's nothing she can do if Kaley chooses to give her lunch away."

I suspected her mother was right. Kaley probably did know what to do, but I wanted to check this out with Kaley to be sure.

> Information alone is not enough to help many children master new or unfamiliar skills. They need to be shown what to do.

"Kaley, what are you supposed to do when other kids ask for your lunch items?" I asked. She parroted back the words her mother told her.

Her mother was right. On an intellectual level, Kaley understood what she was supposed to do, but knowing what to do and actually doing it are two different things. Perhaps her skill training was incomplete. I explored the problem a little further.

"Saying no to big kids is sometimes hard to do," I said.

Kaley nodded in agreement. "I get scared," she said.

"Let's practice saying no to big kids for a while," I suggested. "Perhaps you can learn to feel more comfortable." I wanted Kaley to see, hear, feel, and experience what it was like to do what she was being asked.

I broke the skill down into a few simple steps, then asked her mother to pretend to be one of the big kids. I pretended to be Kaley. I used a book as the lunchbox. When her mother approached and made a pitch for my chips, I said, "No, they're mine. Sorry, but I don't want to trade." We went through this drill several times. I role-modeled different ways to say no.

Then, her mother and I switched roles. I became the big kid, and her mother became Kaley. Her mother role-modeled many different ways to say no and hold on to the lunchbox.

"Now, it's your turn to practice, Kaley," I said. "I'll be the big kid and you can hold the lunchbox." I encouraged her to say no in a loud voice, which turned out to be very soft, and to make eye contact, which she never did; but she did say "no," and she did hold on to the book.

"That was a very clear no," I said. "That will work just fine. Let's try it again."

We repeated the drill many times. Each time, I encouraged her to say no a different way to see which way felt most comfortable. She preferred the simple, two-word approach, "No, sorry," and discovered that she felt most comfortable when she didn't look at me when she said it. She was gaining confidence.

"Ready to try this at school?" I asked.

"I guess so," said Kaley.

I asked Kaley's mother to practice the procedure a few more times in the morning before Kaley left for school and to offer some words of encouragement. We scheduled a follow-up conference for later that week.

"How did it go?" I asked when they arrived for the follow-up visit. I could tell from the proud look on Kaley's face that she must have enjoyed some success.

"It went fine," said her mother. "The practice really helped. Her lunch stayed in her hands all week."

"Congratulations!" I said. Kaley had mastered an important skill, one she could put to good use in other situations as well.

Kaley is a compliant child with an underlying desire to please and cooperate. Her successes came quickly and smoothly. Strong-willed children usually require more time to master new skills, and the learning process is much bumpier. Why? Because strong-willed children learn social skills the same way they learn most rules and skills—the hard way.

As you begin teaching skills to your strong-willed child, your child may make more poor choices than good choices in the beginning. Don't get discouraged. This is normal. Strong-willed children need to experience the consequences of their poor choices repeatedly before they're convinced that cooperation is the better way to go. The learning process is bumpier, but the eventual outcome is the same for all children.

> Strong-willed children learn social skills the same way they learn our rules—the hard way.

All children need our help exploring choices for action, breaking the skill down into teachable pieces, role modeling acceptable behavior, giving them opportunities to practice, and most important, catching them being good and acknowledging their successes. If you follow these simple steps and allow your child to collect the data he or she needs, your child will arrive at the desired outcome. Let's look more closely at each step in the skill-training process.

EXPLORING CHOICES

Sometimes children misbehave because they're simply unaware of other, more effective choices for solving problems or behaving acceptably. Five-year-old Connie is a good example. She sits at the kitchen table drawing a picture, while her younger brother, Tommy, watches and tries to get involved.

Each time Connie puts down a crayon, Tommy picks it up and scribbles on his paper. Her picture takes longer than she anticipated. Connie gets frustrated. When Tommy picks up the next crayon, she hits him and wrestles it away from him. He screams, and their mother intervenes.

"She hit me and took away my crayon," whines Tommy.

"He was taking all my crayons," says Connie.

"We don't hit to get our crayons back," says her mother, matter-of-factly. She sends Connie for a five-minute time-out.

Connie needs a clean slate, but she also needs new skills. After the time-out, Connie's mother explores other choices, besides hitting, for handling the situation differently.

"What else can you do when your brother wants to play with one of your play items?" her mother asks. Connie just stares at her blankly because hitting and wrestling the crayon away from Tommy was the only option Connie could think of. There were no other choices on her menu. Her mother suggests some better choices.

> Sometimes children misbehave because they're simply unaware of other, more effective choices for solving problems or behaving acceptably.

"You could ask him nicely with your words not to use the crayons you want to use," says her mother. "That's one good choice. You could give him the crayons you don't want to use. That's another good choice. If Tommy still doesn't cooperate with you, you could ask me for help. You have three good choices, but hitting Tommy will always get you a time-out. What are you going to do next time?"

"I'll share the crayons I don't want to use," says Connie, "and I'll ask him nicely too."

"Good choices!" says her mother. "Now, let's go back and give Tommy his crayons so you can finish your picture." Connie returns to the table and offers her brother half of the crayons in her tray.

"Good job!" says her mother with an appreciative smile.

As this example illustrates, exploring choices for action is an important first step in the skill-training process. It helps children become aware of their choices. It helps them distinguish between good and poor choices, and it sets the stage for the steps to follow.

> Exploring choices for action is an important first step in the skill-training process.

From a developmental perspective, exploring choices works best with older children and teens because they have the intellectual capacity to consider hypotheticals and think ahead into the future. The method works fine with younger children, but parents usually have to suggest most of the choices. You can use this training step after consequences have been applied or to teach problem-solving skills when no misbehavior has occurred. Carry out the following steps:

1. Explore with your child, in a question format, other acceptable choices available for solving the problem or handling the situation.

2. Review the consequences for poor choices and noncompliance.

3. Encourage your child to carry out one of the better choices.

For example, Tim, age six, arrives home in tears because one of his friends called him names. His mother provides some comfort, then explores other choices for handling name-calling in the future.

"What are some other things you can do if he does this again?" asks Tim's mother.

"I could tell his mother and get him in trouble," says Tim.

"That's one choice," says his mother, "but that will probably make him mad, and he'll probably find other ways to get back at you. What else could you do?" she asks.

"I don't know," says Tim, looking puzzled.

"You could try ignoring him and see if that works," offers his mother. "Or you could tell him that if he does it again, you're not going to play with him anymore that day. If he does it again, you could go home." Tim liked that choice. "What are you going to do next time?" asks his mother.

"I'll try ignoring him first," says Tim. "If he does it again, I'll go home."

"Good choices," says his mother. "Let's practice the skill for a minute." They rehearse the skill a few times until Tim feels comfortable.

"Good job!" she says. "I think he'll get the message."

In another example, ten-year-old Amber completes a time-out for hitting her brother. Her dad takes a few minutes to explore Amber's choices for handling the problem differently next time.

"Hitting Stevie for teasing you will always get you a time-out," her father begins. "How can you handle this problem differently next time?"

"I guess I could ask him to stop," says Amber, "but he never listens to me. I could try to ignore him too, but he makes me so mad when he does that."

"Yes, ignoring someone is hard to do," her father agrees, "but it also works if you can do it. Also, you could ask for my help if he continues to tease you after you've asked him to stop. If he doesn't, then he'll be doing the time-out. You have some good choices. What are you going to do next time?"

"I'll ask him to stop. If he doesn't, I'll ask you or Mom to help," says Amber.

"Good plan!" says her father. "I know Stevie will give you plenty of opportunities to practice."

BREAKING SKILLS INTO TEACHABLE PARTS

An essential part of teaching skills to children is to make each skill understandable. This involves breaking the skill down into teachable pieces, then teaching it piece by piece. When parents neglect to do this, often they experience the type of problems Sean's parents encounter in the following example.

Sean, age eight, has a habit of interrupting. When he was younger, his parents thought it was a stage or phase that would pass with time. It didn't. In fact, the problem got worse. Teachers began to complain. Sean's parents decided it was time to do something about it.

An essential part of teaching skills to children is to make the skill understandable. This involves breaking the skill down into teachable pieces, then teaching it piece by piece.

At first, they tried complaining and criticizing Sean each time he interrupted. That didn't help. The problem continued. Next, they told him to say, "excuse me" when he wanted their attention. That didn't help either. Sean simply prefaced all his interruptions with the words *excuse me* and continued to interrupt.

Things didn't improve until Sean's third-grade teacher recommended a book about setting limits with strong-willed children. His parents read it and realized they had left out an important step in the skill-training process. They developed a new plan and called Sean into the living room.

"Sean, we want you to learn how not to interrupt others," his father began. "Here are the steps we want you to follow. When you want someone's attention, but they're talking or busy doing something, we want you to approach them quietly and make eye contact. Then, we want you to wait for a pause in the conversation, say 'excuse me' once, and wait to be recognized. When they look at you, it's your turn to speak. Do you understand how it works?"

Sean nods.

"Good," says his father, "because we're going to practice this skill from now on. If you forget and interrupt, we'll ask you to go back and try it again. If you interrupt us intentionally, we'll ask you to go to your room for a time-out. Is this clear?"

Sean nods again.

Sean gets his first opportunity to practice the new skill later that same evening. He runs into the room excitedly and interrupts his parents' conversation. His father stops Sean before he completes his first sentence.

"What are you supposed to do when you want our attention?" his father asks.

Sean remembers.

"Now, go back and try it again," says his father.

Sean leaves the room and returns a short time later. He approaches his parents, who are still talking, makes eye contact with his father, and waits for a pause in the conversation. "Excuse me," says Sean. His father looks at him and smiles.

"Thank you," says his father. "What would you like to tell us, Sean?"

Sean and his parents repeated this drill many times in the weeks and months that followed. No, things didn't always go smoothly. Sometimes Sean reacted angrily and became disrespectful when they stopped his interruptions. They always followed through with time-outs. After a few weeks, Sean's successes outnumbered his failures. He was well on his way to mastering an important new skill.

ROLE MODELING CORRECTIVE BEHAVIOR

Sometimes children need to see, hear, feel, and experience the skill we want them to learn before they can master it. Role modeling corrective behavior is a simple but powerful teaching technique that is particularly well suited to younger children and "hard-way" learners. The method is concrete, easy to use, and has varied applications. It can be used to teach problem-solving skills when no misbehavior is involved, or for teaching acceptable corrective behavior when misbehavior is involved.

> Role modeling corrective behavior is a simple but powerful teaching technique that is particularly well suited to younger children and "hard-way" learners.

When your focus is on teaching skills when no misbehavior is involved, use the following steps:

1. Role-model the corrective behavior you want your child to use.
2. Encourage your child to "try it again" using the corrective behavior.
3. Catch her doing it correctly and acknowledge her success.

For example, Becky is a very precocious three-and-a-half-year-old who thinks she's ready to start answering the phone. Her first opportunity comes when her mother is in the bathroom. The phone rings, and Becky decides to answer it.

"Hi, I'm Becky," she says cheerfully. "I'm almost four. My mother is in the bathroom. Sometimes she takes a long time. I'll tell her she has a call." She runs to the bathroom.

"Mom!" Becky shouts, excitedly. "Someone is on the phone. I

told them you're in the bathroom." Her mother realizes it's time to teach her daughter an important skill.

When her phone conversation is over, Becky's mother role-models the right way to answer the phone. "Let's practice answering the phone," says her mother. "When it rings, you're supposed to say, 'Hello, Miller residence.' Now, you try it." She makes a ringing sound and motions for Becky to answer the phone.

"Hello, Miller residence," says Becky.

"Good job!" says her mother. "Let's try it again."

They repeat the drill several times, and each time, Becky does great. "I think you're ready," her mother announces. "Next time the phone rings, and I'm not available, you can answer it. I'm sure you'll do fine."

Now, let's take a look at the second application of this technique. When your focus is on teaching corrective skills after an incidence of misbehavior, use the following steps:

1. Give a firm limit-setting message.
2. Role-model the corrective behavior.
3. Encourage your child to "try it again" using the correct behavior.
4. Catch them being good and acknowledge their success.

Six-year-old Colby pushes his sister in the hallway because she's in his way. His father intervenes. "We don't push others when they're in our way," he says, and sends Colby for a time-out.

After the time-out, Colby's father explores other ways to get people to move besides pushing, then role-models the right way to handle the situation. "When others are in our way, we say, 'Excuse me,' or 'Move, please.' " He role-models the corrective behavior. Then, he resets the scene and asks Colby to try it again.

Colby approaches Kristina in the hallway and says, "Excuse me, Kristina. I want to get by."

"Thanks, Colby," says his dad, with an appreciative smile. "You handled that great!"

A few days later, the family is heading out the door to church, and Colby's dad catches him using the new skill spontaneously. He gives Colby a knowing nod and an appreciative smile. "Good job!" he says.

TRY IT AGAIN

> "Try it again" is a simple, concrete, and highly effective teaching method that provides children with the practice they need to master the skills we're trying to teach.

Learning new skills requires practice. "Try it again" is a simple, concrete, and highly effective teaching method that provides children with the practice they need to master the skills we're trying to teach. The procedure is easy to carry out. After an incident of minor misbehavior, give a firm limit-setting message, role-model the corrective behavior if necessary, then encourage your child to "try it again" using the corrective behavior. Your child is simply given another opportunity to demonstrate that he or she can make a better choice and cooperate. If your child chooses to resist instead, move on to limited choices or logical consequences.

For example, Tre, age ten, runs into his house yelling and laughing. His infant brother is asleep in a nearby room. Tre's mother intervenes.

"Tre, that's not how you're supposed to enter the house when your brother is napping," she says. "You're supposed to use an indoor voice. Now go back outside, please, and come in again the right way."

Tre leaves and reenters the house quietly.

"Thanks, honey," says his mother. "I appreciate it." She says the same thing every time Tre remembers on his own.

Jenna, age twelve, is impatient with her father for insisting that she finish her chores before going off to play with her friends. She completes her jobs, then checks with her dad.

"Can your little slave go out and play now?" she asks in a disrespectful tone.

"Not when you ask me like that," replies her father. "How are you supposed to ask? Let's try that again." Jenna shakes her head, rolls her eyes, and looks at her father impatiently.

"Do you need a little time by yourself to think about the right way to ask?" he asks. He's prepared to follow through with a time-out if necessary. Jenna realizes resistance won't get her anywhere.

"May I play with friends now?" she asks.

"Sure," says her father, "and thank you for asking the right way. That felt much better."

CATCHING CHILDREN BEING GOOD

Children are naturally motivated to learn new skills and to have their successes acknowledged by the people who matter most. They don't require treats, toys, and special rewards to become more skillful. They're already eager to show you what they can do. Skill acquisition is the primary developmental task of early and middle childhood.

> Children are naturally motivated to learn new skills and to have their successes acknowledged by the people who matter most.

One of the most powerful ways to motivate children to learn new skills also is one of the most simple. Catch them being good and acknowledge it. Let's look at how Van's mother does this in the next example.

Van, age six, sees his mom pull into the driveway with a carload of groceries. Without being asked, he runs over to help. He grabs a couple of bags and carries them into the house. His mother appreciates his help and lets him know.

"You're such a great helper!" she says with an appreciative smile. "I can't wait to tell your father." Van beams.

What do you think will happen next time she pulls into the driveway with a carload of groceries? What lesson is Van role-modeling for his siblings?

In a separate example, Tanya's mother has been working hard to help her seven-year-old improve her table manners. They've worked on taking smaller bites, chewing food completely, using her napkin, and clearing her place setting from the table when she's finished. Progress has been slow but steady.

One night, after dinner, Tanya gets up from the table and begins to clear her place without prompts or reminders. "Good job!"

says her father. "I am so proud of you." Tanya blushes with accomplishment.

TEACHING SKILLS FOR CHALLENGING SITUATIONS

Now that you understand the steps that will get you off the discipline treadmill, let's look at how parents apply these steps to improve the challenging situations they encounter throughout the week: trips to the mall or grocery store; visits to other people's homes; phone calls; tattling and sibling quarrels; leaving for school in the morning and arriving home from school in the afternoon.

Trips to the Mall or Grocery Store

Nori's mom dreads trips to the mall or grocery store with her four-year-old. Every time they go, Nori misbehaves. She runs away, hides in the aisles and clothes racks, yells, begs for treats at the checkout line, and throws tantrums when she doesn't get them. The ordeal is exhausting.

A neighbor loans Nori's mom a book that will make shopping trips go more smoothly. She reads it and decides to put the new tools into practice.

The morning before their next outing, Nori's mom calls her daughter into the kitchen and begins teaching Nori the skills she needs to behave acceptably in the mall.

"I want to show you how big kids are supposed to behave when they go to the mall or grocery store," her mother begins. "First, you're supposed to use an indoor voice, the same one we use in the house. Second, you're supposed to stay right next to me while we're in the store. That means no running in the aisles or hiding. If you do that, I'll have to hold your hand or have you sit in the shopping cart for the rest of the trip. Finally, you're not supposed to ask for candy or treats at the checkout line. If you fuss or cry, you'll do a time-out just like you do when we're home, but if you cooperate, we'll celebrate together. Do you understand?" Nori nods. "Good. Let's practice before we go to the mall." Nori and her mother review the procedures and practice the skills several times before leaving.

When they arrive, Nori uses an indoor voice and stays right next to her mom during the entire trip. "Good job!" says her mom between appreciative looks. Everything goes fine until they reach the checkout line, and Nori sees something she wants. She asks in an indoor voice, but when her mom says no, Nori starts to fuss. The fussing turns into crying, then a tantrum.

"Excuse me," Nori's mom says to the clerk. "May I leave my cart here? I'll return in a few minutes and pay for the items." The clerk nods. Nori's mother takes her daughter by the hand and walks her out to the car. No shaming. No blaming. Nothing is said at all.

When they arrive at the car, Nori's mother informs her that she has five minutes, or however long she needs, to get herself calmed down and under control. Her mom pulls out a magazine and begins to read. When the five minutes are over, Nori and her mom return to the store, pay for the items, and leave.

"That went much better," says her mom. "You handled it great this time."

That night at the dinner table, Nori's mom announces that they had a much better trip to the mall. No mention is made about the tantrum in the checkout line.

"Good work!" says her dad. "I knew you could do it."

Nori beams.

Her behavior at the mall and grocery store improves with each successive outing. Sometimes she has perfect trips with no misbehavior. Other times she has to sit in the cart or take a time-out in the car. Her mom always celebrates Nori's successes with some special acknowledgment and follows through with consequences when needed. Nori's mom no longer dreads outings with her daughter.

Visiting Other People's Homes

Whenever Cameron's parents take him to visit other people's homes, their five-year-old acts like a wild man. He runs and yells in the house. He uses language he's not permitted to use at home, and he shows off at the dining table by making bathroom noises. Cameron's behavior is embarrassing. His parents are determined to put a stop to it.

Before their next visit, they sit down with Cameron and discuss the ground rules for a good visit. "When we visit Aunt Margaret today, we expect you to use an indoor voice when you're indoors and walk in the house, not run. If you yell or run in the house, we'll give you some quiet time by yourself to get yourself under control. When we're at the dining table, we expect you to use the same manners you're supposed to use at home. No showing off or bathroom noises. If you do, we'll ask you to leave the table each time it happens. Do you understand?" Cameron nods.

They don't mean it, Cameron says to himself. *They'll chase after me and complain the way they always do.*

When they arrive at Aunt Margaret's house, Cameron goes right to work on them. He runs into the house whooping like a cowboy at the end of a cattle drive. In a matter-of-fact voice, his parents ask him to go back to the car and try it again the right way. He does.

"Thank you," says his mother. "That was much better." His aunt thanks him too.

What got into them? Cameron wonders.

Later during the visit, Cameron decides to show off for his cousins by using unacceptable language. When his dad hears him, he sends Cameron to the den for a five-minute time-out.

I never thought they'd do this, Cameron says to himself. When he resumes play with his cousins, he cleans up his language.

Everything goes well until halfway through dinner when Cameron's seven-year-old cousin starts to act silly. Cameron can't resist the temptation and begins making bathroom noises. Promptly, his mother asks him to leave the table and spend five minutes by himself in the den. She sets the timer.

This is no fun, Cameron thinks to himself. When the buzzer goes off, Cameron returns to the table and cooperates during the rest of the meal. The rest of the evening goes well.

On the way home in the car, Cameron expected to hear all the usual complaints about all the things he did wrong and how embarrassed his parents felt, but not this time. Instead, they expressed their appreciation for all the things he did right. There was no mention of the time-outs. "Yes, it was a much better visit," his parents agreed. They thanked Cameron for doing his part.

Cameron's parents used this same approach on subsequent visits to other people's homes during the ensuing months. Before each visit, they reviewed their ground rules and expectations for a good visit and expressed pride in all the improvement he had shown. They also reviewed the consequences they'd use if things didn't go well. Cameron's behavior steadily improved. His parents began to look forward to taking him on visits to other people's homes.

When the Phone Rings

Have you noticed that a ringing telephone in many homes seems to be a signal for kids to misbehave? They can be playing or eating contentedly, but when the phone rings, suddenly everything changes. Needs that didn't exist a few seconds earlier suddenly have to be met at that moment. Kids whine and fuss and demand their parents' undivided attention.

This is what Holly experienced every time the phone rang in her house. She'd plead with her kids to be quiet, give them angry looks, yell at them, and threaten to take away their toys and TV privileges.

> Have you noticed that a ringing telephone in many homes seems to be a signal for kids to misbehave?

Things didn't improve until Holly decided to take a different approach. One morning at breakfast, she makes an announcement. "I want to show you guys what you're supposed to do when the phone rings," she begins. "You're supposed to use quiet, indoor voices when you talk with each other. If you want my attention, raise your hand quietly, and I'll talk with you as soon as I'm off the phone. If you interrupt me, I will send you to your rooms for a time-out. Is that clear? Now, tell me what you're supposed to do."

The kids repeated her instructions, then Holly and the kids practiced the procedure several times in mock rehearsals.

"Good job!" said Holly. "That's what I want you to do from now on."

The first opportunity for real-life practice happened less than an hour later. The phone rang, and three-year-old April began screaming on cue. Holly was about to pause her conversation and give April a time-out, when her five-year-old son, Chris, stepped in and took April into another room.

"Thank you, Chris," says Holly, when her phone conversation is over. "I can't wait to tell your father what a great helper you were today."

Chris swells with pride.

Holly continued to use this approach in the weeks and months that followed. Chris, her compliant five-year-old, caught on quickly. April, her hard-way learner, required a lot of time-outs and a lot of practice, but her successes were beginning to outnumber her failures.

Tattling

Danielle, age eight, has a habit of tattling on her two siblings. Her parents are constantly refereeing her hassles, and they're tired of it. They decide to take a new approach. They sit down with Danielle and share their new plan.

"We want to help you become a better problem solver with Scott and Kelsey," her mother begins. "When they do things that are not okay, we want you to use your words and ask them to stop before you come to us. If you come to us first, we're going to send you back. If they don't cooperate when you ask them politely, then we'll be happy to help you."

Danielle gets an opportunity to practice the new skill later the same day when her brother borrows her marker pens without asking. She runs to tell her mom.

"Scott took my marker pens without asking," Danielle says.

"Did you ask him to return them?" asks her mother.

"He won't listen to me," says Danielle, hoping she'll get involved.

"Neither will I," replies her mom, "not until you ask him first." Danielle leaves the room and doesn't return. When her mom goes to investigate, she sees the package of marker pens lying on Danielle's desk where they belong.

Danielle's parents used this approach frequently in the weeks that followed and began to notice a change. Danielle tattled less. On one occasion, her mom observed Danielle asking Kelsey to stop bothering her, and Kelsey cooperated.

"You handled that situation with Kelsey very well!" commented her mom. "I'm proud of you." Danielle tried to fight back a smile. She was making good progress solving problems on her own.

Arriving Home from School

Transitions in the day, such as leaving the house in the morning or arriving home in the afternoon, require skills from children that some parents never bother to teach. I know. I was one of those parents who learned this lesson the hard way.

> Transitions in the day, such as leaving the house
> in the morning or arriving home in the afternoon,
> require skills from children that some parents never
> bother to teach.

Each day around 5:00 P.M., I arrived at my sons' preschool and witnessed an amazing event. When my sons saw me enter the room, they greeted me with hugs, then, without being asked, they went over and picked up whatever project they were involved in and put it away neatly on a shelf! Then, they collected their sweatshirts and lunchboxes from their cubbies, and off we'd go.

I wasn't the only parent who watched this event in awe. On several occasions, I heard other parents comment, "I wish I could get my child to do that at home." But all the children did it, and they did it every day!

It was clear from the proud look on the kids' faces that there was something intrinsically rewarding about doing their part. They felt useful and capable, and they beamed when their teachers thanked them.

When we arrived home, my sons returned to their normal behavior. They threw their sweatshirts on the floor, dropped their lunchboxes wherever they pleased, and headed to the kitchen for a snack. Who do you think picked up the sweatshirts and lunchboxes and the messes they left on the kitchen counter? That's right, mom and dad. We spent about twenty minutes every day cleaning up their messes. We were beginning to get annoyed.

One day, after surveying the litter of sweatshirts and lunchboxes, I decided to confront them. "What's going on, guys?" I asked. "You don't leave messes like this at school."

"Of course not, Dad," replied my oldest son, Scott. "They won't let us."

I wanted to say, "We don't allow you to leave messes at home, either!" But I knew it wasn't true. I could see their preschool was doing something we were not: making their expectations clear and teaching children to pick up for themselves.

That night, when the kids were in bed, I shared Scott's comment with my wife. We agreed it was time for our boys to take responsibility for cleaning up their own messes. I built some shelves in the entryway closet so they would have their own set of cubbies like at school. When the cubbies were done, we held a family meeting.

"Guys, Mom and I want to talk to you about some new rules," I announced. "We're going to start doing some things just like school. We made some cubbies in the closet for you. When you get home from school, it's your job to put your sweatshirts and lunchboxes there. When you're done with your snacks, we want you to clean up the mess. That means, put your cups and plates in the sink and put your garbage in the wastebasket. Is that clear?"

"What happens if we forget to put our stuff away?" asked Scott.

"That shouldn't be a problem," said my wife. "You guys remember just fine at school; but if you forget, we'll let you know, and there won't be any playing until you're done."

I expected testing, but when we arrived home the next day, Scott hung up his sweatshirt, put his lunchbox on the shelf, and headed for a snack; then he cleaned up after himself. Ian followed his lead, but required a few more prompts.

That was easy, I thought to myself. Then I realized that their teachers had already done the skill training. My part was easy. All I had to do was hold them accountable and catch them being good.

The testing I expected didn't come until the following week, when the novelty of the new cubbies wore off, or perhaps they really did forget as Scott said they might. Whatever happened, all we needed to say was, "Is that where your sweatshirt goes?" or "No playing until your things are put away," and they picked things up as requested.

Thanks to their preschool, our boys learned the skills of picking up after themselves, and now the habit is well established. We still get tested from time to time, particularly from Ian, and occasionally we need to support our rule with logical consequences, but the boys have accepted the fact that picking up after themselves is their responsibility, not ours.

CHAPTER SUMMARY

Telling children what to do is not the same as teaching the skill. Providing information is an important first step in the skill-training process, but information alone is not enough for many children to master a skill. They need to be shown what to do; and often they need practice and additional instruction before they can fully master the skills we're trying to teach. The process often involves more failures than successes in the beginning.

If you want to get off the discipline treadmill, you have to go to the next step in the guidance process. You have to teach the skills your child needs to behave differently, provide opportunities for practice, catch your child being good, and acknowledge your child's successes.

12

Patience

THE REMEDY FOR ANGER AND FRUSTRATION

What do strong-willed children do better than all other children? That's right. They test our limits, challenge our authority, and wear us down with formidable resistance when we try to guide them in the right direction. How do most parents feel when this happens? Angry. Impatient. Frustrated. And these intense feelings are some of the biggest obstacles to effective limit setting. They cloud our thinking, impair our judgment, make us overreact, and cause us to say and do things we later regret.

To further complicate matters, we live in an era that places high value on speed and convenience. We expect quick remedies and instant solutions to the obstacles we face. As a society, we've become less tolerant of the challenges in life that require patience, understanding, restraint, and big-picture thinking. Raising a strong-willed child is certainly one of those challenges. The expectation of a quick fix only intensifies our anger and impatience.

Some things can be remedied by cranking up the speed, but changing your strong-willed child's behavior isn't one of them. Parents today need a mind-set based on tolerance, restraint, understanding, and big-picture thinking. Patience is the remedy for anger and frustration. Fortunately, patience is a skill that can be taught and learned and applied directly to challenging situations. That's what this chapter will show you how to do. Patience is the key to preserving your sanity as you guide your children through the limit-setting process.

WHAT IS PATIENCE?

Patience is a term with complex meanings. *Webster's* dictionary defines patience as the capacity of calm endurance, tolerance, capable of bearing delay. Other sources define it as the bearing of provocation, annoyance, misfortune, or pain, without complaint, loss of temper, irritation, or the like. Synonyms include: composure, stability, endurance, fortitude, steadfastness, calmness, and courage and strength of character in the midst of pain and suffering. Does this sound like the stuff we need when working with strong-willed children? You bet.

Patience is the remedy for overcoming the intense feelings we feel when we encounter resistance from our strong-willed children. Patience provides us with an opportunity for responding, not simply reacting. Here's the best news. You don't need to be a saint to be patient. Patience is a skill that can be taught and learned by nearly anyone and applied in challenging situations.

One of my most instructive lessons in patience came from my close friend and longtime business partner, Lisa Stanzione, whom I affectionately refer to as the "patron saint of special education." In addition to being a copresenter at my workshops for parents and teachers for more than a dozen years, Lisa has been a distinguished special education teacher and recipient of countless awards for teaching and creative program development. She has an amazing way with kids, and her patience and solid command of effective limit setting have a great deal to do with it.

In the classroom, Lisa is unflappable. Nothing rattles her, and she works with the most difficult kids on campus who do all the usual things difficult children do—test limits, tantrum, disrupt, dig in their heels, power struggle, defy adults, even lose emotional control and lash out physically. Lisa just maintains a steadfast calm, patient demeanor. She sets clear, firm limits and *always* follows through with an appropriate logical consequence when her students make poor choices. Lisa keeps the big picture in view. She knows how to bring out the best in her students and the adults who work with them.

When I ask her how she maintains her calm, encouraging, and resolute demeanor in the face of such extreme and intensely emotional situations, Lisa always reminds me, "They need me to be that way. They're just kids trying to do the best they can. They need to be able to trust and depend on me no matter how bad things get. That's my job. I'm always going to be there for them."

In the classroom, Lisa doesn't need to take any special steps to thoughtfully reflect on what she needs to do. She's always in that moment. She keeps the big picture in view the moment she enters the classroom. She makes patience look easy.

When we get into the car to return home after a full-day's workshop or training event, Lisa becomes more like the rest of us. She and I usually debrief about how the workshop went and about how we, or mostly me, can improve. We're close, and we can be honest with each other. On more than a few occasions, Lisa has pointed out my mistakes during our workshop.

"Slow down, Sparky," she often says. "You schedule things too tightly. It really bugs me when you rush people to get the points. You need to give more examples, provide more practice opportunities, and allow more time for questions." I know she's right, but I'm thinking, *Do you have to be so brutally frank? Where's your patience now?*

Probably most of us know someone who is extremely patient in some situations and less patient in others. Isn't this normal? I watch checkout clerks at the grocery store and marvel at how well they tolerate difficult customers. Most of us are capable of being patient in specific situations, but few of us can be patient in all situations. Here's some good news—You don't have to be patient all the time, but you can learn to be patient with your strong-willed children.

PATIENCE IS A TEACHABLE SKILL

Nearly anyone can learn to be patient in specific situations, but we shouldn't expect it to come as naturally or automatically as Lisa's experience in the classroom. You'll have to work at it. I've taught this skill to thousands of parents and teachers during my career, and I'm confident you can learn it if you are willing to practice a three-step process you'll learn in the next section. You don't need any special qualifications. All you need is a willingness to look at the triggers that hook your anger, then give yourself an opportunity to choose a different, more thoughtful response. Let's begin with triggers.

Each of us has our own special set of triggers when it comes to working with strong-willed children. Triggers are behaviors that really set us off and cause an intense emotional reaction. They're like fire alarms. When they go off, they get our quick attention and shock us into a reaction. At the moment, things seem bigger and more serious than they really are. In most cases, triggers are false alarms because there isn't any fire. They cause us to overreact to our child's misbehavior.

Triggers are great for getting our prompt attention, but they cloud our thinking, impair our judgment, make us overreact, and cause us to say and do things we later regret. Angry triggers are big obstacles to effective limit setting.

What are your triggers? Whining? Fussing? Screaming? Refusals? Stalling? Arguing? Defiance? Challenging? Name-calling? Dishonesty? Tantrums? Eye rolling? Looks of contempt? All of the above?

Whatever your triggers may be, you need to recognize them as red flags or warning signals that you're about to lose your self-control. Awareness is the first and most important step in regaining your self-control. This step begins with an observation. When you think your trigger is being pulled, observe your reaction and ask yourself, *What's going on here? What is my child doing? What am I feeling?*

This can be your moment of opportunity or the beginning of a destructive dance. It all depends upon what you do next. If you recognize the warning signal and observe your anger without acting on it, you can interrupt the usual knee-jerk reaction and give yourself an opportunity to respond effectively. If you simply react to the trigger, you may let your anger and frustration run its course, and risk saying or doing something hurtful to your child or your relationship.

Does recognizing the trigger make the reactive feelings go away? In most cases, the answer is no, at least, not right away. When kids pull our triggers, we react, almost automatically, on an emotional level, but we don't have to allow the intense emotions to take us over. Our moment of opportunity begins the instant we feel ourselves becoming angry or impatient. How long does that moment last? It lasts as long as it takes us to regain our emotional composure so we can respond effectively.

CREATING YOUR OWN THOUGHTFUL MOMENT

Most of us will need to practice three basic steps to create our own thoughtful moment, but how we go through these steps will vary from person to person. Let's look at each step to determine how it will work for you.

Step One: Observe What's Happening

Step One is the important awareness step we discussed earlier. When you think or feel that your trigger has been pulled, observe your reaction and ask yourself some questions so you can become aware of what's happening in that moment: *What's going on? What is my child doing? How am I feeling? Have we been through this before?*

In most cases, you'll discover that your child is testing or resisting the way he or she always does, and you're feeling angry and frustrated the way you usually do. The questions won't make the feelings go away, but they will help you recognize what's really happening in that moment so you can begin to put things into perspective. In effect, the questions provide a moment of clarity so you can begin to change an emotional process that takes you out of control into a rational process that helps you recover self-control.

Step Two: Recover Self-Control

Step Two is a vital recovery step that permits you to follow through with your moment of opportunity. When you recognize that your trigger has been pulled, and you're beginning to feel angry, this is the time to decide to step back and recover or proceed. Think of yourself as a train moving to a switching point that leads to two different tracks: an angry track or a controlled track. This is your opportunity to choose the right track, because the train is not going to stop. It has too much momentum. If you're aware of the choice, you can make the right one.

This important recovery step varies from person to person depending upon your reactivity to your triggers. If you tend to be highly reactive and can't restrain yourself from saying or doing something in anger, then you've already missed the signal, and you're already on the angry track. You can still salvage the situation, but your moment of opportunity will have to begin with a cooldown or an apology of the sort we discussed in Chapter 7.

That's okay. Managing intense feelings is not easy. Learning to be patient takes time and practice. You can use breathing and relaxation exercises to keep you on the right track. You will need to discover for yourself the strategies that work best for you.

Recovering self-control was not easy for me. I have a quick temper and tend to be reactive. When my son Ian pulled my triggers, I reacted almost instantaneously. My face would flush with anger. My voice would get loud and stern, and I'd be ready for battle. When Ian was young, many of my thoughtful moments began with the words, "Pal, I'm feeling really angry, and I need a few minutes to calm down. Have a seat on the couch. We'll deal with this in a few minutes." Then, I would remove myself from the situation, take some deep breaths, and wait for my angry feelings to dissipate.

I found two strategies particularly helpful for restoring my self-control. The first strategy involves a comforting phrase I repeated to myself that put the big picture back into focus. When I felt like exploding, I would repeat to myself, *I'm the adult. He's the kid. I can handle this.* Other times, I found it helpful to separate the deed from the doer by saying to myself, *I love my son, but what he's doing is not okay.*

The recovery process gets easier with time. As Ian got older, and I got more practice, I discovered I needed fewer cooldowns and only an occasional apology. By the time he reached elementary school, I was able to start off in a calm, matter-of-fact manner most of the time. But learning to be patient has always been "a work in progress." I never really got good at it until Ian grew up and left the house.

Parents often ask, *Am I supposed to feel patient and composed when I'm trying to behave in a patient and composed manner?* No. The feeling of composure, serenity, or patience may develop over time, but it's not required to master the skill of being patient. I appreciate what parents mean when they inform me that they don't feel patient when they act patient. That's okay. Your child is not likely to know your internal emotional experience anyway. All he or she knows is that you're behaving in a composed and under-control manner.

Step Three: Respond Thoughtfully

Steps One and Two may seem like a lot to go through to simply to reach Step Three, but in real life, this whole process often takes place in a brief moment. Step Three is the easiest part. Your feelings are under control. Your thinking is clear, and your judgment is good. Finally, you get the opportunity to use the skills you've been learning in this book. If things have already progressed to the point where you need to support your rules with consequences, you simply follow through with the appropriate logical consequence you learned in Chapter 8. Let's look at how several parents apply the three-step method to create their thoughtful moments.

Patience with an Explosive Temper

Tony and his four-year-old son, Marcello, are both strong-willed. Both have short fuses and explosive tempers. They adore each other, but in discipline situations, they are like charged particles in a reaction chamber. Tony came for counseling to learn better ways to manage his explosive temper.

"I don't know who explodes first, me or Marcello," says Tony. "I can't stop myself. I start shouting the moment I see him misbehave, and he starts screaming the moment he sees me coming. It's crazy! I feel terrible after it's over."

From his description, I could see that Tony didn't recognize how far things progressed until he saw how upset Marcello became. Tony's first task is to learn to restore his self-control, then try to salvage his thoughtful moment. We practiced cooldowns and did some relaxation exercises, but Tony decided that what he really needed to do was give himself a five-minute time-out and follow up with an apology. Then, he would try to respond thoughtfully and follow through with an appropriate consequence. Marcello liked the plan.

Tony had an opportunity to practice his plan the evening following our first appointment. "It's time to put away your toys and put on your pajamas, Marcello, and get ready for bed," Tony announces. Marcello is so engrossed in arranging his figures into battle positions that he doesn't realize how much time has passed. His father enters the room to check on his progress and explodes.

"Damn it, Marcello!" Tony shouts. "How many times do I have to tell you? This is the stuff that makes me so mad." Tony sees the tears welling up in his son's eyes and stops himself before he unleashes even more anger.

"Marcello, wait here. I need five minutes alone," says Tony. Marcello looks surprised and scared at the same time. Tony leaves the family room, sets the kitchen timer, and waits to regain his composure. When the timer goes off, Tony reenters the family room. Marcello still has a scared look on his face.

"I'm sorry I yelled at you, Marcello," Tony says, matter-of-factly.

"Will you accept my apology?" Marcello nods. "Thank you," says Tony. "It's time to pick up your toys, put on your pajamas, and get ready for bed." Tony had taken a big step toward learning to become more patient. He and Marcello had taken a big step toward interrupting their angry dance.

Patience with Dawdling and Bad Attitude

Beth is a patient parent, but she also has her triggers. Dawdling and negative attitudes really set her off. Chelsea, her strong-willed daughter, discovered the dawdling trigger at about age three, but things didn't get ugly until Chelsea turned twelve.

Each night after dinner, Chelsea knows it's her job to load the dishwasher and wipe off the counters, but she dawdles and avoids and waits until the last possible moment to get started. Their dance usually begins with a series of prompts.

"It's time to get started," says Beth, matter-of-factly.

"I will," Chelsea replies but makes no move to do so. She knows what her mother will do next.

"We don't have all evening," says Beth, impatiently. "I'm getting upset!"

"Mom, I said I would do it!" Chelsea replies, with the same level of impatience, then rolls her eyes and gives Beth a look of contempt. This is when Beth usually loses her self-control and starts yelling, but not this time. She remembers the skill she's working on and recognizes her moment of opportunity.

Oh no, she found my triggers. We're not going down this path again, Beth says to herself. She walks into another room, takes a few deep breaths, and checks in with herself. *What's going on?* Beth recognizes Chelsea's usual dawdle and attitude routine for what it is. *How am I feeling?* Beth can see she feels angry and frustrated the way she always does in these situations. She takes a few more deep breaths, checks her composure, and returns to the kitchen.

"Chelsea, I love you too much to yell at you about doing your jobs," Beth says, matter-of-factly. "I know you can do a good job if you choose to, but you won't be doing anything else until the job is done. Let me know when you're finished so I can check it over." Beth gives Chelsea an encouraging look and walks out of the kitchen. No yelling. No screaming. No drawn-out power struggles.

What happened to her? Chelsea thinks to herself. *She's no fun.* Chelsea considers dawdling again to see if she can rekindle the flames but reconsiders the plan when she realizes that the time she's wasting is her own.

Patience with Whining and Fussing

It's a beautiful Saturday morning, and Barry, age seven, wants to go skating with his friends. Barry's mom insists that he clean his guinea pigs' cage before he leaves the house. It's a twenty-minute job that Barry agreed to do weekly as a condition to getting the guinea pigs. Barry protests and complains, but his mom holds firm. He tries bargaining. "I'll do it as soon as I get back," he promises.

"You know our agreement," his mom says, matter-of-factly.

"Yeah, well, it's a stupid agreement," says Barry, angrily. His mom doesn't react, so Barry tries the one thing he knows will drive his mom crazy. He starts to fuss in a whiny voice. Barry's mom reacts instantly, but she remembers what she read in the book, takes a few deep breaths, and holds on to her moment of opportunity.

"You can fuss and whine all you want, Barry," says his mom, matter-of-factly, "but you're going to have to do it in your room. I'm not going to listen to it." She sends him to his room for a time-out. Ahh, *Patience feels good*, she thinks to herself.

"This really sucks!" complains Barry. He knows he just added seven more minutes to the twenty it will take to clean the cage.

Patience with Untrustworthy Behavior

Natalie's parents are concerned. Lately, their bright, capable eleven-year-old has been less than honest about her schoolwork. They've noticed the pattern in other areas too. Natalie's grades have fallen from Bs to Cs in three subjects largely because she doesn't complete or turn in her homework assignments on a regular basis.

On the advice of her teacher, Natalie's parents implement a new homework routine to remedy the problem. Each day after school, Natalie is supposed to complete her homework before she does anything else. Her mother checks it over for completion. If it's complete, Natalie is free to play with her friends.

"I'm going to Annie's house," Natalie announces, after arriving home from school. "Ceci is going to meet us there. We have something fun we really want to do."

"Is your homework done?" asks her mom.

"We don't have any tonight," Natalie replies. Her mom is suspicious. Trust and honesty are two of her biggest triggers.

"May I see your weekly assignment sheet?" she asks.

"Well, maybe I have a little," says Natalie, sheepishly, "but I can do it when I get back."

"You know our agreement," says her mom. "Homework comes

first, then playtime." Natalie heads to her room to finish up. Forty minutes later, she returns and passes over two pages of math and one page of vocabulary words for her mom's inspection. As usual, Natalie did a fine job.

"Can I go to Annie's house now?" Natalie asks.

"Okay," says her mom, "but you need to be home by 5:30. Is that clear?"

"I will," says Natalie, as she scampers out the door.

At 6:15 Natalie has not returned. Her concerned mom calls Annie's house and discovers the girls are not there. They went to the park but should have returned thirty minutes ago. Natalie's mom feels panicky. As she heads to the car to look for her daughter, she sees Natalie walking up the driveway.

"Where were you?" asks her worried mom.

"I told you. I went to Annie's house," Natalie replies.

"When I called Annie's mother at 6:15, she said you girls met at the park. You didn't ask permission to go to the park, and you know your father and I don't like you there in the evenings." Natalie's face is flushed.

"Well, I didn't think it would hurt anything," says Natalie. Her mom is furious and about to explode but catches herself, takes a few deep breaths, and asks Natalie to wait in the house.

"I need a few minutes, then we'll talk," says her mom, with tears in her eyes. She recognizes the trust, honesty, and safety issues she has to consider and wants to be sure she chooses the appropriate logical consequences with a clear head. Twenty minutes later, Natalie's mom approaches her daughter in the living room.

"What time did I ask you to be home?" asks her mom.

"Five-thirty," replies Natalie.

"What time did you actually arrive home?" asks her mom.

"About 6:30," says Natalie, remorsefully.

"Natalie, the real issues here are about honesty and trust," her mom begins. "You deceived me about your homework, where you went, and about what time you would be home. Your father and I must to be able to trust you if we are to give you the freedom and privileges you have. You need to earn back the trust that's been lost.

"I will continue to check your homework each day before you play for the rest of the semester. You can have your friends play at our house after school, but you won't be permitted to go to their homes or anywhere else for the next two weeks. After that time, you can resume your play privileges at your friends' homes, but we will check to make sure you're really there. If you're not, this privilege will be suspended for even longer. If you want to go anywhere other than where we agree, you must have our permission. If you don't, we will suspend the privilege for even longer. When we say we want you home at a certain time, we mean it. If you show up late without notifying us, we will suspend this privilege for even longer. Finally, we love you. We won't take any chances with your safety. Is all this clear?" Natalie nods.

Can you see yourself exercising this level of patience with your strong-willed child? Mastering this skill is well within your capability if you're willing to practice the three-step procedure. Don't expect it to be easy or to happen quickly, but it will happen if you persevere. Patience is the remedy for overcoming anger and frustration.

CHAPTER SUMMARY

The gift of patience is one of the greatest gifts you can share with your strong-willed child. When you give your patience, you share your best inner qualities—your clearest thinking, your best judgment, your loving understanding, and your most thoughtful guidance. Fortunately, you don't need to be a saint to be patient. Patience is a skill you can learn. In fact, you don't need any special qualifications at all. Nearly anyone can learn to be patient. All you need is a willingness to recognize your triggers and follow a simple three-step procedure: (1) observe what's happening, (2) recover your self-control, and (3) respond thoughtfully. What we do is what we teach. When you practice patience, you teach an invaluable skill that can be passed on to future generations.

13

Understanding the Change Process

The idea of a quick fix is very appealing. We all want our children's behavior to improve as quickly as possible, but we also need to recognize that these patterns didn't develop overnight. Retraining takes time, not only for children, but also for parents.

On an intellectual level, you may recognize that the methods you've learned in this book will lead to the type of change you desire, but the new guidance tools may not feel comfortable to you or your child in the beginning. Your child will likely resist, and you will probably be tempted to give in to your compelling desire to revert to old bad habits and do things the way you always have. This chapter will prepare you for the changes that lie ahead. You'll gain a better understanding of the change process and develop realistic expectations to keep you on track.

WHAT YOU CAN EXPECT

When you begin applying the methods in this book, you will stop misbehavior quickly, but changing your child's beliefs about your rules will take time. In the meantime, you'll likely encounter an initial increase in testing and resistance from your child. Don't be alarmed. This is temporary and very normal. It doesn't mean your methods are ineffective. It simply means your aggressive researcher has a lot of data to collect. The initial retraining phase, usually the first eight to twelve weeks, is a period of heavy data collection. Hang in there. Be consistent. Allow the teaching and learning process to run its course.

> Your child's beliefs about your rules and how you're supposed to behave are based, in most cases, on years of experience.

After all, your child's beliefs about your rules and how you're supposed to behave are based, in most cases, on years of experience. Your child is not likely to change well-established beliefs overnight just because you said things are going to be different. History, in this case, works against you. Children will need to experience the change for themselves over time before they'll revise their beliefs and accept the change as fact.

During this retraining, you should expect your child to test frequently and do everything he or she can to get you to "behave the way you're supposed to." If you danced in the past, you should expect your child to try to hook you with tempting baits to get you back out on the dance floor. You'll probably need to rely heavily upon the tools you learned in Chapter 7 to stop the dance before it gets started.

Consequences will play an important role during the initial retraining period. You'll need to use them frequently to interrupt power struggles, stop misbehavior, and to teach your child to tune into your words and take them seriously. Make friends with these wonderful tools. They're your ticket to credibility. The more consistency you achieve between your words and your actions, the quicker your child will learn to tune into your words and cooperate.

Monica is a good example. Her parents attended one of my workshops looking for more effective ways to deal with their twelve-year-old daughter's defiant and argumentative behavior. They soon recognized that their approach was permissive, their limits were soft, and their consequences were late and ineffective. They sat down with Monica and announced that things were going to be different.

"We're not going to repeat or remind anymore when we ask you to do what we ask," said her father. "We'll ask once. No arguments or debates. No lectures or raised voices. If you choose not to cooperate, we'll be using some new consequences." They explained logical consequences and time-out.

I'll believe it when I see it, Monica said to herself, skeptically. Based on all her previous experience, she had no reason to take their words seriously.

But Monica's parents kept their word. When they asked her to do something, they stated their request once, firmly. When Monica tuned them out or tried to argue, which she did most of the time, they used the check-in procedure or cutoff. No more repeating or reminding. No more arguing or debating. If she continued to resist, they followed through with logical consequences or time-out.

The methods worked. For the first time, Monica was accountable for her poor choices and behavior. She began to understand that she, not her parents, was responsible for her misbehavior. But her persistent testing didn't stop right away.

In fact, she intensified her resistance during the first month and pushed most of her conflicts to the point of consequences. She was collecting a lot of data. When her parents held firm, Monica made comments such as "You're not fair!" or "I hate you!" to wear her parents down and get them to give in. It didn't work. They held firm.

About six weeks into the retraining, Monica's parents noticed a change in her behavior. The change was subtle at first. She tested less and cooperated more. She was beginning to tune in to her parents' words and take them seriously.

> You can tip the scales in your favor by being consistent, but expectations of a quick fix will only set you and your child up for needless disappointment.

Monica's initial increase in testing is a normal part of the learning process. After all, her parents told her that the rules had changed. How else would she know that they meant what they said? Testing was the only way she could be sure, and when she tested, her parents provided her with the data she needed to arrive at the right conclusions. Their new tools were changing her behavior.

Changing your child's behavior will be the easy part. Changing your child's beliefs about your rules will take more time. How much time? This depends on a number of factors: your child's age, your child's temperament, your consistency, how much history you both need to overcome, and how much data your child needs to collect. Younger children (three to seven years) have less history to overcome and generally require less data. Older children (eight to twelve years) have more history to overcome and require more data.

Most parents report a noticeable reduction in testing during the first eight weeks to twelve weeks. Some children require longer. You can tip the scales in your favor by being consistent, but expectations of a quick fix will only set you and your child up for needless disappointment.

UNDERSTANDING THE CHANGE PROCESS

Family therapists and other helping professionals recognize that families try to maintain a state of balance or equilibrium in the way they communicate, solve problems, and relate with one another. This balance defines a comfort range for acceptable behavior—the family's normal way of doing things.

> Change, even positive change, is stressful. Resistance is a normal and expected reaction to change.

Punitive, permissive, and mixed training styles and family dances are often part of this comfort range. They're familiar and accepted patterns that most family members are reluctant to give up even though these patterns cause upset and stress. When these patterns are disrupted, family members often respond with resistance and attempt to restore the balance that has been disrupted. Change, even positive change, is stressful. Resistance is a normal and expected reaction to change.

The methods you've learned in this book will stop misbehavior and interrupt your family dance, but they may also upset your family equilibrium for a while. You should expect some resistance from all family members, even yourself. Your strong-willed child, in particular, will likely do everything he or she can to get you to revert to your old bad habits. At times, you'll probably be tempted to give in to the pressure.

> You can't change your child's behavior or beliefs
> unless you're willing to change your own.

How do you resist the pressure? By staying focused on your goals and by making a commitment to see the process through. Learning the methods in this book is retraining for parents as well as for kids. The new tools will take you to your goals, but you have to use them with consistency to get the results. You can't change your child's behavior or beliefs unless you're willing to change your own.

First- and Second-Order Changes

Behavior change in families usually comes in two forms. Family therapists refer to the first form as first-order change. This type of change involves a temporary adjustment in the behavior of family members without any lasting impact on their beliefs about family rules. First-order change is superficial and brief. When the change is discontinued, old patterns of behavior return.

For example, if you use the methods in this book for two to three weeks then stop, you'll stop your child's misbehavior; but the temporary change will have little impact upon your child's beliefs about your rules. Your child will likely resume his old pattern of behavior as soon as you discontinue the new methods. Why? Because your child didn't collect enough data in the form of experience to change his beliefs. The learning process didn't go far enough.

If you're willing to see the process through and provide your child with the data he needs to change his beliefs, you can move beyond superficial change to second-order change, an enduring change that becomes a new part of your family's normal way of doing things. Second-order change requires consistent application of your methods over time.

> First-order change is superficial and brief. When
> the change is discontinued, old patterns of behavior
> return.

You should be well on your way to second-order change during the first three to six months of this program. You'll notice less testing, quicker cooperation, and a decreased need for consequences. This is your clue that the change process is shifting into another gear. Your child's beliefs are beginning to change. Change is fragile at this point because the learning is incomplete. If you begin to slip and revert to your old ways, you'll likely encounter renewed testing.

However, if you stay on course and remain consistent with your methods, you and your child should begin to reach a new level of comfort and acceptance in the weeks and months to come.

Second-order change, an enduring change that becomes a new part of your family's normal way of doing things, requires consistent application of your methods over time.

ENJOYING THE REWARDS

If this book has fulfilled its mission, you should have the information and tools you need to improve the match between your guidance methods and the temperament and learning style of your strong-willed child.

You understand that setting limits involves an interaction between three primary factors: your child's temperament, your own temperament, and your limit-setting approach. You can't control your child's temperament, but you can shape and guide it in the right direction with the right tools.

Setting limits involves an interaction between three primary factors: your child's temperament, your own temperament, and your limit-setting approach.

You have the right tools, and you can manage your own temperament. Two of the three factors are solidly within your control, and you can influence the one that isn't! Now you're in a position to make a big difference. You've prepared yourself with awareness. You understand the major obstacles to effective teaching and learning: punitive, permissive, and mixed training approaches; soft limits; negative motivation; and family dances.

You've added many new tools to your guidance toolbox. You know how to set clear limits, give clear messages, reduce testing, eliminate power struggles, and stop misbehavior with effective action. You've learned how to manage resistance, how to inspire cooperation with positive motivation, how to teach problem-solving skills, and how to use patience to overcome your anger and frustration when your child pulls your triggers.

> With the proper guidance and direction, your strong-willed child can grow up to become a responsible, cooperative, respectful, and dynamic individual.

You've looked ahead at the change process that awaits you. You've anticipated many of the obstacles in your path, and you know what to do to overcome them. Your preparation is complete. The next step is to put your knowledge and new tools into practice and begin enjoying the rewards of your efforts.

The immediate rewards will be fewer power struggles and quicker cooperation. You'll be stopping misbehavior you couldn't stop before without going through all those exhaustive dances and without injuring feelings in the process.

The long-term rewards will be the most satisfying of all because you'll be laying a foundation for cooperative and satisfying relationships for years to come. By your example, you'll be teaching the skills your child needs to be successful not only at home, but also out in the world. With the proper guidance and direction, your strong-willed child can grow up to become a responsible, cooperative, respectful, and dynamic individual. Enjoy setting limits!

SUGGESTED READING

Adler, A. *Superiority and Social Interest.* Evanston, Illinois: Northwestern University Press, 1964.

Adler, A. *What Life Should Mean to You.* New York: Capricorn Books, 1958.

Ames, L. B., Ph.D. *Questions Parents Ask: Straight Answers from Louise Bates Ames, Ph.D.* New York: Clarkson N. Potter, 1988.

Ansbacher, H., and R. Ansbacher. *The Individual Psychology of Alfred Adler.* New York: Harper Touchbooks, 1964.

Bandura, A. *Social Learning Theory.* Englewood Cliffs, N.J.: Prentice-Hall, 1963.

Brazelton, T. B., M.D. *Infants and Mothers: Differences in Development.* New York: Delacorte, 1983.

Budd, L. *Living with the Active, Alert Child.* Seattle, Wash.: Parenting Press, 1993.

Chess, S., M.D., and A. Thomas, M.D. *Know Your Child.* New York: Basic Books, 1987.

Dinkmeyer, D., and R. Dreikurs. *Encouraging Children to Learn: The Encouragement Process.* Englewood Cliffs, N.J.: Prentice-Hall, 1963.

Dinkmeyer, D., and G. McKay. *Raising a Responsible Child.* New York: Simon & Schuster, 1973.

Dinkmeyer, D., G. McKay, and J. Dinkmeyer. *Parenting Young Children.* New York: Random House, 1989.

Dodson, F. *How to Discipline with Love*. New York: New American Library, 1987.

Dreikurs, R., and L. A. Grey. *A New Approach to Discipline: Logical Consequences*. New York: Hawthorne Books, 1968.

Erikson, E. *Childhood and Society* (2nd Edition). New York: Norton & Company, 1963.

Ferber, R., M.D. *Solve Your Child's Sleep Problems*. New York: Simon & Schuster, 1985.

Glasser, W. *Control Theory*. New York: Harper Collins, 1984.

Kohlberg, L. *The Development of Children's Orientation Toward a Moral Order: Sequence in the Development of Moral Thought*. Vita Humana 6 (1963): 11–33.

Kohlberg, L. *Stage and Sequence: The Cognitive Developmental Approach to Socialization*. In D. A. Goslin (ed.), Handbook of Socialization Theory and Research (pp. 3478–3480). Chicago: Rand McNally, 1966.

Losoncy, L. *Turning People On: How to Be an Encouraging Person*. Englewood Cliffs, N.J.: Prentice-Hall, 1977.

Minuchin, S. *Families and Family Therapy*. Cambridge, Mass.: Harvard University Press, 1974.

Piaget, J., and B. Inhelder. *The Psychology of the Child*. New York: Basic Books, 1969.

Satter, E. *How to Get Your Kid to Eat . . . But Not Too Much*. Palo Alto, Calif.: Bull Publishing, 1987.

Turecki, S. and L. Tonner. *The Difficult Child: A Guide for Parents*, Revised Edition. New York: Bantam Books, 1989.

Wadsworth, B. J. *Piaget's Theory of Cognitive and Affective Development* (4th ed.). New York: Longman Publishing, 1989.

INDEX

ABOUT THE AUTHOR

Dr. Robert MacKenzie is a family therapist and educational psychologist with more than thirty years of experience helping parents and teachers solve children's learning and behavioral adjustment problems. He is the author of two previous books, *Setting Limits*, and *Setting Limits in the Classroom*, and numerous magazine and newspaper articles. Dr. MacKenzie provides family counseling, parent education, and teacher training. He consults privately with hospitals, school districts, teacher-parent organizations, and a wide variety of community service agencies. He leads more than fifty workshops each year nationwide on his Setting Limits program. Dr. MacKenzie lives in Davis, California.